No Easy Road

NO EASY ROAD

*A Study of the Theories and Problems involved
in the Rehabilitation of the Offender*

BY

SALLIE TROTTER
M.A.(Edin.), D.S.St.(Edin.), S.R.N.

London
GEORGE ALLEN AND UNWIN LTD
RUSKIN HOUSE · MUSEUM STREET

PRINTED IN GREAT BRITAIN
11 on 12 point Baskerville type
BY NOVELLO AND COMPANY LTD
BOROUGH GREEN · KENT

*To all the men in grey or navy-blue who have
told me that 'this time they would make it',
I affectionately and prayerfully dedicate this
book, as well as to all those who in future hope
for the same goal. I have kept the promise I made
to you in 1962 to write it. I wish you all success
in your much more difficult task.*

Foreword

'The prisons of this country are not open to the visiting public. The general reader is not therefore able to weigh, in the scales of personal experience, the practical value of such criticisms and proposals as are laid before him. Thus it is of peculiar importance that the credentials of critics and reformers should be subject to the most rigid scrutiny. The psychology of a man in confinement differs fundamentally from that of a free man: the vision of the theorists penetrates obscurely the barrier that divides the two. Books upon penal institutions therefore lose all authority if, as is so often the case, they prove to have been written by those without practical experience of men in prison. . . . With regard to the spate of books written by ex-prisoners, it is sometimes difficult to understand how even the most credulous of the community can be carried to the length of apparent unquestioning acceptance of what are, for the most part, grotesquely distorted pictures of prison life in this country. Men are listened to with grave attention, when, emerging from an imprisonment which in itself has been merited by an offence of fraud or cheating, without a vestige of evidence, they make the most serious allegations against the character of officers and the administration of prisons.'

With these words Leo Page opens his book, *Crime and the Community*. If *No Easy Road* requires any justification, Sir Leo's succinct words adequately describe the need for its production

The author had the privilege of being the first woman social worker in Britain appointed to work inside an all-male prison, with more freedom than had hitherto been offered to any other person not strictly of the prison staff. As head of a small but important department, I was made responsible for the welfare and rehabilitation of over 1500 men, none of whom was a first offender.

Most books on prisons have been written by men: by ex-Governors, chaplains, lawyers, sociologists (some not even qualified), magistrates, prison visitors, prisoners and others. Readers interested in this highly controversial social problem have also been inundated with a flood of official reports from committees predominantly male, prepared, submitted and edited by men.

Thus certain facets of prisons and the men in them, through no fault of these writers, were never apparent to them in the way they were to me, a woman.

'Nobody ever sends *me* flowers,' was the Governor's comment to me when I received a very beautiful mixed bouquet from a grateful prisoner, recently discharged. The remark might have been laughable had it not been so pathetic in its underlying emphasis, high-lighting as it did, the vast barrier between the prisoners and the head of the disciplinary hierarchy.

The first part of the book is an account of some of my experiences inside Wandsworth prison during the years 1960-1962.[1] The second part deals with some of the theories of others and my attempts to analyse them. The third part is reserved for my own ideas.

Because of the Official Secrets Act and the laws of libel, but most of all because of the Hippocratic-like views of the professional social worker, I have been careful to 'scramble' case-histories so that, though the incidents are based on fact, no individual is intended or can be identified. The men described, with their problems, could be found in their hundreds in Wandsworth and indeed in every prison in the country.

Only descriptions of the prison and some of the incidents already well-publicised by the press have been mentioned. The same applies to the second section, where already known or published theories and books are reviewed.

The ideas expressed are my own and do not necessarily coincide with those of the Home Office.

S.W.B.T.

---

[1] The author was Senior Prison Welfare Officer at Wandsworth from September 1960 till December 1962. Many changes have of course taken place since that day of which this book cannot take account.

Acknowledgments

I am indebted to the Home Office for permission to reproduce extracts from various reports and to *Woman* for giving us permission to use their photograph as the frontispiece.

I am glad to have this opportunity to acknowledge the debt I owe to Brigadier Paton-Walsh, former Governor of Wandsworth Prison for the patience and understanding he showed in a novel situation.

My gratitude goes also to my friends Mr Gale, until recently Governor in succession to the Brigadier and to Col. R. Shebbeare, Governor of Shrewsbury prison, whose help, support and friendship made my task possible; and to all the prison staff for their friendly co-operation in the work of the Welfare department which made our task lighter and a pleasure instead of a nightmare. Included in my gratitude are the heads and staffs of the many and varied statutory and voluntary agencies whose hard work and understanding teamwork made our efforts at rehabilitation of the men possible and worthwhile.

I wish to thank also the most loyal and hard-working people whom anyone could know, to whom I was 'Mum' as well as 'the Boss'. The members of my own small department were my friends as well as my colleagues and staff. I am the richer for the good times and fun we had together.

To my old friend of many years' standing, James Hodge, the Scottish legal publisher, and to Dr Letitia Fairfield I am most grateful for their vetting of the first draft of this book. Their frank criticisms and encouragement enabled me to produce it in its present form.

Most of all, I am obligated to my family for their encouragement, understanding and patience. Without their help I should have been unable to spare time to write this book.

Because I was known better by my name before my remarriage, I have retained this throughout the book.

S. W. B. CRAWFORD

Contents

PART I

Chapter 1

H.M. PRISON WANDSWORTH

'It is not for nothing that H.M. Prison Wandsworth is known among prisoners and prison staff alike as the "toughest in Britain, Dartmoor not excepted." '[1]

The men inside are none of them first offenders, covered in guilt and ashamed at the disgrace they have brought on themselves and those dear to them. Many are among the most dangerous criminals in the country. Many have been 'in the business' from childhood. They have graduated through approved schools, Borstals or probation, or from prisons which take first adult offenders and later from other prisons for recidivists. Their language and standards are not those of the law-abiding citizen outside. Life inside the prison walls is regimented and unnatural.

This vast Victorian prison, its bricks grimed with nearly one and a half centuries of London soot, lies sprawling behind a twenty-feet high brick wall. Embracing an area as large as Trafalgar Square, it is a blot on the pleasant common and the tree-lined avenues surrounding it.

All the senses are assaulted as one steps over the wooded strip through a small doorway in the main gate on to the cobblestones in the forecourt. The surface, unkind to feet used to the smoother modern road-surfaces of asphalt and cement, is of stones laid down when the Black Maria was drawn by horses.

Wandsworth's forbidding and awe-inspiring gate, with its steel-studded doors of blackened oak and portcullis effect, in its Roman archway, has been made through press, television and films, probably the most notorious entrance to any prison in the world.

1 *Daily Mail*, June 26, 1961. Peter Lewis, *I Saw the Sickness of Wandsworth*.

Built in 1848 for about 750 men and women, Wandsworth held at the time of my arrival on that dull morning in September 1960, over 1500 men (and was to house nearly 1800 while I was there). Many of those men spent the major part of their imprisonment three to a cell. A prison cell consists of a cheerless, brick-lined area thirteen feet long, seven feet wide, and eight feet six inches high, with a small window seven feet up with tiny panes, some of which are broken and all of which are barred and cross-barred. The steel door has no handle, but in the middle is an inch-wide hole (the 'Judas-hole'), with a cover which can be slipped aside to keep the occupants under observation.

Beyond the cobbled forecourt, guarded by a steel-barred gate, lies the prison yard, a strange misnomer for such a large expanse of cobblestones, asphalt, pavements and flower-beds. In the midst of this area are several blocks, most of them four storeys high and standing foursquare against all comers, defying entrance with their thickly-barred windows.

There, too, are the visiting 'boxes' (an appropriate title), the wood-shop, the engineering department, (periodically issuing a warning hiss of steam), the other 'shops'[2] huddling beneath the shelter of the wall, the officers' mess, the bathhouse and outside latrines and, far to the right, the prison hospital.

The Main block dwarfs all others, with its administrative offices facing the entrance gate.[3] Climbing the steps, I noticed an iron ring in the wall at the foot of the stairway. This was once used by visiting Prison Commissioners for tying up their horses.

On entering the administrative wing I received my first surprise—a pleasant one, because this spacious hallway, with walls and doors painted in pastel colours, was such a contrast

---

[2] Shops are where the prisoners work at making mailbags for the G.P.O., clogs, mostly for the Gas Board and broom-handles and where they do shoe-repairing, laundering and tailoring.

[3] This book is a description of things as I found them during my stay. I am glad to report that on a recent visit I found the 'boxes' gone—to be replaced by a large and attractive visiting room. There is a new administrative block. The cobblestones are replaced by asphalt. The former 'Admin.' hall is now the social workers' department.

to the grim outside. I was soon to learn, however, that I had not yet entered the prison proper.

Of all the senses, I think hearing and smell are those most assailed by Wandsworth prison.

The noises of this vast city within a city are not unlike those of a busy railway junction in war-time, with the constant movement of troops. There is an endless flow of men from one block to another, or to the shops or hospital, or to and from 'Reception'.[4] There is the echoing sound of thousands of feet clattering over the flagstones in the wings, as the men exercise on wet days, or the drone as they march round the yard in fine weather, their voices and footsteps magnified by the precipitous walls all round them. One hears the occasional shouts of officers, the jingle of keys, the thunderous slamming of steel doors, the hissing of steam from the Engineers' block or from the heating plant in the middle of the yard. One is aware of the machine-gun rattle of a load of coke being delivered to the plant, the whine of an electric saw from the wood-shop, the heavy vibration and rumble of a stream of trucks bringing supplies in and out of the prison gates, usually to the kitchen or hospital. Finally there is the shrill of the alarm bell, followed by a wary silence, the prelude to a startling rush of officers to the trouble spot, accompanied by a clanging of doors as other prisoners are locked up securely.

Yet there are other sounds which are more familiar and reassuring. It may be the clatter of a bucket and the sound of scrubbing as a man washes the stairs and corridors outside our office; pigeons coo up and down the wings, for the glass dome of the Main block where our department was, has broken panes through which the birds fly to live as pets and companions to prisoners and officers alike. Seagulls call from the common, visiting us undeterred by a twenty-foot wall. An incredibly lovely though ironic sound descends from the chapel, to those walking in the grounds in the evening, of a male-voice choir composed of prisoners rehearsing with great lustiness many well-known hymns. I usually stopped to listen as I passed through the dark shadows from one block to

[4] The block where prisoners are admitted and discharged.

another. It often warmed my heart when I was tired with working until late in the evening. I felt: 'Those men cannot be wholly lost!' Yet it made me sad as well. It is a sound I shall never forget.

Paradoxically, it is not this constant din which alerts prisoners and staff and causes them to hold their breath and to make pulses beat more quickly. It is lack of noise! For noise in Wandsworth is a reassurance that all is well. A sudden stillness, a wary, crouching posture of the prisoners passing in front of officers, and all the staff knows that trouble is imminent. The first time I sensed it, I did not understand what it portended.

Greeting a P.O. (Principal Officer) brightly one morning on my way to my office, I remarked: 'My! Isn't it peaceful in here this morning?'

The smile vanished from my face as the officer, a man with years of experience, looked gravely over his spectacles at me, his usually cheerful, plump face solemn and unsmiling, and replied: 'Watch out, Mrs Trotter. There's always trouble when it's quiet in a prison.'

His diagnosis was correct. That weekend in June, 1961, the press had a field day reporting sensational stories of one of the largest mass breakouts that the prison had ever known. Hitherto, I had always thought the term 'smell of fear' was literary licence, but I have smelt it in Wandsworth and know it is no flight of fancy. Even the yelling, swearing and screaming of a riot, or the sullen rumble of a sit-down strike, or the banging of tin mugs and pots on doors on the eve of an execution, though all scarifying, do not produce this aura of fear. By then, so to speak, the 'boil has burst', and everyone knows where they stand. The intense stillness before an outbreak of violence and the terror of the unknown, with ignorance of where it will strike, produce, as one young officer once told me, 'a salty taste in the mouth and a clamminess in the palms as you feel for your truncheon.'

Many officers had known war service and were familiar with the sensation. To me it was an unpleasant novelty, in spite of the fact that I had been nursing near war-time London

20

and had experienced unusual adventures with dangerous criminals in Canada, including two riots in a women's prison, not mine fortunately! Yet this very novelty acted as a challenge. I like to feel that my bearing in front of officers and senior staff was one of the factors of my acceptance by both. Never was I more thankful of the histrionic training which both nursing and social work demand!

Smells, mostly unpleasant, are a pervasive feature of all large prisons and Wandsworth is no exception. Having worked in hospital wards, and with many years behind me of visiting in the most sordid slums in numerous large cities, I had a fairly strong resistance to odours, though I have a keen nose. I needed that immunity in my new post!

Each morning and evening there is the aroma, and, since taste is so closely connected to the olfactory sense, almost the taste of stew or soup or baking bread. Those pleasant odours temporarily erase others not so tempting, including the all-penetrating smell of cats. (The staff do not know how many there now are in the prison.) There is a stench at certain hours when 'slopping out' takes place, with approximately 150 men on each landing having to empty their 'potties' in two recesses, each containing only two toilets of the stall type and a sluice. One meets too, the acrid smell of sweat and bodies too infrequently bathed.

Such was the setting of my new job amid many hundreds of men in drab, grey woollen battle-dress, mostly ill-fitting (later changed to a smarter navy blue). They were guarded by smartly uniformed officers with brass buttons gleaming (the colour and metal making the only distinction from police uniform), each officer erect as a guardsman. It is to the credit of the prison service that I never saw a sloppy officer the whole time I was in Wandsworth. Their smartness ought to have been an example to the prisoners in their care, which I gather was one of the ideas of the Home Office. Whether this was so need not be discussed here. Certainly the uniform helped most officers by boosting their morale. Many wore war ribbons with justifiable pride.

So important is the rôle of those men that I shall devote an entire chapter to them later in this book.

Chapter II

A PIONEER POST RAISES PROBLEMS

My appointment as Senior Prison Welfare Officer[1] to Wandsworth Prison created a sensation, greatly to my surprise, both inside and outside the prison, by its novelty and daring. For it was the first time in this country that a woman had been appointed to hold such a post. The placing of trained and full-time social workers inside the local prisons of England and Wales was anyway very new.

'Are you not afraid?' 'What do criminals look like?' 'How did you come to get the job?' 'How did the prisoners react to having a woman in their midst?' 'What do you plan to do?' 'What does your job entail?' 'What is prison welfare?' These questions and many others I was asked and indeed am still asked.

To the first question, originally asked by a reporter, I gave a very simple answer: 'No. If I were, I might just as well pack up straight away.'

This was not bravado. I did not waste time telling the reporter the background to this answer.

My experience in the Navy and as Governor of a women's

---

[1] This title roused great confusion in the minds of most people, and still does as it tends to be associated with material welfare, as supplied by the former local Discharged Prisoners' Aid Societies, not casework and rehabilitation. The fact, too, that the Maxwell Committee thought that the National Association of Discharged Prisoners' Aid Societies would be a suitable central authority and did not visualise the social workers as probation officers working also as members of the prison staff, raised still further perplexity. This situation had of course its advantages, but also its disadvantages. Since January 1966 the status of the prison welfare officers has been made clearer. They are now amalgamated into the probation service and are probation officers on secondment. I shall therefore in this book after answering the third question above, talk of prison social work and prison social workers rather than the inaccurate term 'welfare'. It is a pity that at the time of secondment, prison welfare officers were not also given the more accurate title which gives a clearer picture of their function.

prison in Canada had taught me that I had little to fear from the mass of men in Wandsworth. Those men could hold little terror for anyone who, like myself, had worked as a probation officer in Toronto. There, on one occasion, I had had to sprint, like a female James Bond, down a narrow street towards a convent. Clutching my hand during the flight was a terrified young probationer who had been a 'gangster's moll'. We were pursued to the very door of the convent, the Home of the Good Shepherd, by a car full of thugs, some probably armed. These gangsters had already threatened to snatch her back and to 'fix' me and the Mother Superior into whose care I had given the girl for protection and sanctuary the month before.

I walked round the landings of Wandsworth with less feeling of uneasiness than in a certain street in Toronto, where on a bright Sunday afternoon I found it safer to walk in the middle of the road, fortunately fairly clear of motor traffic, than on the sidewalk. The probationer I was calling upon had been the 'madam' of a brothel, who supported her blind mother by this dubious means. She lived in a typical 'red light' area. It was she who had expressed concern at my visiting and had advised me to walk where I did, advice from an 'expert' I knew better than to ignore!

I had been inside a large women's prison at the outbreak of a serious riot, the suppression of which all but required the use of tear gas. I had, on another occasion just missed being witness to the stabbing of the Deputy Governor on a staircase by an enraged woman who had stolen a knife from the vegetable kitchen. These and many other far-from-routine experiences enabled me to say with truth that I was indeed not afraid of the prisoners in Wandsworth. Further I really like people and suspected what was later confirmed, that there would be some redeeming feature in most of those men.

'What do criminals look like?' In the first place, it has long been proved that the nineteenth century Italian, Cesare Lombroso, was mistaken in his theory of an anthropological criminal genus. Criminals can to some extent be grouped (and for the purposes of research have been), but there is no way of identifying them by their physical appearance.

At one of the first talks I gave outside the prison, I was illustrating this point. My illustration had an amusing sequel.

One of the professional staff of Wandsworth had asked me to talk to the young people of his church, and I had agreed with pleasure.

The hall contained a larger audience than I had expected, including older 'post'-teenagers of both sexes, with the staff member beaming encouragement from the back row.

When I came to the point that there was no such thing as a criminal face, I drew the attention of the audience to a mild, pleasant-faced man seated half-way up the hall at the middle aisle. 'For instance, that gentleman there,' said I, pointing to him, 'could easily just be out of Wandsworth after serving a sentence for False Pretences.'

I was trying to lead up to my friend, whom they all knew, just to play a little joke on him. However, my jest was held up for a few minutes as the audience laughed heartily, clapping and cheering. Puzzled at the reaction, and thinking, 'Surely it's not so funny as all *that*!' I continued, accusing my friend of perhaps being a pickpocket. At this there was further laughter, including a booming guffaw from my friend himself, but not so much as at my remarks on the stranger.

At the end of the lecture, when people came up to shake hands and talk to me, the strange gentleman was brought forward and introduced.

'This is the Reverend ———, our minister!'

The clergyman accepted my red-faced apology with a grin, and everyone around laughed again at the idea of their minister being a 'con' man.

The points I had made went home, however, and the audience gave a number of examples showing that they had had bitter experiences of men and women who had claimed to be other than they were.

'How did you come to get the job?' This question I found one of the most difficult to answer without sounding egoistic and pompous.

I replied to an advertisement in a well-known journal. The background was this. Prison welfare officers as they were then confusingly called and still are (Cf. footnote on page 23), were appointed as a result of a committee under the chairmanship of Sir Alexander Maxwell. This committee investigated the work of the various Discharged Prisoners' Aid societies in England and Wales, as the welfare state had by then, made so many statutory provisions for citizens, including prisoners and their families.

In 1953 the committee published its report, known as the Maxwell Report. The rôle of fairy god-father, hitherto played by the Discharged Prisoners' Aid society officer, who gave five shillings at the gate accompanied by an admonition not to get into trouble again, had not reduced recidivism and was in any case superseded by the work of the National Assistance Board and employment exchanges. The problem of crime was growing so acute, and the causes were much deeper than 5s. could treat or cure. The Maxwell Report recommended that trained social workers should be appointed full time in local prisons, to discuss with prisoners all their problems, social, material and otherwise. The social workers would prepare detailed case-histories on what the Maxwell Report called the 'special cases' and would refer them to the local Discharged Prisoners' Aid society with recommendations for further treatment. The prison welfare officiers with the rank and salary of probation officers and of Senior probation officers, for Senior prison welfare officers, were if trained and experienced in social work, to hold the position of professional advisers to the societies (Clause 107). It followed almost as a corollary that as our work grew we were also a useful source of reference and advice to anyone else interested in the rehabilitation of the discharged prisoner. It was hoped that the new service would appeal to probation officers.

It was several years before the Maxwell Report recommendations were put fully into effect. I came on the scene in September 1960, when there were more than sixty prison welfare officers in the country, of whom five were Senior prison welfare officers, covering the largest local prisons. I applied for two posts; one as P.W.O. in Wormwood Scrubs; the other as the sixth Senior post in Wandsworth; thinking as I wrote, that the latter appointment post would go to a man, Britain being a man's world. I did not then know that I was to enter yet another pioneer post, my third. However unfair it may seem, a woman applying for a position normally held by men has to have higher academic and other qualifications than the men applicants, and to have held higher executive and administrative posts.

I like to think, however, that personality plays as important a part as paper qualifications, or is even more important. I was widowed and a young mother, which perhaps gave me an understanding of problems which men regard differently or never sense. From early girlhood I had always had the almost physical ache to be of service to people and had certain codes of living strengthened by my background as a daughter of the manse, lawyer's wife and student for six years of philosophy, ethics and other social studies. I had to start everything from the bottom, even nursing, to gain training and experience.

In case all this sounds too grim and pompous, may I add that physical characteristics have had their influence. I have always been happy as a woman and felt that femininity should come first and career second. I love pretty and beautiful things. Being small, grey-eyed and blonde, I have usually appealed as the helpless little woman (as indeed I am inwardly). This I found probably my greatest weapon in winning the prison officers and the prisoners to my side. Without trying, I seemed to succeed in a way few of my male colleagues had so far been able to do. I also have a saving sense of humour, which in a position of such responsibility is as necessary as technical know-how. I was to need it. In certain taut situations I was saved by my wonderful welfare staff who, when I was angry or in despair at the obstacles I had to surmount, made me see the funny side of some of the effrontery we had to encounter.

I was therefore very surprised, immensely flattered and then sincerely humble when, before my short-list interview with the board of senior N.A.D.P.A.S.[2] officials and Prison Commissioners who were to examine candidates on July 18, 1960, I was asked by the General Secretary of N.A.D.P.A.S. at a meeting

[2] National Association of Discharged Prisoners' Aid Societies (Incorp.)

in his office on July 7th whether I would consider taking the senior appointment, if I was offered it. It was then I learned that I should be the first woman in this field, but, as the General Secretary persuasively pointed out, the Maxwell Report, which of course I had by this time read, did not specify that prison welfare officers had to be male. I agreed that if it was offered, I should accept the post, nervously suggesting that I hoped I should not remain the only woman in the service. When I replied on July 11th to the written offer I spent the weekend before the board interview with stage-fright symptoms at my boldness in facing such a challenge, the biggest in my life.

On the morning of Monday the 18th I dressed happily and confidently. At first I thought of wearing a very prim and proper felt hat, which usually depressed me. Every woman will know the type I mean, bought in a foolish moment of thrift which in the end is extravagance. It did nothing for me or for what looks I have, but it was 'suitable' for interviews. I looked glumly in the mirror, then thought: 'be blowed! I'm going to wear one of my pretty hats so that I can feel myself and forget about the impression I'm making! Besides, they might as well see me as I am, and if they don't like me, or think me frivolous, then the job isn't for me—not what I want.'

I like to think that my pretty straw hat (which I kept as a souvenir, being an unrepentant sentimentalist except in my professions), with its little gesture of defiance, tipped the scales in my favour with the group of important men round the table shooting questions at me. I know that, though inwardly I was shaking, it gave me the necessary self-confidence to answer their questions apparently competently.

Queries about my job and what it entailed cover so much that I shall try to answer them in a separate chapter. What I can do now is to clarify what prison welfare or social work is *not*.

On my second day in the prison Chief (Chief Officer) popped his head round the office door just as I was reading the morning mail and asked: 'The Rabbi wants to know,

Mrs. Trotter, if you can supply a ram's horn for the service on Saturday? It's their Feast of the Passover, and the prisoner who played his own is going out tomorrow.'

What a poser for a social worker and a Gentile at that! However, I smiled sweetly at Chief, tongue in cheek and replied: 'I'll scout around, Chief.'

I had not a clue as to what a ram's horn was, but I did not dare let Chief, of all the prison officers, know what a silly, useless creature this woman in the prison was. 'No place for a woman anyhow' I could almost hear him muttering.

I sat at my desk wondering how on earth I was going to produce this strange instrument for the Rabbi whom I had never even met. Then inspiration came. I remembered being introduced by the Governor the previous evening to a meeting of Prison Visitors. One of the visitors was Jewish, and he had seemed interested in, and sympathetic to, my appointment. Hastily I telephoned him at his office. He had given me his card with an offer to help any Jewish prisoner in Wandsworth. Very kindy, on hearing my request, he said I was to leave everything to him. I did.

The Rabbi got his ram's horn for the service, and my reputation with the prison staff was still safe! I never made enquiries as to how the instrument was sent into the prison. My belief that I was under trial by the prison staff was later confirmed by Chief's milder attitude and his comment weeks afterwards that he wouldn't have known how or where to find a horn and I must be very smart! I chuckled inwardly as I joked:

'All part of the service, Chief.'

A little less amusing, because of its source, was a very erroneous idea of our job. I had been working in Wandsworth about a year and was invited to the opening ceremony of a building which has to remain undescribed. The guest speaker was a senior magistrate. At the reception afterwards I asked one of my outside colleagues, a probation officer, if he would be kind enough to introduce me to this magistrate, because I wished to hear his views and thought he might be available to help us with the prisoners. Hitherto, I had not had the opportunity to apply to magistrates for help in this country.

On being told of my 'rank', this gentleman looked uninterestedly around after I had been left alone with him by my friend. Then he asked: 'And is your job to see that the prisoners keep their cells tidy and have decent meals?'

I replied demurely: 'Hardly.' I laughed silently at the image of myself as a sort of matron of a boys' school.

Thinking of some of my prisoners; 'Some schoolboys!'

The magistrate's attention was distracted by someone else. While I was left to wonder how many other magistrates in this country had not read the Maxwell Report and were unaware of our existence. Yet they were sentencing men to prison daily without knowledge of what social rehabilitation for the offender meant.

Nor were we, as some prisoners and staff thought, a cleaning service for suits for their discharge, nor amanuenses to write letters indiscriminately for them.

They were allowed only one carefully censored letter a month.

As to how the prisoners and staff reacted to a woman in the prison, I propose to answer that question in the next chapter.

Chapter III

REACTIONS IN WANDSWORTH PRISON

How did the staff and prisoners react to having a woman in their midst?

Let me take the reader into prison to study situations which arose from my first day until my departure two and a half years later.

In the first chapter I have given a picture of the background. In this chapter I hope to provide more details.

The main block, like those of a number of other Victorian prisons, is internally like a gigantic wheel with a polished metal grille on the floor of the central hall as the hub round which the Chief Officers stand whenever there is movement of men, which is frequently. Like the spokes of the wheel the various four-storeyed wings sprout from this centre with long corridors whose farthest reaches are shadowed in gloom. Staircases of metal and stone spiral upwards on each wing to the top landing. Between the wings on each storey is a wire mesh stretched across landings, which themselves have cells on either side. The grim purpose of the nets is to break the fall of any would-be suicide or to protect anyone on the ground floor from falling objects.

Round the hall are arranged various offices: the Chief's, the censors' and the medical room where men are examined before discharge and where others not ill enough for the hospital are seen daily by one of the medical officers. A glass box at the side of the hall acts as the quarters of the Centre Principal Officer who, like a sentry, never leaves this post of observation unmanned.

On the upper landings are various classrooms, where in the evenings prisoners receive instructions in numerous subjects from teachers of the Greater London Council (in my time

London County Council) under the supervision of a full-time resident Tutor Organiser. There too are the Roman Catholic chaplain's office and the chapels. Our office was on the second floor of B wing.

Over all towers the glass dome of the roof with some of the panes broken and others still bearing traces of wartime blackout paint. No amount of light-coloured paint dispels the gloom of this huge building, with steel-doored landings whose only light comes from electric bulbs twenty-four hours a day.

* * * *

To begin with, I had the powerful backing of the Governor's approval. In these initially hard days, I was indebted to him for his support, though we did not always see eye to eye on the rôle of the social workers in his prison. In another prison I might not have been so fortunate, as some of my colleagues found, especially if, as happened later, they were women.

Already interested and involved in prison after-care and rehabilitation, the Governor accepted me from the first day as one of his senior staff. He assured the Welfare Organiser, who brought me to Wandsworth to be introduced, that I should have the status and privileges of an Assistant Governor, like the others heads of departments, the medical officers, the psychologists and the chaplains.

The Organiser must have breathed a sigh of relief at this Governor's attitude. Another Governor in my initial training had shown his disapproval of the whole project by writing at his desk with his head lowered the whole time he was addressing me and firing questions. This technique is usually calculated to make the person interviewed nervous and aware of disapproval as well as impressed with the importance of the interviewer.

When it was the turn of the other potential prison welfare officer, my junior but a man, to be interviewed, this Governor chatted politely to him about music, turning his profile to me and the Senior prison welfare officer who had brought us to meet him.

I was neither nervous nor impressed by such ungentlemanliness. I knew I had to take a firm stand against such treatment if my sex was to be accepted by other Governors, or even perhaps by this man. The next day, I refused to attend a teaparty in the Governor's office which he had arranged for our benefit. The Senior P.W.O. was frantic, as he had the unpleasant task of explaining my absence to the Governor. He begged me to change my mind, but I held firm. I must be one of the few in prison history who has dared to snub so powerful a person as a prison Governor! In normal circumstances I should not have troubled to show my displeasure, but on this occasion I felt it necessary to establish that women were entitled to the same respect as their male colleagues.

On my return to Head Office in London I reported my action, fully expecting to be told I was not 'suitable'. I explained my motives and offered to resign if the officials thought I had been wrong. Fortunately, I had been able to explain before the Governor reported. They agreed with me, and I heard no more of the matter. Weeks later, when I was on friendly terms with the Governor of Wandsworth I asked him if he had been told of my action. He grinned and said that, before my arrival his colleague had telephoned him

I had little difficulty with either the Deputy Governor or the Assistant Governors. Within a few weeks I was laughing, joking and discussing with all but two Assistant Governors the problems of prison administration and reform. I had their full co-operation in dealing with the prisoner's problems, and they soon seemed to think that the idea of a social worker in the prison was more sinister that the reality.

Naturally, we did not always agree at first, but our differences, which were few, were amicable, and, as time went on and I established myself in their good opinion, they gradually came to accept my experience. Only the two Assistant Governors refused to accept 'interference' from a social worker, especially a woman. They wished to 'rehabilitate' their prisoners independently of the official welfare department. As the scheme had had the blessing of the Home Office before my appointment, there was little I could do except to protest to N.A.D.P.A.S., (National Association of Discharged Prisoners' Aid Societies), who could not do much either. I counted myself lucky that such an attitude in this vast prison was rare, and I got down to the rest of the work.

Gradually the hostile staff imitated some of the ideas I had put into effect in the rest of the prison. It amused my staff and me, as well as numerous prison officers, that while the hostile officials were decrying my presence and work, and were often untruthful in their tales about us, they still imitated my introduction of 'Associates' to befriend discharged prisoners and my pre-release classes.

They then proposed to extend their scheme to the main prison. This neither I nor the prison officers wished, as it was a duplication of our work and not as efficiently carried out, since they had neither the resources nor the authority with outside agencies which we had. So I persuaded N.A.D.P.A.S. that there could not be two queens in one hive. The Prison Officers' Association took independent action, and the scheme was confined where it could do little harm.

My experience as a medical social worker opened the door for me in both the Senior Medical Officer's department and the Senior Psychologist's office. It was a novelty for them to have a medical social worker with nursing training, and I was asked on my second day if I would be their 'almoner'. I felt honoured and also relieved. Yet another hurdle was overcome. My visits to the hospital and talks with the staff, both medical and nursing, are among my happiest memories of Wandsworth.

The Church of England chaplain was a grey-faced, anxious-looking man harassed with overwork. Hugh Klare[1], whose book I did not study until I began research for this book, comments:

'Not all chaplains have welcomed the gradual development of social work in prison. Education and welfare used to be the exclusive preserve of the Church, and chaplains would often

[1] Hugh Klare *Anatomy of Prison* (Hutchinson 1960).

use these as a way of making contact with prisoners, and, from this point of vantage, seek to reach or awaken religious feelings. Moreover, some chaplains did and do consider it part of their Christian duty to have concern for the whole man and not just for his soul.'

I set out to win over the chaplain and his staff, encouraging my colleagues to do the same. Though he did not at first see it, we were talking the same language and we needed him. I gave him a copy of a thesis I had prepared, and this was the beginning of a more understanding attitude. I had weekly informal discussions with him on plans for solving particular problems, and he agreed that for two sets of people to treat the same men for the same difficulties was of little use to either the men or our departments. The men, too, were inclined to set one advice against the other—like a housewife comparing supermarket prices. We made full use of the material help which was in the chaplain's hands. Gradually he saw that we each had something to offer the other, and that we were all working towards the same goal, which was that as many men as possible under our care should not return to prison.

Ultimately we became the best of friends. One day he remarked in our office that he was glad the Welfare department was there, because now he got more time to expand his spiritual duties. He saw that giving up what Hugh Klare called his 'initial lever' did not lower his status in the prisoners' eyes. One of the reasons for this may have been that, knowing our own limitations, we always referred to him men who seemed to need spiritual help or who wanted his assistance in discussing questions like joining the Church, being married or having their children baptised.

I felt I was really accepted by the senior staff when they, including the chaplain, started calling me 'Sallie' instead of the more formal 'Mrs. Trotter', I was 'Sallie' even to the new Governor who arrived a year after my appointment. I had not asked to be called by my first name, though all the

35

male staff addressed each other by theirs. My cup of happiness was full![2]

This friendly relationship with senior staff was all very well, but what of the attitude of the prison officers? Before I entered Wandsworth I had been much more nervous about the reaction of these men than about those of the prisoners or even of the Governor.

During my Induction course in another prison, my colleague had jokingly informed me, not without some truth, that it was not the Governor who ruled the prison but the Chief of the officers and the Centre Principal officer (the officer who sits in the centre and directs the movement of prisoners and prison officers to different areas).

When I was a naval nursing sister, attached during the war to a base hospital, I had had in my wards a Chief Petty Officer (responsible for the male nurses) to whose opinion we officers listened with respect, even the Surgeon Commanders, so I knew what my colleague was trying to tell me.

From the beginning of my life in Wandsworth, therefore, I set out to gain the respect and co-operation of these officers, for I knew that, if they were actively hostile to our work, their 'men' would refuse to fetch prisoners for us or to hand over the prisoners' applications. To have brandished the threat of reporting to the Governor would have only made matters worse. Yet though in two years we had a series of Chief Officers, each one was without exception, a very fine man, expert in his job and just as anxious to avoid friction as I was. Each knew that this would create just the atmosphere inside the walls which trouble-seeking prisoners would seek to exploit.

My prison welfare officers and I set ourselves to learn all we could about Standing Orders, Security and Prison Regulations —I sought the Chief's advice on all such matters. We were later helped by being sent by N.A.D.P.A.S.[3] to Wakefield

[2] I learned from prison officers too that some prisoners talked of me to each other as 'our Sallie' though never to my face. They also had a rather charming nickname for me.

[3] National Association of Discharged Prisoners' Aid Societies.

Staff College on a conference course. This is where the prison officers are themselves trained, and there we learned from Training Officers all the complicated ramifications of running, and working in, a maximum security prison.

In Wandsworth we were careful to take no chances. Though I had the privilege, both by the terms of my appointment and by receiving the keys of an Assistant Governor from the Governor, to open prisoners' cells in the main prison, I never did so. I always requested the Principal Officer of the wing to ask an officer to do this for me and to have the man talk to me either on the landing or in my office. I had three reasons for this. Firstly, it reassured the prison staff about my safety. Secondly, in a prison where the majority of the men were locked for hours at a time three in a cell with no comforts, I felt it would be an unpropitious start to an interview about a social problem disturbing to a man, if I embarrassed him by walking in when he was crouched in a corner on a 'potty', literally with his pants down! As I had been a nurse, it would have caused me little embarrassment, but I could visualise the man's resentment and humiliation. These I should have had to overcome before beginning an interview, and it is extremely doubtful if I should have succeeded. When every second is valuable to an overworked department, this would never have done. Nor was it any use to knock on an inch-thick steel door, hoping for an answer. Thirdly, as a woman, I wished to give neither prisoners nor staff any cause for talk which could harm my reputation and hence my work. None of these difficulties, of course, applied to my two male colleagues, who could unlock doors and talk to the men in their cells.

After the senior officers had approved us, the prison officers quickly became our friends and colleagues. Many a time I was moved when they said: 'Anything for you, Mrs. Trotter.' To my initially incredulous delight they showed they meant it. When male welfare officers from other prisons came to see me about men with whom they wished to keep in contact, they used to wonder how I managed to have prisoners lined up for me without any trouble. They remarked a little sadly that they were left to fend for themselves in their prisons and to fetch men themselves, which of course took up valuable time. Of course I used to laugh off their questions and say it was because they did not have such long eyelashes as I to flutter at the officers. I hope however it was because I genuinely liked and respected most of the officers. One gave me a clue: 'We were expecting a superior attitude when we heard all about you before you came, but you treated us as equals and with friendliness.'

The prison officers, so often called 'warders' by press and outsiders and 'screws' by the prisoners are frequently maligned and misjudged men. Many of them are as dedicated in their desire to help the prisoners to 'go straight next time' as any social worker or do-gooder. They are unarmed except for a leather truncheon, but the way they controlled hundreds of dangerous and violent men gained my respect, accustomed as I had been in Canada to seeing armed guards in the male prisons.

* * * *

What of my own staff?

On my arrival, this consisted of two prison welfare officers, both men, and two girl typists. These, as female staff, were stationed well outside the prison itself in a small office, a converted muniment room on the ground floor of the chaplain's house. All the other secretaries belonging to the Governor's, Steward's[4] and Treasurer's staff were also outside the prison proper in the Administration entrance hall offices, though they were inside the external walls of the Main block. To reach my clerical staff we had a ten-minute journey from our office, and we sometimes had to spend as much as twenty minutes getting there. (There was no telephone in the typists' office.) Our only means of communication, other than leaving the prison, was to telephone the Accountant's office, but as this was like all others, a very busy department we seldom did so, being cautious to keep everybody's goodwill.

The reason it took us so long to reach our clerical office was simply that we were working in a maximum-security prison,

[4] Now known as Administration Officer.

and each communicating gateway and door within the prison had to be unlocked and relocked carefully. The Main Gate through which we had to pass to get in or out was the responsibility of a Principal Officer known as the 'Gate Officer'. Not even the Governor could go through except by the action of this officer, and if, as frequently happened, he was talking on the telephone or answering the queries of prisoners' relatives or admitting a truck, everyone had to wait until he had done. We accepted this as necessary, but it was frustrating and a serious drawback to our work. Later I felt it should be avoidable and I knew something would have to be done as soon as possible.

I had therefore, two secretaries and three prison welfare officers, including myself, with whom to handle the 'after-care' of over 2000 men annually from the day of admission till well after discharge from Wandsworth! I did not need a time and motion study expert to tell me that to tackle this task I had to make the best use of what facilities I had and fight for more and better ones.

I was fortunate in my two colleagues, though the health of one worried us and created a constant threat to my efforts to improve the service we were trying to offer the prison. Both men, having had some practical experience in social work, were studying for their Diplomas in Social Studies. How they or anyone else thought they could stand up to the strain of such hard work I did not know. We needed the constitutions of Olympic champions. With such a vast effort to organize, everyone had to be on the job all the time. There was no forty-hour week for us. I found, too that one colleague had worked himself, as a selfless, practising Christian, before my arrival, to breaking point by being unable to say 'No' to anyone. The result was that the department had become a sort of dry-cleaning agency, a second-hand clothes shop, a shoe-repairing, messenger and letter-writing service, a store of the prisoners' clothing and property. In fact it performed almost everything except its true rôle, which was to supply social casework. We were even expected by prisoners and staff alike to act as flower-purchasers for prisoners' wives!

Many of the tasks which properly belonged to other bodies and departments inside and outside the prison had been imposed on us, with the idea that this was 'welfare's' job and the other departments were overworked already. Everyone had this mental indigestion because of the gross overcrowding of offenders in the prison. The result was that social work as such could not avoid being other than virtually nonexistent. The two prison welfare officers had worked out an amicable arrangement between them of seeing such men as they could. If one of the social workers was not available, the other saw the men and if the files were not on his own desk, he would find them on the other's or outside in the secretaries' office. As the girls were not permitted inside the prison, the two men did their own filing whenever they could spare time. The reader can guess how often that was.

One of these men was quiet of speech, with a shy smile which was often misinterpreted by officers and prisoners as a sneer. Wild rumours flew round the prisoners that he was an 'ex-dick' (detective). With his size and shoulders he looked not unlike one. I had to spend some time beating down this rumour and with time I was able to talk to him about his manner and to suggest that he tried to conquer his shyness and thaw out. He might, I suggested, find his work easier as a result. He took my advice, and gradually as my own staff altered, he became very popular with them, full of humour and laughter at which I should hardly have guessed when I first arrived. As long as he was in Wandsworth he remained my right-hand man. He found however that his interests lay more in the home conditions of the men and later transferred to a post which gave him greater opportunities for field work. We all missed him, but perhaps I most of all.

*   *   *   *

How did the prisoners react to having a woman in the prison?

Apart from some initial misunderstandings of our rôle and our work, the prisoners behaved, to my relief, much better than I had hoped. In fact, I never ceased to be deeply touched by the respect and care for me which these so-called hardened criminals showed.

Almost in the first week one of my colleagues reported that two men in a cell in the main prison had been asking what I was like. They had urged him: 'You will take care of her, won't you? There are some pretty desperate types in here.' In over two years, I found only three men in that prison whom I had to reprimand.

From the beginning I treated those men as men, as I had done in Canada. I did not address a prisoner as No. 1111, but as Mr. Smith, and I called some of the younger ones by their Christian names. In our office, no man had to stand to attention, literally on the mat, at a given distance from our desks, as was the case when prisoners appeared before the prison staff. Each man sat in a chair, relaxed and informal, and was permitted to smoke. This might sound to a disciplinarian a breach of prison authority, but, as the Governor himself realised, such treatment is essential to create the atmosphere of mutual confidence leading to effective help in rehabilitation.

Time and again, too, we found that prisoners preferred to talk to a woman about their problems, especially if these were of a domestic nature. They felt, they said, that, as a woman and a mother, I should be better able to understand their wives' attitudes. I made a great effort not to undermine that confidence.

Occasionally, when I had my own office, separated from the Welfare department room, where my colleagues and secretaries sat, I had to deal with a man who had broken down either before or after we discussed his problem. It is a shattering experience at any time to see and hear a man weep, but in a prison setting it was poignant and harrowing.

Whenever a man was distressed I said: 'That's right. Have a good cry. It'll do you good. Have you a handkerchief?'

I would hand him a bundle of paper tissues from a box I had learned to keep on my desk for such situations, and after a vigorous blow of his nose he would apologise for his outburst. 'I'd never cry in front of a man!' he would say, and I believed him and felt very humble each time it was said.

The men who put on a tough exterior before even my male prison welfare officers or the chaplain felt they could release their pent-up emotions in my presence just because I was a woman and would not think them 'cissie'.

The first time it happened was with a really hard 'professional' robber. I told the man, who was ashamed and full of apologies, not to be sorry. A telephone call on the spot about the health of his child, who was in hospital, reassured him and he went back to his cell in a more tranquil frame of mind. Each day I either saw him or left a message as to his child's improving condition.

The bewildered Wing Officer amused me some weeks later by asking if I had hypnotised Joe, because for the rest of his sentence he was polite to the officers and no longer a violent trouble-maker. As the secret was Joe's and mine, I merely grinned and replied: 'Maybe.'

My presence was a safety valve, of which the prison staff somehow gradually became aware. The Governor and Wing Officers would occasionally refer a man to me in the hope that I could release him from his anxieties, and so disciplinary action could be avoided. Such a prisoner was either becoming violent as a result of his inability to solve his difficulties from inside the prison, or he was showing symptoms which might lead to his breaking prison discipline. Without help he might bang on his cell door and shout, or assault a prison officer or fellow prisoner, or even take the desperate step of trying to make a 'breakout'.

The men soon learned that the social workers, by virtue of their training, knew of more statutory and voluntary agencies, employers etc. and had more influence with them than anyone else inside or outside the prison. They discovered that, by applying to one of us for help, they could remove many of their difficulties without resort to violence, with its accompanying and inevitable embittering punishment.

*   *   *   *

As our work grew and the men realized that we were not their enemies, they found in me a safety valve of another kind. There is a human wish in all but the worst of us to give as well as to take, and now we became the recipients, as well as welfare officers. Those who had been helped by me began to show their gratitude by making little gifts for me and for my office—leather blotters for our desks, a leather case for my desk diary, felt dogs, paintings and pencil drawings done in the Art class in the evenings. My desk was always fragrant with flowers sent by discharged prisoners.

One spring evening a man who was still serving his sentence, but was on parole from the prison hostel, came to my office holding two bunches of daffodils, one for his wife, whom he was going home to see at the week-end, and the other for me. To my surprise he handed the bouquet over with the words: 'You've earned it, Mrs. Trotter.' Yet what I had done for this man seemed to me such a little thing.

On a day when I was feeling rather depressed, because we certainly had our formidable obstacles, a young West Indian apologetically handed to me a Christmas card in the 'centre', as the main hall was called, saying humbly that he wished he could have given me a 'real one' but that this was the only material he had. I looked down at my hand, into which he had furtively tucked it, being afraid he would get into trouble with one of the officers for passing a 'kite'[5]. There I saw depicted on toilet paper a golden Star of Bethlehem, above a manger containing a baby, all drawn with wax crayons, and the words 'Merry Xmas to Mrs. Trotter' printed in a childish hand at the foot of the 'card'.

From that moment and throughout the day I was so happy and proud that I could have sung aloud. I treasured that humble card more than any elaborate shop purchase glittering with tinsel. In the evening I again met the prisoner and told him how his card had cheered me and made my day. He went off, beaming happily, his white teeth gleaming in his shiny black face.

I must, I think, be the only woman who can proudly show a dressing-table set of brush, mirror and comb, presented to her by prisoners out of their own savings. It was given to me by the men of the hostel on the occasion of my remarriage. Each had only £1 weekly pocket money and the sacrifice of

[5] An illicit note handed from one prisoner to another.

canteen and cigarette money was considerable. They had asked the Hostel's Principal Officer to make the purchase for them, after having obtained the consent of the Governor. I was very touched. The Governor and the officers gave me a present, too, a barometer which has a place of honour in our hall; and each time I pour coffee from my Pyrex jug I am reminded of the happy times I had with my own little staff, who made that gift.

If my presence did nothing else in that grim fortress, I like to think it had a softening influence on both officers and men. I was told by high authority that swearing among the prison officers had caused the Prison Commission considerable anxiety. After my arrival, I was aware that it existed, but, the officers had the courtesy not to swear in my presence at least. Though I do not like it, I would have understood swearing by prison officers, for I am sure that it is as much a release for many of them as shouting and banging cell doors is to the frustrated prisoners.

As for the prisoners, I made some of them think as they had never been able to think before. Whether this aided their eventual rehabilitation is not for me to say. There is no easy road to this goal for either guide or seeker.

Of course, not everything was as rosy as this chapter may have made things seem. My picture would not be truthful if I did not show something of the other side of the coin.

Chapter IV

PRISON WELFARE

What is prison welfare? This question is not answered easily or briefly. There are so many ramifications, so many disciplines, so many people involved.

The question was asked me often, and, though I could give some reply in a half-hour or hour's lecture, I was never satisfied. This book is the product of that dissatisfaction. I hope each chapter may show a different facet of this most complicated of the social services.

In this chapter I propose merely to give a general picture of most of what is involved, limiting my description to adult prisons only. Social welfare, as distinct from prison welfare, which is still in its infancy, is, of course, almost as old as the history of man himself. Archaeology shows that ancient empires had systems of welfare and schemes of health and hygiene that were enforced by religious or political laws. Nearer home, social welfare as we know it today grew up side by side with the evils of the Industrial Revolution, supplementing many of the old Elizabethan Poor Laws.

To anyone interested in social economics, political economy or economic history, all social studies inseparable from the history of the growth of the Welfare State in Britain, there is a wealth of literature available. What is however particularly noticeable is the much slower growth of literature about practical social reform in prisons in this country—as compared with others, particularly the United States.

As this is not a historical study, I cannot go into the development of welfare in the prisons of England and Wales, but there is nothing new in the idea. As soon as the theory that imprisonment should not be purely punitive but reformative, was postulated by Elizabeth Fry and John Howard, modern prison welfare began, and here let me add a very important comment. Some people think that such social work is coddling the wrong-doer. Let me assure the reader that it is more difficult for a man to shed a lifetime of crime than it is for him to be born. Birth is involuntary, but rebirth has to be of his own volition, battling at first with strong inclination and temptation. The impetus must come from within himself. All we who work with him can do is to stand by; sometimes with a metaphorical pair of forceps for the delivery!

Prison welfare can be regarded as something limited in function, applied principally to the needs of the prisoners while they are incarcerated. It can be a concern for their food, their living conditions, their clothing, their opportunities for religious observance, what they do with their leisure hours. Or it can apply to their requirements after they have been released, and to help them to find a place to live, a job, money. A somewhat wider view would include assistance in a man's anxieties about his family.

Modern penology ought however to adopt the larger concept discussed in philosophy. Each prisoner should be considered as an individual with mental and moral, as well as material and economic, requirements.

Even with large numbers therefore, a satisfactory form of welfare for prisoners must include work and education projects which are, together with highly skilled psychological and social-casework techniques, geared towards the man's future place in society. This outlook is becoming more generally adopted as most likely to produce lasting results. As I hope to show in a later section, prison welfare—or rather prison social work to use the more correct term—prison policy and after-care cannot be isolated from one another. They are a partnership towards a common end, the rehabilitation of an offender and his acceptance into society.

This brings us to a brief look at the many people involved and interested in prison welfare. I do not think there is any other profession which has such a variety of applicants and personnel. This is due partly to its strong emotional appeal, partly to the vagueness of function mentioned above.

Yet it is just this variety which creates confusion in the mind of the public, with its growing awareness of what is going on in all forms of social welfare. This awareness led to the Young-husband Report[1] which sets down minimum and maximum standards of training in social work, and which may yet be implemented, and applied to prisons.

There are the humanitarians who wish to supply the material needs of prisoners. These include business men, members of various church organizations, recognized voluntary societies and others. They can and do fill a vital rôle in rehabilitation of the offender. Their success is greater if they realise their limitations, and understand that they are part of a larger team, which has persons with more specialized training who ought to be available to advise them.

Sir William Clarke-Hall wrote about the qualities of a probation officer:

'To enter upon this most difficult work equipped only with a religious or humanitarian desire to "do good" and without devoting careful study and much thought to the subject is not calculated to produce a good probation officer.'

These words might also be applied to welfare or social workers handling prisoners' problems; for, like the probation officer, they are dealing with sentenced offenders, but with people who often have much more complicated behaviour difficulties than probationers.

Quite early this need for some kind of skill was recognised. Hence the prison chaplain's traditional rôle, which combined religious duties with welfare work, because he was sometimes the only qualified professional man, apart from the medical officer, within the prison precincts. Recently in some instances the prison psychologist or psychiatrist has been involved in the same idea. He is regarded as an adviser on not only psychological problems but on those of social and economic welfare, and has accepted this rôle.

[1] Report of the Working Party on Social Workers in the Local Authority Health and Welfare Services, 1959.

More and more, however, in many countries has grown up an awareness that social pathology requires a different type of training from that given in divinity college or school of psychology or medicine; hence the increasing demand for trained social workers. These are expected to have not only wide and varied practical experience but a specially disciplined mind and personality and a training in casework techniques which only a university can supply.

Yet even with trained workers confusion arises, as different standards of academic and practical training are provided by different universities. In some a Diploma or Certificate in either Social Science or Social Studies is a non-graduate course involving mostly academic, and few practical subjects. In others a Diploma in either course is awarded, quite correctly, only on the basis of a post-graduate year of specialised study. The student must present a thesis and spend many months of practical work in varied fields and several towns. The degree course prior to this consists of subjects relevant to social studies; perhaps philosophy, psychology, moral philosophy, economic history or political economy. (I count myself fortunate that I was accepted by a university which demanded this higher standard.) An M.A. in English or French would not make an eligible candidate.

Eileen Younghusband expresses it thus:

'There is a body of knowledge to be learned, skills to be acquired and wisdom to begin in training and mellow through the years of professional practice which distinguishes the trained caseworker from the "good, sensible woman with an all round experience of life who has travelled about the world a bit and who is widely but not in my view wisely believed to be 'just as, if not more valuable' than the specialized social worker."'

This definition takes no account of the fact that the social worker may himself have 'travelled about the world a bit'. Moreover, such definitions do not quite clarify the confusion which exists about the qualified social worker. Various shades of academic and practical experience are often classified to-gether as if they were all of the same value. This is most obvious perhaps in advertisements for professional or official appointments. Here is a typical example: —

Chief Welfare Officer————Co. Council
Male or Female—Degree *or* Diploma in Social Studies/Science *or* practical experience, *or* relevant knowledge. Salary £1200—rising to £1400 p.a. Starting salary at level of experience and/or age.
Welfare Officer. Qualifications as above. Salary £850 rising to £1200 p.a.

Can one wonder that professional services cannot recruit the best in the field? Or that there is a brain drain to countries which show appreciation of hard study and experience by giving a bonus to every set of qualifications after one's name? In Canada I had three bonuses to the salaries for the posts I held.

With such a complicated set-up in Britain, it is little wonder that the lay person is often mistaken and confused.

*　　　*　　　*　　　*

There are three forms of welfare for prisoners.

1) *Statutory Aid on Discharge.* This is concerned with issuing travel warrants, subsistence money for a journey to the nearest Labour exchange and clothing so that a man goes out of prison respectably clad. These duties are the direct concern of the Governor's prison staff. The social workers only report a man's needs.

2) *Voluntary Aid on Discharge.* This applied, when I came to Wandsworth in 1960, to all men serving sentences of less than four years. The Criminal Justice Act, 1961, when fully imple-mented will extend compulsory after-care to include many formerly given voluntary aid.
Compulsory after care will cover:

    (a) men serving a term of four years or more,

49

(b) men serving a term of six months or more, who have served at least one previous sentence of three months or more or a sentence of corrective training, preventive detention or borstal training,

(c) men serving a sentence of six months or more, who were under the age of twenty-six at the commencement of their sentences.

The Government White Paper, *The Adult Offender*[2], reports that since 1964

'the transfer of the Local Aid Societies' responsibility for after-care has been proceeding smoothly. Of the 36 local Discharged Prisoners' Aid Societies in existence at the time of the publication of the Advisory Council's Report[3], 28 have now handed over their after-care responsibilities to some 60 probation committees and it is expected that the transfer will be very nearly complete by April 1966[4].'

The White Paper also announced that the prison-welfare service was now to be integrated with the Probation and Aftercare service, 'and in future all Prison Welfare Officers will be Probation Officers on secondment.'

3) *Prison Welfare itself.* For this officers are appointed under the terms of the Maxwell Report as trained social workers employed inside the prisons for three purposes:

a) 'to pick out those prisoners who are most willing and likely to benefit from friendship and assistance after their discharge.'
b) 'to help those prisoners during the period of their imprisonment by making enquiries on their behalf, about family matters or other matters which are causing them anxiety: to do what they can to mitigate the numerous difficulties which beset a man or woman whose social ties have all been suddenly

[2] *The Adult Offender*, Home Office, Dec. 1965, Cmnd. 2852, H.M. Stationery Office.
[3] *The Organisation of After-care. Report of the Advisory Council on the Treatment of Offenders*—Home Office, 1963.
[4] H.M. Stationery Office.Now completed.

snapped by a sentence of imprisonment; and by such means to establish with the prisoner a relationship of confidence'

c) 'and on the basis of the knowledge gained by such a relationship to prepare case-histories of selected prisoners and constructive plans for their assistance after discharge for submission to the Society to whose care they will be released.'

A tall order for the small number of prison social workers at present in England and Wales!

In Wandsworth we recommended, (a) 'special cases' initially to the local Discharged Prisoners' Aid Societies; but as our contacts with other professional social workers in statutory and voluntary societies increased, we referred our 'special cases' directly to them, to probation officers, medical social workers, local-authority social workers and so on.

The men of (b) were called 'welfare applications'. They asked their Wing Officers daily, by means of special forms, for permission to see their welfare officer.

The (c) prisoners were closely connected with the (a) front, and we prepared case-histories on them.

All other men serving over three months we saw one month before their release to discuss their plans after discharge. We had to see those serving for less than three months, unless they were 'special cases', only at the sitting of the Discharge Board, as the former Discharged Prisoners' Aid Society officer used to do. This was necessary because of the overwhelming caseloads. As, however, between us we knew each man in the prison, we were generally able to assess when such short-sentence men needed extra attention, and then we saw them with 'welfare applications.'

*   *   *   *

We gradually acquired within the prison the reputation of being a speedy source of reference. We were of use to not only the prisoners but to the prison senior staff with their problems about what action to take on certain men. Often an offer from us to do what we called a 'Supervised welfare visit' relieved the Governor or his Deputy of the need to order disciplinary action which they were anxious not to take. This involved interviewing, for example a man and his wife in a private office with no prison officer present. Officers, of course were present at the usual visits in the 'visiting boxes' in which we were not involved.

I was not unnaturally proud that we had established among both prisoners and staff a reputation for reliability and sincerity. When, as fortunately happened seldom, we could not help, we confessed this honestly, pointing out that this was not because we were unwilling but because we had not the resources.

In December 1960 I introduced into the prison 'Associates' from the Blackfriars Settlement. This was a revolutionary step which the National Association of Discharged Prisoners' Aid Societies had initiated with the Warden and staff of the Settlement. The Settlement had been formerly the Women's University Settlement in Blackfriars where I had received part of my training as a social-work student. N.A.D.P.A.S., together with the reconstituted Blackfriars Settlement, had gathered together a group of volunteers from all walks of life who wanted to help in this work of after-care. N.A.D.P.A.S. prepared a leaflet for their guidance, and the Settlement inaugurated a series of classes.

The greatest contribution made by those Associates was that they had no connection with prison or with social work. They were ordinary citizens who were to play their part in restoring the discharged prisoner to ordinary life in the community. This was of especial value if by his criminal life an ex-prisoner had lost all outside contacts. The Associate would be there at the prison gate to be a genuine friend to the man, helping him over the rough patches which confronted him on his release.

We found in our pre-discharge interviews that a considerable number of men were in just this isolated situation. These men, lonely and bitter, often committed further crimes either for lack of a friendly contact or because they turned back to the world of criminals, the only persons who would accept them.

At Wandsworth we therefore considered that the Black-friars Settlement offered something of value hitherto un-available. There were a few flaws to begin with. Some Associates misunderstood their function, thought they were unofficial social workers, and did not refer social problems to the Warden or the prison social worker. However, these were gradually ironed out amicably.

*   *   *   *

In March 1961, after many preliminary enquiries and discussions with prisoners, with the Governor and with the Tutor Organiser, I commenced a series of after-care Pre-discharge classes. These were much appreciated by the prisoners. Some attended for two 'terms'. Later, too, the Blackfriars Associates took part by attending the lectures. Afterwards they held small group discussions in our office with the men whom they had 'adopted'.

In time, as our more intensive and detailed plans for the men's discharges developed, the committees of the local Discharged Prisoners' Aid Societies realized that their officers were more urgently needed to do outside work than to work in prison. We asked them to make home visits and after-care arrangements, following the recommendations of the Maxwell Report. So the committees ceased to come to the prison, and this gave me another morning and afternoon which I much needed for pre-discharge interviews.

Prisoners not unnaturally had a great many domestic and marital problems. These were, as I have already mentioned, often alleviated by our Special supervised welfare visits If I had had more staff, this valuable part of our work would certainly have been increased. We did the best we could in the time we had.

Another difficult problem in pre-discharge interviews became easier as time went on. This was the question of employment on discharge. Previously, prisoners had had only the representative of the Ministry of Labour from the local labour exchange to provide prospective jobs on release. His services were valuable, especially to a man who lived outside London, for then the agent could refer him by correspondence to the employment exchange of the town to which he was going, but the help was limited.

My television interview, shortly after my appointment, interested a number of employers, who offered to take ex-prisoners on their release. My pre-discharge classes also attracted employers, who came individually to talk to the men or appeared on a panel with other speakers.[6]

Other sources of employment were the Prison visitors some of whom were, or knew, employers willing to take on the discharged prisoner. The Blackfriars Settlement, the New Bridge Society, N.A.D.P.A.S., which had a social worker who had built up a register of employers, and the after-care officers of the Discharged Prisoners' Aid Societies who also began to provide several employer contacts, helped us as well. Our net was spreading wider with each month.

Set amidst the disciplinarian and administrative background of the prison was the most important and interesting part of our work—the actual interviews and discussions of the men's problems. It goes without saying that a man's rehabilitation began from the day he entered the prison. The Reception Board, where a social worker sat beside the Deputy Governor and the Chief, provided our first contact with him. Unless his difficulties were immediate and causing him great anxiety, we let him have twenty-four to forty-eight hours to settle into the prison routine. A willing and efficient Principal Officer on the reception or Induction wing—the wing where new admissions were sent—informed the incoming prisoners of our existence and prepared a list of those who wished to see me. This was brought over each morning to the 'Main' to be collected by one of my secretaries. Later, I initiated a series of weekly afternoon meetings, taken by a colleague, to let the men ask questions about problems which were perturbing them. These meetings were later found difficult to fit into

[6] Appendix I.

the prison routine, and we discontinued them, returning to my weekly visits.

From the Reception board on, as long as any man was in Wandsworth, our assistance and advice were available. Six weeks to one month prior to discharge we discussed with each man serving a sentence of over three months his plans for re-entering the civilian community. For almost a year we had at first struggled to see each man, even if he was in for only ten days for drunkenness. Presently, however, as our work expanded and attempts at rehabilitation of the special cases took up more and more of our time, often several months with one individual, we had to husband our meagre resources. A selection had to begin somewhere, and, I decided that the most suitable material (c) cases of the Maxwell Report, would be found among those serving longer sentences.

For the remainder, we made routine discharge arrangements similar to those formerly made by the D.P.A. officer. They were seen by the labour exchange official. Applications for National Assistance were made, if necessary, and they were fitted out with clothes. This outfitting became tedious work with the vagrants and drunks or 'copperkits' as they were known in prison slang. This came from the fact that their clothes on admission were often so filthy, even verminous, that they had to be destroyed in the prison boilers. Sometimes, too, I warned the D.P.A. officers, who were at first responsible for the supply of clothing to voluntary discharge men (i.e. men not on statutory parole or licence), that these drunks would go out in a set of replacements, carrying some of their old clothes (unless they were 'copperkits') in a bundle under their arms. A week or so later they would reappear in their old clothes, having in the meantime pawned the D.P.A. outfits to buy drink.

With such men, we had to show commonsense and face reality. They were not the stuff of which the Maxwell Report 'special cases' were made.

*   *   *   *

An excerpt from our annual report in 1962, the last I

prepared before I left, may give the reader some idea of the gargantuan task which faced three social workers and three secretaries.

'The following tables show the day to day work of the Welfare Dept.'

Receptions	Discharges	Responsibility of local D.P.A.S.	Responsibility of C.A.C.A.[8]	Responsibility of Borstal After-Care
3901	2273	2203	58 (seen by Central After-Care Officer)	12

1) *Applications*—5513. All dealt with. Many for the collection of property from "left luggage offices" or redeeming of suits from pawn shops; in a fair number of instances we were able to alleviate the men's anxiety and their wives' distress over debts by contacting H.P. firms, Gas & Electricity Boards etc. In very few cases did such companies refuse to take a sympathetic view.— With men serving long sentences, however, there is no doubt that the lightening of a burden of debt on the wives' shoulders, even if temporary, helped the wives to endure their remaining many problems.

2) *Supervised Welfare Visits*—155. The main topics discussed in these were housing, the children, economic and marital difficulties (especially reconciliation).

In addition, 264 home visits were paid by various organisations and persons, who later came to discuss with the prison social workers, the problems which confronted the families.

3) *Home Visit Reports*	W.V.S.	100
	Royal London & Sussex D.P.A. Societies	144
	Others; Probation officers, medical social workers, health visitors etc.	20
	Total	264

[7] Annual Report for the Year ended 31st December, 1962. Welfare Dept. H.M. Prison, Wandsworth.
Central After-Care Association.

Letters received by Welfare Dept. on behalf of the prisoners	2800
Letters sent out	2250
Telephone calls received	3000
„ „ (internal & external) made	3400

4) *Pre-Release and After-Care*

Of 2203 men discharged for the year 1962, 196 were Special Cases. This figure includes 10 compulsive alcoholics referred to St. Luke's Rehabilitation Centre; 38 men referred to Blackfriars Settlement for Associates; 32 referred to the New Bridge Society for Associates.

Of the balance of men discharged this year, 13 were referred for After-Care (voluntary) to probation officers; 3 were taken to hospital; 7 certified insane; 4 referred to the District Rehabilitation Officer of the Ministry of Labour for placement on the Disabled Persons' Register; 2 recommended for Government Training Centres (included in the 196 Special Cases); 12 declined to be interviewed; 823 were routine discharges (i.e. men serving sentences of less than three months); 1145 were discharges having served sentences of over three months. Discharge arrangements for these included:

1.—Assisting with accommodation which is dealt with in a later section;

2.—Recommending to the Discharge Board the need for travel warrants in certain instances;

3.—Suggestions for fares and subsistence to the prisoners' money clerk;

4.—The arranging for employment (also in a later section);

5.—Asking the D.P.A. Societies for special help with
>   tools—20 men.
>   clothing on release—840 men.
>   working clothing—66 men.

6.—The provision of Associates for those men who wished and needed them—75—of whom 7 were members of Alcoholics Anonymous.

5) *Accommodation.*

This grave social problem and one of the most difficult and pressing of all after-care functions was handled more intensively by the prison social workers than in previous years. The previous year's figures, of which I had written. "Out of 2302 men for whose discharge arrangements the P.W.O's, were personally responsible, 1200 were of no fixed abode before and at the time of the pre-release interviews", constituted a challenge which we could not dismiss lightly.

We therefore tried very hard to approach this problem from as many angles as possible.

The following table shows how we tried to improve on last year's situation:

Private landlords	32	Golbourne Centre	3
Referred N.A.B. 'recommend		Houses (Exch. flats)	11
money for private rooms'	744	Housing Area Managers	
Church Army Hostels	68	finding council houses	6
Salvation Army Hostels	124	Voluntary Hostels Conference	1
Rowton Houses	126	St. Martin of Tours	1
L.C.C. Homes	48	Divisional Case Committees	2
Part III Accommodation	9	Reconciliation with wives who	
Langley Houses	3	had homes or lived with	
Norman House	3	in-laws	5
Blackfriars Settlement	5	Single men who had parents'	
St. Luke's House	10	homes etc. to go to	48

Out of 2203 men discharged we were therefore left with a smaller core of 992 men of "no fixed abode"; a still far from satisfactory figure.

6) *Clothing.*

This is still a difficult administrative problem. The present system of a team effort between Reception P.O., After-Care officer and the Prison Welfare Dept. functions, but all feel it is unsatisfactory and only handled like a first-aid station. The vexed question of fitting-out the "copper-kit" each weekend he is discharged still remains, with cost looming high.

7) *Hostel.*

37 prisoners were paroled from the hostel this year, of whom 11 were failures; the reasons being given as drunkenness, misconduct in the hostel, failed to return from parole, in possession of unauthorised goods.

8) *Employment.*

This has been handled by the P.W.O.s.[9] according to the
men's requests and needs.

Referred to the Ministry of Labour representative who called at our request each week;	410
Of this number—were found employment within a week or so;	82
Referred to the New Bridge;	32
Referred to St. Luke's Alcoholics Rehabilitation Centre, all of whom were found jobs quickly;	10
Obtained jobs through pre-release classes with employers;	6
Contacted by P.W.O.s by letter or telephone and agreed to employ the men recommended;	119
Referred to the Royal London and Sussex After-Care officers for help with employment on release;	781

An abortive attempt was made on the part of the S.P.W.O.[10]
in early spring to relieve one of the causes of "gateitis" from
which these men suffer. It was felt, as a result of a group
discussion on the pre-release classes, that the men were very
insecure with only a letter of introduction to the Ministry
of Labour or a recommendation to the After-Care officer on
release. There was a need for the morale-boosting knowledge
that a man was going out the day of his release to a job. An
employers' board to meet a month before the men were
discharged appeared a good thing for certain men.

Mr. H— with his wide experience . . . . . (P.W.O.)[11] offered
to select for the Board the likeliest cases. He went to tremendous trouble ascertaining all previous employments; writing
out to employers for references and dealing with such correspondence in addition to his normal work. One meeting with
the prison staff was held, in which these cases selected were
still further weeded out. Unfortunately, lack of co-operation
from other organisations we had hoped might be interested
to help us in this project caused it to die a premature death.
We could have built up independently a register of suitable

[9] Prison Welfare Officers.
[10] Senior Prison Welfare Officer.
[11] Prison Welfare Officers.

employers to serve on this board. Unfortunately, we just have neither time nor staff, and it seems an unnecessary duplication of effort when there are others interested in the field of after-care who have regular contacts with suitable employers and who had been invited to sit on the board with us and the prison staff.'

*   *   *   *

Some of the cases illustrated below are 'scrambled' from a random selection of our daily work. To have given the actual instances might have led to identification and distress. They represent the type of man who came before us by the dozen each week. To save the reader the irritation which mere initials or numbers cause, and to add a sense of reality to their situations, I have given the men Christian names. These are only fictitious. So also are the sentences and number of previous convictions and any other names and events described. The offences and types of employment are however representative.

1. STEWART: aged 36 years. Date of birth 3/6/25
   Nationality: British. *Occupation:* Capstan operator.
   Address: 110 ———— Street, Ilford (address given on admission).
   Marital Status: Married. *Religion:* Agnostic; wife R.C.
   No. of Children: One.
   Offence: Office-breaking w/intent   *Sentenced to* two years.
   Committed from Bow St. & C.L.S. (County of London Sessions)
   Description. Light brown hair, blue eyes, pale complexion, 5 feet 10 inches, slim build. Would be quite good-looking if it were not for surly expression; slim, sensitive hands well-kept.

This man seems at first unlikely to benefit from an 'Associate', as he has a long record of serious criminality, including one sentence of C.T. (Corrective Training). However, after a long session with him, I think he might well benefit from assistance on his discharge. His marriage, fifteen years before to Anne (now aged 32 years), was a 'shotgun' affair. Their daughter, aged 14 +, is at present in a Roman Catholic home, while his wife, a nursing aide, works. During this sentence, she has now said she wishes to have no more to do with him and has moved to an unknown address. He had not wanted to marry her, though he was quite fond of her, as he felt too young, but her parents, staunch Roman Catholics insisted. His own family, father, mother and brother, washed their hands of him. His father was a leading light among the Plymouth Brethren, and was very angry at the whole situation. His mother had died of cancer shortly after Stewart's marriage. His father blamed him for this; and said mother had died of a broken heart. The father had his own tobacconist-sweet shop business in Harrow, but has finished all dealings with Stewart, who is the elder son.

At the beginning of the interview, this man was very surly and taciturn, but he gradually unfolded the story of his marriage. He claimed very bitterly that he was going to divorce his wife for desertion. He stated, again on the surface rather bitterly, that he did not care about either her or the child. He blamed 'society' for his wife's desertion. After further discussion, Stewart gradually talked out his anger and frustration against society, which he claimed 'had never given him a chance'. He had been unlucky in his jobs. Though he was a capstan operator, he had not been in this skilled occupation for years, as he was in and out of prison.

He had lately, been feeling that he was too old for a criminal's life, and that he would this time make an effort to go straight on discharge, but now, with his wife's ultimatum, he had nothing much to look forward to except a long sentence of preventive detention. He said he might as well make such a sentence worth while and would set about obtaining a gun on his release. This was probably bluff, but the social worker could not take the chance. Further talk showed that underneath all this aggression was a sensitive nature which had been deeply injured. In the end, he himself was laughing at his childish remarks and threats.

Recommendation and Prognosis: This man is without doubt immature. He feels very rejected and lonely, and might, if no interest and warmth is shown towards him, become dangerous. Despite his threats of violence, he admitted that he felt he could benefit from having someone to tide him over his initial weeks after discharge, particularly to smooth his way with statutory authorities such as the National Assistance Board and Ministry of Labour. With these he at first refused to have anything to do, saying that they always made him nervous and 'mad' with their 'snooping'. On the surface he appears to reject every type of social contact, but he has obviously been deeply hurt by his father's attitude, his mother's death and his enforced marriage. He reacts rather in the manner of a goaded animal, lashing out blindly and irresponsibly.

Stewart may seem a difficult or even a doubtful case for after-care, but it struck me that his emotional needs are greater than those of many who do not make life so difficult for themselves. I feel that he should be encouraged to accept responsibility and be treated as trustworthy. Then he might respond. Otherwise it is certain that, if nothing is done for him, he will commit some further violence against society or an individual, which might end in something very serious indeed. I recommend a sympathetic and very patient Associate. Stewart is intelligent, so will appreciate intelligence in the Associate.

The reader might like to know that from such unlikely material we had one of our 'successes'. There were a number of setbacks. Stewart was given a skilled job with an understanding employer and earned £28 a week, but soon gave it up. The Associate and I then realised that good money was not the answer in Stewart's case.

The Associate was interested in welfare work among seamen, and one evening took Stewart to see a hostel. Stewart himself became very interested, and several weeks later was made an Assistant Warden. He earned less than half of what he could in his skilled trade, but this, as he said, was compensated for by a feeling of doing something useful which gained him respect.

In assisting others worse off than himself, he found some value in life. The job has helped to damp down his hostility, aggressiveness and self-pity. Then he acquired a girl-friend who knows his past. They want to marry. She is willing to wait. Stewart thinks his wife may be able to obtain a divorce, as, though she is Roman Catholic he is, or says he is, an atheist.

Three years later, the longest time since his marriage that Stewart has stayed out of trouble, he is still a free man.

2) JAMES, aged 32 years. *Date of birth:* 30/1/28.
   Nationality: British. *Occupation:* Window-cleaner.
   Address ————, Lambeth, on admission.
   Marital Status: Married. On good terms with his wife.
   Religion: Methodist
   Number of Children: Three, Twins, James and Robert, aged three years, Diane aged 18 months.
   Offence: Larceny; Obtain credit by Fraud. *Sentenced to* 9 months.
   Committed from Thames and County of London Sessions
   Number of Previous Convictions: three
   This man, who has few marital difficulties, stated that he had got into trouble this time because, through ill-health (he suffers from chronic bronchitis), he was unable to carry on his small business of window-cleaning. He and his family were threatened with eviction from their flat for arrears of rent. He therefore bought some furniture on hire purchase and resold it privately to pay the back rent. He has not been in trouble for two years since he started his own business.

His reason for taking up this type of work was that, on his previous sentence for theft, his wife and twins had been put into Accommodation Part III[12] and had all been ill with dysentery. He was anxious that they should not be put there again, especially as the baby Diane was delicate. Though he was self-employed, his unemployment benefit had not been enough. He had not claimed National Assistance. (These

[12]Hostels for mothers and children in need of urgent temporary accommodation provided by Local Authorities under Part III of the National Assistance Act. Husbands find their own lodgings until the entire family can be re-housed and/or find permanent accommodation.

statements were later checked with the local National Assistance Board office and found to be correct). Although bronchitic, and this is known to his doctors' he had not attended a Chest Clinic since he had been advised to five years before by a prison medical officer. He had thought that working in the open air would improve his health.

He is returning to his home and family on release. He is not sure whether he will continue with window-cleaning, though he has been helped with equipment for this by his former probation officer. He admitted that he had not contacted the officer when he was in difficulties over rent, but the officer had seen him after sentence in the County of London Sessions.

The social worker contacted the Senior medical officer of Wandsworth to ask if he would see this man for a check-up. Later, the hospital reported that his chest X-ray was negative to tuberculosis and lung cancer, (James smokes moderately). The sputum also is negative. James was seen by a visiting chest consultant who will write to his doctor recommending that he should be referred to the local Chest Clinic on his release.

Recommendations and Prognosis: This man appears genuinely to be making an effort to try to support his family in a more honest manner than previously and should be encouraged. He is a worthy case to assist with after-care. The probation officer has been contacted by the social worker, and agrees that he will continue his support. James also asked if he could have the address of the Discharged Prisoners' Aid Society, although the prison social worker had told him that the probation officer would be coming to the prison to help him about his plans and that the local Chest Clinic medical social worker was also willing to help him and his wife. The prison social worker would give James a letter of introduction to her.

I felt that, though sincere, James had not shown much intelligence in his trouble. He had not applied for help with his rent difficulties to the National Assistance Board, who already knew the family, and he had not contacted the probation officer until it was too late. He appeared to me to be in need of friendly support for some considerable time until he could learn to deal with his problems in a more sensible way.

During this sentence, the National Assistance Board, the W.V.S.[13] and N.A.D.P.A.S. have been assisting the wife to manage with her young family. James's fear of them being put into Accommodation Part III was thus alleviated. I think James has learned his lesson.

3) ERNEST, aged 30 years. *Date of Birth:* 30/9/28.
  Nationality: British   *Occupation:* Labourer
  Address: Caravan Site, Somerset (since admission).
  Marital Status: Married. *Religion:* Nil.
  Number of Children: One
  Offence Burglary and Larceny. *Sentenced to* three years.
  Committed from County of London Sessions.
  Description: Fair hair, grey-blue eyes, fair complexion, Pock marked, scar on left cheek, height over 6 feet, work-roughened hands.
  Previous Convictions: 8
This man, who is a rather weak type is married to a girl ten years younger than himself. She is on probation for shop-lifting.

A great deal of social work has been done on this family by many social agencies, including the Welfare Department, the probation officer of Christine, the wife, the Royal London Discharged Prisoners' Aid Society, and the W.R.V.S. In spite of this, social prognosis on this case does not seem too good because of marital difficulties, due perhaps to personality clashes.

Ernest is dominated by his mother who has made a great deal of trouble in his marriage. She considers Christine too young and too flighty for her son. Christine seems a little higher in intelligence than her husband and mother-in-law, and if left alone could probably be a good wife and mother. This is the opinion of the probation officer. A Supervised

13Now W.R.V.S. (Women's Royal Voluntary Service).

C

welfare visit by the prison social worker confirmed this view.

Christine is an orphan, whose parents were killed in a car-crash. She was brought up by a grandmother and aunt who were 'square'. She ran away from home with Ernest, and lived with him for a year before his mother's offer to provide them with a room in her house (she is a widow) enabled them to be married. Christine had not wanted to live with her mother-in-law, but Ernest wanted to marry and also keep his mother company; so Christine agreed.

A County probation officer assisted considerably in the potential rehabilitation of this family by finding a caravan, where Christine now is with Barbara, and where Ernest can go on his release. It is in a different county from the mother-in-law's, and we hope that, without her influence this young wife may be able to make a more useful citizen out of Ernest.

The caravan is on a registered site, and, though not very large, is clean and sufficiently comfortable during the spring and summer at least. As there are no heating arrangements, it will be necessary for the family to move in the winter, but at least it will give Ernest some time to look for better accommodation.

Other occupants of caravans on the site are very friendly and willing to help Christine and the baby. A neighbour, who is elderly and sensible, seems to have a good influence on Christine.

In his pre-release interview Ernest was informed of the new address and asked what job he could do. The County probation officer had already informed the social worker that, although it was mainly an agricultural county, there was a lot of work available in the building trade and in connection with various road schemes.

Ernest said he liked agricultural work and can drive a tractor. He would like to try for a job on a farm, particularly if he could get a house with this. He has also done road repairing, brick-laying and plastering. He should not therefore find it too hard to gain employment. He will be seen by the Ministry of Labour representative here and be given a letter of introduction to the nearest Employment exchange.

Christine said she also would make enquiries locally about farm work. As they have no furniture, a house would be a difficulty, but the W.R.V.S. have promised to assist, if they can, with this.

Recommendations and Prognosis: The prospects look promising but, in view of this man's rather unstable and shiftless character, it will be a hard struggle for his young wife. Christine says she loves her husband, but Barbara comes first now, and, if he does not go straight this time, she will leave him. Ernest is aware of this threat, and says he is really going to 'make a go of it'.

Later

A few months after his discharge, we learned, to our disappointment if not to our surprise, that Christine had run off from the caravan because Ernest said he could not find work. With the summer season in full swing, we doubted this. The National Assistance Board was 'turning nasty', and Christine had found country life too quiet and dull.

She was later picked up by the police at Redhill, Surrey, along with Barbara, homeless. She had hitch-hiked all the way, and was making for London. A Court Supervision Order had been made for Barbara for two years, as the authorities felt the child was in need of care and protection.

Ernest is back 'inside' in another prison on a charge of theft, in association with two other men whom he says he met in a 'pub'.

*   *   *   *

To achieve this increasing volume of work by the department we had, of course, to overcome the obstacles usually met with in any pioneer job. We also had others to deal with which were peculiar to the work itself and to its special setting.

Some of those obstructions are described in the next chapter.

Chapter V

OBSTACLES

Obstructions to our work were of three kinds:

a) Those connected with prejudices, rumours and mis-apprehensions about our duties. It was, I found when I arrived, one of my tasks to act as a sort of publicity agent, to correct those and to give a more accurate picture.

b) Those which were more purely administrative, connected with the expansion of our department and functions.

c) Those which were concerned with the problems of the men themselves.

Like a gardener taking over virgin land, I had first to clear the prison of 'weeds', of wrong ideas and theories, before, as it were, planting our own ideas. I had firmly to remove misunderstandings about our duties and, if one can call it this without sounding snobbish, our status.

To prison officer and prisoner alike, I discovered very quickly, we were the despised D.P.A. (Discharged Prisoners' Aid Society), which was, in the opinion of many, a mixture of do-gooders and 'queers'. In whatever way the D.P.A.S. had let themselves acquire this reputation for 'do-gooding', which failed to meet the requirements of modern times, the hostility towards such worthy societies was very real and had to be faced.

I had to exercise all the qualities of a pioneer. If my attempts to win co-operation and understanding by friend-liness and tact failed (and fortunately, as I have shown, they seldom did in Wandsworth), I had on occasion to 'get tough'. In spite of all my inner shrinking and dislike of such an attitude, I had to show that I held certain principles and that I intended, for the good of the men I had come to help and for the reputation of the Welfare department, to stand by them.

Our office door, under which scurrilous letters were from time to time thrust, had a card outside bearing in large letters N.A.D.P.A.S. These letters might have been the plague cross on a mediaeval door. Few were the prisoners who, of their own accord, sought help on the other side. I had the letters removed and the words 'Welfare Department' substituted.

On two occasions within a month of my arrival, prisoners whom I approached in the wings spat sideways on to the slate floor and said: 'You're the D.P.A. We don't want none o' your ruddy charity here. What the hell use is 5/- to us on discharge?' Then, I suppose because I was a woman, they added: 'No disrespect to you ma'am!'

I reassured them by agreeing to their surprise that 5/- was indeed no use, but added that this was not at all that my colleagues and I were in the prison to dispense. I took each man to an empty classroom nearby and gave him a talk on what we intended to do. I said that we did not regard the men about to be discharged as objects of charity. We hoped that, before they left, they themselves, with our help, would acquire the means of keeping out of trouble. The means were not merely cash but an altered outlook on themselves and the community. We wanted them to have a suitable job to go out to and, wherever possible, a reunited family to welcome them back. I informed many men who resented (and I felt quite rightly) the 5/- given by the Secretary of the Royal London D.P.A. after the Discharge Board meeting, that I should see what could be done about stopping it! This of course drew some squeals of protest from the very men who were trying to make trouble, but certainly stopped the grumbling. I left it to the bush telegraph of the prison to spread the word round that the men had better think twice before they mixed up 'their Mrs. Trotter' with the D.P.A. or ran down those worthy bodies in her presence.

The Governor, though he was apparently charm and co-operation embodied, informed me on one occasion, when I sought his help about hostility in a hard core of the prison, that my department was concerned with 'welfare' (whatever *that* meant!); not with rehabilitation of the men. The Governor was too important a man to be antagonised at a time when I needed his full support in nurturing the tiny seed of qualified social work within the prison. I did not argue further, but set about enlisting his help in making my task easier by providing proper staff and better accommodation. I felt the other matter of our function could wait until our reputation was more firmly established inside and outside the prison walls. Obviously a direct approach was useless. Nor had I any intention of losing the respect and trust we had already gained from officers and prisoners in the rest of the prison by carrying out the policy suggested to me by a responsible authority: 'If you can't lick 'em, join 'em.'— about joining activities I felt were misguided.

The Royal London D.P.A. itself took some winning over. The chairman, when we had our weekly Discharge Board meetings on Wednesday afternoons, was rude enough to speak pointedly past me across the table to my assistant, a friend of his, about the problems of the men to appear before the board. My assistant himself had been careful to introduce me and to place me in the senior position at table, beside the chairman. I was disappointed at such prejudice. As happens so often, this obstacle was removed—by the retirement of the chairman. His successor was much friendlier and willing to discuss ideas and improvements.

I had similar discourteous treatment from the Secretary at first. In our office in the mornings before the daily discharge board, he used to discuss the cases with my colleague. Without seeming peevish, I could say little, and tried to hide my fears that such obvious disapproval of my sex and appointment would jeopardise my plans for a more effective programme of after-care. Presently however, the Secretary also began to be more friendly.

*　　*　　*　　*

Obstacles

A very powerful body in the prison and indeed within all prisons is the P.O.A. (Prison Officers' Association).

On my first day, when I was in the Governor's office, the chairman and secretary of the Wandsworth branch asked permission to come into the office to meet and welcome me. The chairman explained to me who they were, and said I could rely on their help and co-operation. I thanked them with a smile and assured them that I appreciated their offer. I was ignorant at this time of just how necessary it would be for me to win over, not only individual prison officers, but the total body as a unified force. I was soon to be enlightened.

On May 26, 1961, about eight months after I had entered Wandsworth, I was startled and somewhat amused when a newspaper article was shown to me in the prison. Several times during the day prison officers showed me notices from various papers. The P.O.A. holds an annual conference, at which the Press is present. There, as with trade unions, the members have complete freedom to air their views and grievances, and make suggestions for improvement of their conditions.

This year they and the Press created a sensation. The Wandsworth delegate was reported as expressing a fear of violent sex attacks on women welfare officers in prisons. The poor prison officers, he said, had to work harder because they had to ensure that the women were not attacked by prisoners. He also feared that keys might be lost by women, and prisoners try to escape, so causing danger to prison officers. In support, a Dartmoor officer was quoted as saying the 10 per cent of women prison staff were off duty recently as a result of attacks. He conveniently forgot to add that not one of those was working 'inside' the prison, nor were they working for the prisoners' welfare, nor indeed with the men as their 'guide, counsellor and friend', as I was in my rôle of probation officer. They were secretaries to the Governor's staff.

My first reaction and that of my staff was laughter at the absurdity of the comments. My faith in the prisoners' regard of me was to have startling and moving confirmation that day and the next. I was however concerned lest the

Governor should be adversely influenced in his decision to give me keys. A woman social worker in Pentonville, though appointed seven months before, still had been refused any keys in spite of all the pleas of her male Senior to the Governor.

I telephoned the Governor after a series of telephone calls from the Press, asking for my views. To all them I had given the trite but self-defensive phrase, 'No comment.' It was a great relief when the Governor assured me pleasantly but firmly that he himself had accepted the responsibility of giving me keys, and it was not for the P.O.A. to query this decision. As for my losing keys, he was sure that, as a former prison Governor, I knew better than to be so careless. I was glad to telephone N.A.D.P.A.S. head office to tell the staffs of the Governor's statement and to leave them to deal with any Press enquiries.

Throughout the day prison officers came to my room to repudiate indignantly their delegate's opinions. They claimed that he had ventilated only his personal ideas, and that he had been given no authority by them to make such provocative statements. I was obviously so amused by the ludicrousness of the complaints that the officers were reassured. I was not offended nor going to leave the prison then and there, as one or two had expected.

Nor did the prisoners let me remain long in doubt as to how *they* felt. That afternoon I interviewed, alone, as was customary, a very violent robber, with whom I had not had previous dealings. I wished to discuss with him his plans for his release in a month's time. He was a 'professional', who soon made it clear that he had no intention of altering his way of life. I hid my slight disappointment at an unfruitful interview, although it was only what I had expected. With a mischievous grin I suggested, as he left the classroom where the interview was being held: 'Next time, make it worth your while. Try the Bank of England! Then you won't be back inside here and have to put up with me!'

Rather taken aback at this response to his previous aggressive surliness, he turned to me with one hand on the door.

'You know, Mrs. Trotter, I had heard the other men on the landing talk about you and was curious. I thought you might like to know that, if you went round with an escort of prison officers amongst us, you wouldn't have half the respect you do. It's just because you *do* treat men as though you relied on them for your protection that you are safe. It's a lot of ———— nonsense what that ruddy screw said in the papers'.

Then he added, regretfully I felt, 'If I had had a mother like you, I might have given up this life long ago, but you can't alter me now.'

I thanked him thoughtfully. Later I told the Governor, for I felt that he too might like to be relieved about my safety. I, perhaps foolishly, had always felt I could trust the prisoners as far as my person was concerned. My trust was never once shaken.

The next two days saw still further touching reactions from the prisoners. I was returning from one block in rather a hurry. It was lunchtime and I had to go to my office to escort my secretaries through the prison to the canteen, and I had already been held up. I did not worry for myself, but I never liked any of my staff to be kept waiting.

As I was passing through the wing where the men had their meals in 'open association'—that is, they were not locked up in their cells, as in the rest of the prison, but sat at long refectory tables—one man came forward diffidently. 'Can I see you a moment, Mrs. Trotter?' he asked humbly.

I was about to say, rather impatiently, that I would be back in the wing at 2.15 p.m. and could see him then at more leisure. Then something made me hesitate, I noticed a look on his face, a stir amongst a group of men clustered behind him. I suddenly sensed a tension, a waiting to see what I was going to say or do. At any rate, I was to be glad I had paused.

This man, whom I knew only by name, suddenly shook me out of my impatience. 'Mrs. Trotter, I'm speaking, as I've been asked to by the prisoners, on behalf of them all. I want you to know that you need never be afraid of us. We realise that in everybody's eyes we are bad men, and we admit this. But the papers are wrong. There are things we would never do. In fact, if any b—— so much as hurt a hair of you, the screws wouldn't have to worry. We'd fix him before they even got near. So *please*, please don't be afraid.'

I was so taken aback and moved that I thought for one horrible moment that I was going to weep. However, the men were waiting for my answer. I saw their faces, almost like those of children, anxious to please and be assured that I did not hate them.

I took a deep breath to calm myself and thanked them all, showing how touched I was by their spontaneous approach. I assured them that I had known I had nothing to fear from any of them; that in fact I was probably far safer in here than on Wandsworth Common. This roused a laugh of relief and some murmurs of agreement and approval.

Another man, emboldened by my attitude, stepped forward and told me: 'And here's another thing you don't know, Mrs. Trotter. A number of us always warn any newcomers what to expect from us when they see you walking round the prison in your red coat and they start making wolf-whistle noises.'

I said that I had not been at all anxious, and in fact had been amused by the wolf whistle. As a final joke, which had in it a warning hint, I laughingly said that, if anyone felt like getting my keys from me, he had better know some judo! As we were all well aware, none of them knew this art. Uncertain whether I was bluffing or in earnest, the men also laughed and made some further joking repartee.

Only after I had locked the gate on them and walked through the prison yard to the 'Main' did I find I had to blow my nose vigorously and swallow a strange lump in my throat.

That afternoon, not to be outdone, the men of another wing also told me, in as touching a way, that they felt similarly towards me. These hardened men were anxious to show that they had soft hearts where I was concerned; to express their appreciation of what they regarded as my courage in working among them—a small feminine figure who tried not only to help them practically but to bring a touch of colour and the outside world to them in a monastic setting of uniforms. If I had been an athletic battle-axe type, I do not think I should have produced this result. Perhaps the Selection board had thought of this when it chose me for the post.

I entered the small office, a converted cell which had been first a cell then the officers' cloakroom. The Wing officer and some prisoners had decorated it for my use, even putting up curtains. They had also obtained a rug and linoleum from 'stores' to cover the stone floor of the original cell, so that my feet would not be cold.

I was about to ask the first man who was sitting outside to come in for his interview, when three others, who were not on my list for the afternoon, asked if they could speak to me before I started work. This was a most unusual request, but I invited them in and asked the first man if he would mind waiting.

The three entered the room looking sheepish, one holding his hands behind his back. When I enquired what I could do for them, the spokesman brought his hands forward. He held a shoebox containing a bouquet of artificial pink and red roses which some of the men on his wing had made from crêpe paper the previous evening. Handing them over, the man, suddenly shy, said: 'We only wish they were real, Mrs. Trotter!'

That was all. His supporters smiled, but made no remarks. Words were not needed. I knew that, whatever the P.O.A. might say or fear, the newspaper articles had struck some chord of chivalry in those recidivists. They had won over the prisoners to protect and respect me in a way which I had never dared to hope. Years of effort on my part might never have achieved this. I still have those paper roses, somewhat dusty now as they stayed on a locker in my office all the time I was in Wandsworth. My only regret was that the newspapers never got to hear of how the prisoners' really felt about a woman in their midst.

I could afford to be generous. On a landing, weeks later, I met the officer responsible for this unlooked for increase in my prestige with both officers and men. I had not seen him since that sensational day; whether by chance or intent on his part I do not know.

Now I took the opportunity to show I bore him no ill-will. After all, the incident had been taken more seriously by the staff and prisoners than by me.

I gave a mock pout and said I was disappointed. He who had offered friendship and help when I first met him had let a conference and the Press know how he really felt about my presence in the prison. I hoped, I said, that he had changed his attitude. I had taken care that the whole prison staff should hear of my reassuring experiences with the prisoners. To show I meant friendship, I did something I rarely do. I put my hand forward to shake his. He took it. I think he had been made to feel rather a fool over the whole business. He had lost face with his own colleagues, and I could not help being sorry for him. I was as relieved as he was that this was the end of the matter. I never had any further trouble from this officer. In fact, he became most helpful.

*   *   *   *

b) Difficulties of a different nature faced me administratively, as they face everyone who has to build up a department. Seldom, however, can problems have had the peculiar slant which working in a maximum-security prison gives to attempts at organisation.

Our department, small as it was, had one great advantage over all others in the prison in that we were more or less autonomous. This benefit had been given by the Maxwell Report.

Clause 102 runs: 'The Committee thought that on the whole the balance of argument was against appointing these officers as members of the prison staff. The governing consideration which led to this conclusion was, that in order to keep alive the sense of interest and responsibility among members of Aid Societies, the status of Prison Welfare Officers should make it manifest that they will be the agents and advisers of the Societies, whose help and charitable assistance we are all so anxious to retain.' Cl. 107 adds: 'When a Prison Welfare

Officer is appointed who has had training and experience in social work, his position will be that of a professional adviser to the Society or Societies whom he serves. His proposals as to the best way of dealing with cases of selected prisoners will be submitted to the appropriate society.'

This made things both easier and harder for us. As employees of the national voluntary society, N.A.D.P.A.S., and consultants to the local Aid societies, as the Report had foreseen, we had a greater freedom and elasticity in forming policy applicable to our particular prison. Each prison has its own difficulties, almost its own individual personality, and what works well in one would be a hopeless failure in another. We were freer than if we had been under the direct control of the Governor or the Home Office. We were given licence to experiment with and express ideas which civil servants, fenced in with bureaucracy could never attempt.

I took great care, however, never to abuse this privilege or to let any of my staff do so. To all intents and purposes, while we were inside the prison we were prison staff, and became integrated with the rest. I discussed with the Governor, every step I planned and obtained his approval before I took any action or notified N.A.D.P.A.S. Head Office of any proposals. We stuck strictly to the prison rules, with one important exception for which I won the Governor's agreement. We had other social workers from outside—probation officers, medical social workers, psychiatrists, associates, National Assistance Board officers and potential employers—up to our office inside the prison, instead of at the gate or in the Administrative Entrance hall as was required with all the other staff. Even with this important concession, I was careful to bring the Centre Principal Officer and the Gate Officer into the picture. I had asked for this privilege because of the inconvenience to ourselves, prison officers and sometimes senior staff when we had to spend time searching for a room in which to interview those busy workers. They like ourselves, had no time to waste.

All this ease of interviewing did not come at first, naturally.

Three main inter-connected obstacles, faced us at the beginning. The most obvious and formidable was simply the vast
numbers of men. When I came to Wandsworth, the numbers
were as I have mentioned, about 1500. In more than one week
in the following year it reached nearly 1800. Never at any time
were the numbers below 1,200. Between 2,000 and 5,000 men
were discharged in a year and passed through our hands.

Probation officers and other social workers have stated that
a caseload of 60 for each social worker is about the maximum
if effective and professional work is to be carried out. A
hundred stretches the work to capacity; after that it is just
impossible.

I had previously been accustomed to working within the
60-100 capacity. In Wandsworth there were three of us and,
to begin with, two secretaries with an average caseload of 500
men each. Not one of them, obviously, had hitherto been
successfully rehabilitated.

I had accepted this challenge, however, and refused to be
drowned in this tidal wave of numbers. I prayed, not blas-
phemously, for a second miracle of the loaves and fishes for
the five thousand, and got down to assessing the situation.
How could three people working in a new field be of use to
so many and to the prison authorities in their struggle for
penal reform? No one was keener on this than I, and I
determined to contribute something, no matter how little.

The ideal would have been to have had one or two prison
social workers responsible for each landing (84-100 men), but
this would have meant a minimum staff of 32 professionals.
If I had been given ten more, and six or seven more secretaries,
this would have created perhaps worse problems, because
accommodation for such a large staff would have had to be
found, and the Treasury would have had to approve salaries.
I sighed for dreams and decided that I should have to work on
the assumption that our staff was not likely to be greatly
enlarged in the near future. The three of us, together with
N.A.D.P.A.S. and the Royal London and Sussex D.P.As,
would also have to meet to discuss how far the Maxwell
Report could be implemented with its blithe assumption

that with such numbers we could prepare detailed case-histories.

Clause 126 runs: 'To prepare such case-histories, it is neces-sary that the officer charged with this task shall not only have the time to make the requisite inquiries, but shall have had some training in the technique of such work. This work calls not only for judgment and insight into human nature, but a special skill; and this is one of the reasons why we recommend that persons appointed as Prison Welfare Officers should have had suitable training and experience.'

Skill and experience we all had, and we were anxious to use them, but the operative word in this clause was 'time'. This, with such numbers, we could not have. In the meantime some-thing would have to be done about improving our accommoda-tion, and we must build up good relationships with, and help from, the prison staff and outside agencies.

As I mentioned earlier, it was a hopeless situation to have the secretaries working outside the prison. It was frustrating, time-consuming and embarrassing. Our Welfare office in the 'Main' consisted of four former cells knocked into one room. It had, before my coming, been furnished sparsely with two desks, two chairs, two wastepaper baskets, and two filing cabinets. Two recesses were filled with dreary dusty telephone directories and street guides. A worn, threadbare carpet lay on the tiled floor and a broken iron fireplace smoked badly in the winter. The décor was chipped brown paint and custard-yellow enamelled walls.

Each of the wings had four landings, each nearly a quarter of a mile in length, one wing even longer. We walked literally miles in a day within the perimeter of the prison wall. All this promenading had to be reckoned with in the time allotted to our interviews.

We had to fit interviews with the men into the life and movement of the prison. For example, in the afternoons we had only the two hours between two and four p.m., and then the men had to be released to the centre prison officer, sent back and locked in their cells for tea. Our rate of discharges for the month was about 180 men. Each welfare officer could see only six to eight men in an afternoon to discuss their most vital problem; what they were going to do on discharge. When I came, we had a single office on B2 landing available for our interviews. The confidential nature of our work meant that only one social worker could have the office; the rest had to visit the cells, a slow and unsatisfactory method.

Nor was every afternoon free for those important sessions. As the excerpt from my 1962 annual general report showed, telephone calls had to be made, and letters and case-papers dictated. Queries from the Governor, chaplain, medical officers and other senior staff had to be answered; and special visits by wives and relatives fitted in.

Those poor 180 men for discharge! Their release plans were likely to be most desultory and perfunctory.

I had always enjoyed preparing detailed case-histories. Did those who suggested this realise the time they take? With enquiries into family background, into previous employment and probably education and health, each case-history takes at least a week to prepare, with a minimum of two hours' un-interrupted typing (with three carbons). Even if we had had no other functions, it would have been a quite impossible task.

My main problem was somehow to create a department which did ten times the amount of work it was at present doing, but without prostrating members.

Obviously we needed more time. We could not obtain it by increasing the staff; but we could utilise that staff in a more time-saving way and increase our accommodation so that three officers could interview in separate rooms. This would give us a chance to do at least three times the amount of welfare and social work (for the two, as I hope to show in Section II, are by no means the same).

We also badly needed more secretarial help, as well as some-one to take enquiries off our hands. In the present set-up we lost a great deal of assistance and information because we were busy in the prison or outside dictating in an office without a telephone. Meanwhile the Welfare office itself was seldom occupied. In my first week I received good-natured complaints from the medical officers and Assistant Governors that when they telephoned our office they could never get an answer.

For a second time a Principal probation officer from London rang me up for information on one of his former probationers, who was now serving a sentence, and I had to apologise and say that I could not give him the answer immediately. The file was outside, twenty minutes' away in the typists' room. By now I had had enough of this chaos. I telephoned the Governor to ask to see him urgently. I put my need before him, and begged him to help me to have the secretaries transferred to our office 'inside' on B wing. I pointed out, in case he needed further fodder to placate the Prison Officers' Association, that as I, a woman, was already inside, the first breach in this monastic establishment had been made. I promised that those girls would never have to come face to face with a prisoner; that one of us (the social workers) would escort them through the prison at all times; and that, when we were not in the office, they would be shut in with Yale and mortice locks operated by them from the inside.

I explained that we should be saved hours in the day, and that, by having the girls in the office where the filing cabinets were, we should always have the files available at a few moments' notice. Also, whenever either external or internal telephones rang, the secretaries could give information or take messages. In addition, they would be under my direct supervision, and we hoped to get much more secretarial and clerical work done.

The Governor was most sympathetic, and said he did not see why this should not be done, especially if the precautions offered by me for the girls' safety were carried out. He promised to arrange matters with Chief, and also to provide a party of prisoners to remove the girls' office furnishings from the chaplain's house into the B-wing office.

I slept better that night than I had done for weeks, feeling that I had made the first crack in the hard, impenetrable shell of the task I had undertaken. We should be rather over-crowded, but it was a start, and, with the prison social workers rarely all in the room at the same time, it should not be too bad. I hoped also that the Governor and the Prison Officers' Association would presently supply me with a separate office of my own in which to interview both prisoners and important contacts for after-care, such as Principal probation officers and others.

Within six months most of my dreams came true. Thanks largely to the Prison Commission, N.A.D.P.A.S., the Governor and Steward of the prison, we had a secretarial pool of three secretaries, new and highly efficient. They were handpicked by me for qualities of team-spirit, good-nature and conscientiousness, which were as important to our work as efficiency in typing and shorthand.

I had my separate office, adjoining the main one. Both were decorated in pastel colours of my choosing, and there were a new fireplace, new carpet and an armchair for visitors in my room.

We were given the use of two classrooms, empty each afternoon in the 'Main' and an outside office for special supervised welfare visits which the Governor encouraged. In these we were often able to sort out a man's difficulties with his wife before they were beyond repair, or in these too he would be interviewed by a potential employer. In another block, I had, in addition to the converted cloakroom, the use of the empty library mornings and evenings for interviews.

Administratively, I divided our work territories into the wings of the prison, giving three to each of us, with the hospital as an extra to myself. The filing system was drastically altered and simplified. It took the secretaries and myself a week to put it straight. After that a telephone enquiry took only minutes to answer. Senior staff, who often sought information from us, could now be helped on the spot. My dream of making the department do ten times the work was being gradually realized. Yet there was less strain on all of us.

My arrival had been too late to help my two assistants. The health of one necessitated his transfer to a lighter post. I was sorry to lose him. The other stuck by me till we were well established. New staff, after a series of 'temporaries' supplied by the Head Office of N.A.D.P.A.S. was needed to create a stable organisation. The 'temporary social workers', though willing, were not enough. Teaching them 'the ropes' also took up valuable time. I had to wait nearly another year for the staff I wanted.

In spite of all the challenges which we had to meet, the atmosphere in our office was at last happy. Prison staff began to realize this, and, whenever they had a 'free' moment, developed the habit of 'dropping in', usually at the time of our 'tea-break', ostensibly to discuss the prisoners' problems. The laughter in our office often seemed to act like a safety valve and a tonic. There was no pomp or formality to deter the prison officer. Yet, if the Deputy Governor, a frequent visitor, came to discuss some matter with me, we could combine necessary business with the informality which was so relaxing to all of us, surrounded as we were by gloom and constant tension which could not be slackened outside the door of our office.

With better accommodation, more efficient staff organisation and hours of time saved in the day, we could get down to concentrating on the benefit of the prisoners, whose welfare and after-care were our principal concern.

To show our gratitude to everyone, we gave in 1961, a Christmas party (open-house style), the first of its kind inside the prison. We invited all the prison staff to our newly decorated rooms. Many officers dropped in throughout the afternoon, those on duty who could be spared for a few moments of unusual relaxation. Owing to prison rules, the party had to be strictly non-alcoholic; but it seemed to be appreciated. Even the Governor came upstairs, bringing with him a visiting Governor from abroad. The visitor was impressed with our friendliness and happy atmosphere. We hoped afterwards that he did not think we were frivolous all the time.

c) Problems of the men.

A surgeon in hospital delegates to the nursing staff the

less specialised tasks of applying dressings and bandages and giving medicines and sedatives. So, as social workers, we had, because of our small numbers, to devise ways of delegating the important but simpler tasks of welfare which did not require specialised training.

One of the most controversial of these was to see that the men's clothing on release was respectable, clean and adequate. Hitherto this duty had been performed in the Reception block (where the men were admitted and discharged) by the Reception Officer and his staff together with the Discharged Prisoners' Aid Society's after-care officer. The Royal London D.P.A. had a large cupboard in 'Reception' where they kept a stock of new and second-hand clothing obtained with a Government grant and supplemented by much-needed voluntary contributions.

Once the D.P.A. officer had left the prison to concentrate on outside after-care, as recommended by the Maxwell committee in their Report, we were faced with this problem of clothing supplies. Thus we could very easily have found ourselves in the position envisaged by Gordon Rose.[1]

'The Committee was, in fact, a negotiating body, the object being to find some compromise which would allow the Commissioners to appoint trained social workers in the local prisons and raise the standard of work of the Discharged Prisoners' Aid Societies without arousing their opposition, or making them feel that they were losing their liberty or functions . . . The result was a bargain in which the Commissioners were recommended to appoint trained social workers as prison welfare officers. These officers however to be appointed by the National Association of Discharged Prisoners' Aid Societies, not directly by the Commission; and the Discharged Prisoners' Aid Societies got more money to ensure that all of them had a Welfare officer as well as a Secretary. The prison welfare officer would work inside the prison and would dispense material aid on discharge which would now come from the Exchequer, and the Discharged

[1] *The Struggle for Penal Reform* by Gordon Rose. (1961, Stevens & Son Ltd.).

Prisoners' Aid "Welfare" officer would be responsible for contact with the families and the prisoner after discharge.

'Thus the trained social worker *inside* the prison was to be given a job which was very largely routine work under pressure, with little opportunity for casework; and the untrained D.P.A. officer was to deal with the difficult human problems of prisoners and their families. It is not surprising in the event that they found it difficult to obtain social workers of the standard they had hoped for the job of Prison Welfare officer[2] . . . . and more important, the D.P.A. officers still very largely retained the old ideas of how the work should be done.'

Rose omits the very important clauses I have already cited about the duties of the prison social worker (Clauses 99, 107 and 126) and our status as advisers and consultants to the D.P.A. societies. Yet there is no doubt that many D.P.A.s resented being, as they felt, ousted from their work inside the prisons, and interpreted the function of the new social workers in much the way that Rose describes. In Wandsworth too, before and after my arrival, the enemies to our department being established in the prison to the jeopardy of other ideas about rehabilitation were quick to jump on this idea and

[2] This statement of Gordon Rose written in 1961 requires a slight qualification to avoid any misleading impression. The Annual Report of the National Association of D.P.A. Societies for the same year (1961) in Appendix 2 (page 23) describes the qualifications of the prison welfare officers as follows.
'*Qualifications and Experience of Prison Welfare Service Staff (as at 1st December 1961)*.
'Of the 54 social workers on the NADPAS staff listed on pages 5 and 6:
  18 hold a Degree, Diploma in Social Science or have taken a post-graduate course and each has had not less than 3 years social work experience.
  2 have not less than 3 years social work experience and are now taking an extra-mural Social Science Diploma course.
  5 have taken the Home Office Probation Division long course or have served not less than 3 years as a probation officer.
  2 have not less than 3 years social work experience and have taken a Diploma course without qualifying.
  23 have not less than 5 years appropriate experience acceptable to the Selection Board.
  6 have experience outside the foregoing limits which has been considered by the Selection Board as particularly suitable (including younger officers with social work qualifications but less than 3 years social work experience.'

spread it around. It was one of the obstacles I fought and fought in certain wings. It was reported to me by a friendly Wing Officer on one occasion that 'Mrs. Trotter had been put in her place.' They were to find out that neither Mrs. Trotter nor any of her staff were willing to accept a subservient role to any untrained workers, whether they belonged to voluntary societies or to the prison staff.

In Wandsworth, while we had to endure less hostility from our two D.P.A. societies, they still took the opportunity of sloughing off responsibility for the men's clothing on to the Welfare department. First one, then a second of my officers took this on at the expense of their true work and health.

We had a series of discussions with the Governor, the head office of N.A.D.P.A.S. and the Royal London D.P.A., and it was finally agreed that, although the prison social workers had been instructed by N.A.D.P.A.S. to make recommendations as to the clothing required for each man about to be discharged, this did not mean that they should spend considerable valuable time each morning sorting out stock and handing it over to the Reception officer. Nor could the social workers really be expected to continue to take time off from their more important duties to do book-keeping for the Royal London D.P.A. We could not be expected to make entries of articles and their cost in a book belonging to the Royal London society.

After many months of trying to devise a scheme which would satisfy all parties, we finally agreed with the prison staff and the Royal London D.P.A. that the Reception Officer should be responsible for the men's clothing, and the D.P.A. should give him the key to their cupboard. After all, the Reception Officer saw the condition of these men on admission, and could be trusted, as a responsible senior officer, to know what would be required for their release.

In a similar way, it was agreed that it was the prison's responsibility to arrange for the dry-cleaning of suits and repairing of shoes. This was already arranged for other prisoners not under the aegis of the 'voluntary after-care authorities.' These were the several hundred men serving

sentences of four years or more and under statutory supervision on discharge.

This was a tremendous help to us. We had now gained
an extra five mornings a week to see men about their welfare
applications, and worries about their wives and families,
hire-purchase debts and so on. Before that, the officer who had
been looking after the D.P.A.'s clothing arrangement had had
to stay till 7 or 8 p.m., an inconvenient time for the officer
to do his real work of rehabilitation. Now his improved health
and alertness permitted him to carry out this job with more
energy and happiness.

With our present staff the work of preparing case-histories
on approximately 1,500 men was quite out of the question.
Also, as we found on studying the record kept of each man on
his reception, it was not strictly necessary. The Maxwell
Report had advocated the preparation of case-histories for
'special cases', not for every single man as many outsiders,
including research workers and other social workers, seemed
to think. Ah, but how, the critics might answer, would the
prison social workers know which men to select unless they
prepared histories on all? The answer is that prison social
workers were appointed for possessing just such training and
capabilities as enabled them to make the choice.

It was pretty obvious to all in the prison that old Joe Bloggs,
aged 72, who had for years been discharged on a Friday only
to be readmitted on the Monday for yet another sentence for
drunkenness, was not likely to be a 'special case', 'willing and
likely to benefit from friendship and assistance from the
D.P.A.s after discharge.' He required more specialised treatment, and then only if he himself wished to be cured of his
affliction.

So we started a plan of interviewing about discharge plans,
only those men who were serving sentences of over three
months. Shorter sentences than that did not give us opportunity for professional casework on rehabilitation. By such
means our monthly list of discharge interviews was reduced
by nearly one third. Instead of having 150 men to interview,
we had 100.

We were greatly helped also from sources of after-care which the Maxwell Report had not visualised. These were more professional than the D.P.A.s who, because they did not always grasp the necessity for teamwork, often appeared to operate independently of our recommendations. In some instances they wasted what must have been their valuable time by reinterviewing an ex-prisoner, and taking that prisoner's word about his past and future.

This was especially the case with those most difficult of cases, the confidence tricksters. We gave the correct report on these men, with comments from their army, prison and psychological records, and cautioned the D.P.A. to beware of their claims to noble ancestry, public school and university education and professional training. Yet on more than one occasion we had to read through the after-care officer's repetition of the man's story with sentimental, sympathetic comments. Sometimes, particularly if the man had been previously known to another professional worker such as a probation officer, the after-care officer had to admit he had been fooled, and then wrongly 'took it out' of the ex-prisoner.

We had no such frustrations with our professional colleagues in the probation and medical fields. More and more frequently we found it more satisfactory from the ex-prisoner's angle to refer him back directly to those workers who already knew him or his family. We referred the ex-prisoners to probation officers, medical social workers, psychiatric social workers, Family Welfare officers, the District Rehabilitation Officer of the employment exchange, marriage guidance counsellors, wardens of hostels. We approached in fact, any and every statutory, and voluntary body available, together with employers, trade-union officials, railway and coach left-luggage offices, hire-purchase firms and housing area managers. By building up professional contacts, we were at least trying to give each man the after-care most suitable to his need.

This direct approach also saved the after-care officers of the D.P.A.s, overworked like ourselves, a great deal of unnecessary labour. A recommendation alone that such-and-such a man might do better under the care of a probation officer, who would visit his home in the course of his rehabilitation, would have been a ponderous and roundabout way of tackling the problem. Instead, probation officers and men met in our presence in a 'Special supervised welfare visit' and discussed with us their plans for the future.

The top-heavy tidal wave was beginning to be harnessed as a source of power instead of destruction.

*   *   *   *

Of course we had our critics, even our enemies. We would not have had it otherwise as it gave piquancy to the challenge, though, being human, we sometimes became irritated and hurt. Occasionally I had to placate and console my colleagues in the department, who knew they could always count on my support. Sometimes, when I was upset, my staff would comfort me until we all once more saw the funny side of the hostility and ended up in bursts of laughter. For a long time those afternoons of tears and laughter will remain with me.

We were told by N.A.D.P.A.S. head office, none of whose senior executive staff were trained social workers, that, it had been informed by other 'welfare' workers that they managed beautifully to cope with 900, 1,000, 3,000, 10,000 men. We too, said head office, ought to be able to do this within the compass of the forty-hour week. That bright comment nearly lost me both my social workers, who wanted to return to fields where their services were understood and appreciated. I replied to the speaker on the other end of the telephone line that, whatever those workers were 'managing', it was certainly not social work. It was similar to the old ineffectual procedure which really washed its hands of the prisoner's main problems.

The small section of the prison staff who never accepted me, my staff or our work took up more energy than we could really spare, as we had to spend a good deal of time with anxious prisoners who had not had their problems solved. This section of staff had been taught before our coming to regard themselves as the social workers for the men; indeed as sociologists. All had been informed that they were to carry out the function of probation officers (which, according to the Maxwell Report which they had not read, was our function), namely, to 'guide, assist and befriend the prisoners.'

Some officers were openly hostile and made our work well-nigh impossible. They even resorted to deliberate falsehoods to make mischief. They had no desire to hear about what we were trying to do and refused our repeated appeals for their help and co-operation in doing 'real' social work. This, I in vain essayed to show them, would be more interesting and rewarding than their 'scheme'. I was once indeed reproved by N.A.D.P.A.S. head office, almost to the point of being dismissed, because I would not associate my department with this 'scheme'. We had the authority of the Maxwell Report for my stand. Clause 100 states:

'In this task' (i.e. the selection of suitable prisoners for rehabilitation and attending to their problems while in prison) 'the Prison Welfare Officer would be assisted by all members of the prison staff (including the Governor, Assistant Governor and Chaplain) and also by the Prison Visitors, whose special knowledge of individual prisoners and of their hopes and interests will often enable them to make valuable contributions to the formulation of plans for after-care.'

This group refused to accept that after-care and indeed in-care were the responsibility of the officially appointed social workers, and they utilised amateur and less desirable contacts. They consistently believed that 'welfare' in Wandsworth was 'just the D.P.A.' and was concerned only with clothing and money for the discharged prisoner. How, I asked, could you co-operate with persons who would not co-operate with you? To this question N.A.D.P.A.S. could give us no answer. What made me anxious was that the conflict affected most those prisoners who needed and wanted our help. They were unable to have it because, when they asked to see me, my department was not notified.

The hostile group told the prisoners that 'Mrs. T.' was 'no good', and they had better see Mr. So-and-So. The prisoners, however, all of whom had been first in the 'Main', knew better. Some plucked up courage and insisted that they should see me, and not Mr. So-and-So, thus risking punishment for contradicting an officer. Others took the more drastic step of applying to the new Governor for transfer back to the 'Main', although they would lose many privileges such as open association, all sorts of group discussions and, 'open' meetings with their wives in a pleasant visiting room.

However, we became in time a necessary part of the prison, and more and more officers and their seniors referred men to us, especially as we showed our respect for their great experience in sensing the prisoners' reactions. For example, they knew that, if a man had received a disturbing letter from his wife, it was better to ask him at once if he would care to discuss his problem with the prison social worker. Before our arrival, they had waited until the man had become so anxious and overwrought that he reached a stage of violence in his frustration, rage and inability to solve his problem for himself.

Later, when the Chiefs and Wing Officers knew that I was interested in alcoholics, and had contacts to assist in the problem, they referred such men as they considered might be rehabilitated to me for the prolonged intensive casework in which I specialised.

Chapter VI

THE PRISON HOSTEL
AND THE HOSTEL SCHEME

No picture of Wandsworth prison would be complete without a description of one of the greatest potential 'open sesames' to the outside world for some of the prisoners. It is a single-storeyed building, opened in 1959, which houses twelve men.

Outside, the paintwork is in gay pastel colours. Inside, though not exactly a home from home, the hostel is a considerable improvement on the wings of the main prison. It contains a small kitchen where the men prepare their meals,[1] a cosily furnished living-room with radio and television, the 'usual offices', as estate agents euphemistically term them, and a large dormitory.

The hostel, together with one in Pentonville, was originally intended for men from Dartmoor serving terms of four years or over. Within nine months of their discharge, those men were transferred to the two London prisons to enable them to go out daily to work on parole from the hostels. By June 1960 twenty-seven men from Dartmoor had passed through the Wandsworth hostel, but eight were failures in that they broke parole and committed further offences.

In that month, because of a change in government policy, the supply of Dartmoor men stopped and the hostel became empty. The Prison Commissioners decided to use it for the Wandsworth men who were serving similar sentences. The senior Assistant Governor (No. 1) on what was known as the 'rehabilitation wings' became Warden, assisted by an enthusi-

[1] In October 1962 permission was given by the Prison Commissioners for the hostel to have a cleaner from the main prison. His duties were to clean the hostel and to cook the men's meals. This arrangement was put into effect in November 1962, and enabled the hostellers to have a hot meal ready at night on their return from work and also to have breakfast prepared for them before they left in the mornings. I understand that the cleaner now comes from another block.

astic and efficient Principal Officer. Such was the position
when I arrived in Wandsworth.

* * * *

Among the many prison boards on which I was supposed to
sit was the Hostel board. If I had myself sat on all prison
boards, I should have had little or no time to do social work,
let alone administer the department. I had therefore delegated
the work on some of them, such as the Reception and Discharge boards each morning, to my male colleagues, and
received afterwards written records of the men seen.

The Hostel board, however, seemed to me very important
as well as personally interesting. I hoped to find it similar
to the one for which I took the chair in 1957 in the Rehabilitation Clinic in Ontario. In October 1960 I sat on my first
Hostel Selection board, in the visiting magistrates' room. I
soon felt bewildered and useless.

In the chair sat the Governor. Round the table were ranged
a number of gentlemen; some staff, others strangers to me.
Moving round the prison among hundreds of men, I had
ceased to feel 'odd man', or rather woman, 'out'. This formidable all-male board at a long polished rectangular table was
much more awesome. I felt very self-conscious, especially with
the strangers. What such a terrifying array of masculine
authority did to the poor prisoners I hate to think. I was
soon introduced to the other members.

One was a magistrate; another a probation officer; a third
the manager of the local labour exchange. Besides those
visitors and the Governor, there were the Assistant Governor
in charge of the rehabilitation wings and the hostel, a new
young Assistant Governor who had arrived the day after me
in Wandsworth to work in the rehabilitation wing, the
Chief, the Principal Officer for the hostel and rehabilitation
wings, the Church of England chaplain, and the Senior
psychologist. Lastly, there was myself, seated between the
magistrate and the Chief.

All those staff had certainly contributed towards the work

of the hostel, knew the men about to be interviewed, and so could give valuable information to the board. It was difficult to see how the board could have been much smaller. It seemed to me, however, top-heavy and far too intimidating. On the other hand in its favour was the fact that the larger numbers probably gave a fairer assessment of the men's eligibility than, say, a more prejudiced board of three would have done.

The function of the board, which was held two-monthly was, to select up to twelve men from a short list of fifteen to twenty. They were to be prisoners from the rehabilitation wings whose discharges fell within the right dates, and they would fill the vacancies caused by others discharged from the prison via the hostel at the end of their sentences.

In front of each member was a pile of slips of paper containing the name, age, marital status and offences, together with the date of discharge, of each of the candidates. These had been prepared by the Principal Officer.

All the men who appeared at the bottom of the table one by one throughout the long afternoon were serving sentences of four years and over. They were the responsibility of the Central After-Care Association, not of our department (hence the presence of the probation officer). This was a division of duties which never seemed logical to me, to the men or to some of the prison staff. The Central After-Care officer came only once a month to see the men about their discharge arrangements, and did no daily work at all, as we did, on their social and marital problems. That anomaly has now been removed.

At the first meeting I found I knew none of those men before us nor anything about them which would help me to assess their eligibility for parole from the hostel. I knew nothing about their employment capabilities, whether their wives and families would welcome them on week-end leaves, what were the parole risks of their drinking habits or other weaknesses, what the men planned to do on discharge. As a caseworker, I felt that these were questions which should be asked. With such a large board I had no time to put more

94

than one of these queries to each man. Each board lasted over four-and-a-half hours, wearying everyone.

After attending a number of such meetings, and feeling less and less useful, to either board or men, I attended one which was interviewing eighteen men for ten vacancies. We had a mixed bag, according to the men's records. There was a rapist who had had previous convictions for indecent assault on females and was also a confidence trickster. Another prisoner had been guilty of robbery with violence and a not proven murder in another country. There were two or three perverts, one man up for buggery with his stepson, with previous convictions for attacking small boys, and a number of others with records of serious violence. Only two had prospects for rehabilitation and were good risks from the point of view of the prison authorities, who have to take the responsibility of turning those individuals loose on society six months prior to completion of their sentences. I am afraid I annoyed the Governor that day because, with Scottish stubbornness, I dug my heels (stiletto!) in, and refused to accept such men, especially the rapist and the prisoner who attacked little boys. I refused to take the risk of their committing further offences while they were on parole, which I might have been accused of being instrumental in recommending. Fortunately, the Senior Psychologist supported my view. I came out of the meeting shaken but determined to find some method which would avoid time-wasting arguments by the board.

Before the next meeting I had a number of discussions with the Governor, the Assistant Governor who was the Warden of the hostel, the Central After-Care Association and N.A.D.P.A.S. head office. I made certain offers which were accepted.

As a result, two weeks before each subsequent board meeting, I saw each applicant. In the relaxed peace and privacy of my own office in the rehabilitation wings. I obtained answers to questions I had thought of at that first meeting—and to others. With the written consent of each man, I sent a letter to his wife to ask whether, if her husband was given the chance of a place in the hostel, she would welcome him home on week-end leaves. I received most enlightening replies. Most accepted, but some wished to have nothing to do with their husbands. These made the husbands a parole risk. Their potential indignation might push them to commit offences, even if they did so only to annoy their wives. Such details were incorporated in my report on each man.

Reports by myself, the Principal Officer accompanying me, and by probation officers on the homes which were visited were also included. At the next board meeting, the members had this additional page of information to digest about each man. Some groaned good-humouredly, but the magistrate politely thanked me at the end of the meeting.

The length of the meeting had been cut by more than an hour. Afterwards, the teasing staff admitted that 'Sallie's social précis' were a good idea. I felt that at last I had contributed something positive both to the hostel board and to the prisoners' welfare.

These précis, which became a feature of the selection of the men, were gradually made easier for me. During the discussions, I had asked why men serving shorter sentences of two-and-a-half years and more could not be considered for the hostel. A number of them seemed to offer a likely source of rehabilitable material, selection being based not merely on length of sentence but potential effort to go straight on release! They were our 'special cases' according to the terms of the Maxwell Report and by no means always selected by the Assistant Governor for the 'rehabilitation wings'. With the peculiar telepathy which seems to accompany ideas on prison rehabilitation, such thoughts had already been in the minds of the Assistant Governor and the Prison Commissioners.

As a result, eligibility for the hostel was extended to men serving from three years upwards.

Men who obtained the much-coveted privilege of admission to the hostel began rehabilitation several months before their official discharge. Living in the hostel, they went out to jobs offered either by the manager of the labour exchange, who interviewed them after they had been accepted by the board, or by the Assistant Governor Warden or the Principal Officer. Both of these, keenly interested in making a success of the hostel, had built up valuable contacts with numerous local employers, who looked with a friendly and humanitarian eye on the hostellers. They earned full wages according to their ability, and had their insurance cards stamped. This removed a great disadvantage to the discharged prisoner—the un-stamped insurance card. At the end of the week each man handed over intact his pay-packets to the Warden and Principal Officer.

After the deduction of certain charges, including expenses and pocket money, the balance of his wages was compulsorily saved for his discharge. Compulsory savings could be held as 'prisoners' money' with the prison cashier or paid into a Post Office savings account on behalf of the prisoner. The savings books were not left in the prisoners' possession.

The first deduction was an amount equal to the National Assistance Board payment for the maintenance of the prison-er's dependants. The Board was notified, so that its book was withdrawn. This amount was sent directly to the dependants. If there was a balance remaining after all charges had been made, the prisoner could, if he wished, send additional money to his wife or dependants in excess of National Assistance Board standards. It is to the credit of these men that most of them did this.

A second deduction was made weekly towards any amount payable under a Court Order for compensation or costs. If a man had children in the care of the local authority or otherwise maintained, for example, in an Approved school, a further deduction might be made. A third charge included £2. 7s a week for lodging, toilet requisites, laundry done in the prison and all meals except dinner on working days. A sum to cover the cost of fares and meals taken at work was also estimated.

Finally, a man was given pocket money, which was normally 30s a week. If there was insufficient balance, pocket money could be allowed to fall to 10s weekly, but, if it came to less, instructions had to be sought from the Prison Commissioners, who generally did not let it fall lower.

Men were also supplied with work clothes and a basic minimum kit of tools to the value of £3, where necessary. They were granted week-end and public holidays' leave on parole, and the local associate—for example the probation officer, who had paid the home visit to report on conditions to the hostel board—was informed of a man's leave.

Once a man was admitted to the hostel, he was severed from all contact with the main prison. Everyone, staff and hostellers, worked very hard and enthusiastically to show the worth of this form of rehabilitation. There was the same spirit among the men as I found among the women in Canada, a feeling that one had to prove one was worthy of the trust that the authorities and the community had shown. If a man betrayed that trust and committed a further crime, there was the feeling that he had 'let the side down'.

There were two major ways in which an otherwise excellent and invaluable scheme could have been improved. One was by extending its scope. Twelve men seemed such a pitifully small proportion of more than 1,500 prisoners. The other was by a more careful selection of cases.

The numbers could have been increased by using the rehabilitation wings as an extension of the hostel.

The unsatisfactory selection of cases was not the fault of the hostel board. This had to assess only what candidates were put before it. The fault lay further back in the original selection of men for the two rehabilitation wings, which were the source of supply for the hostel.

Unfortunately, the Assistant Governor and Principal officer who were initially in charge, and who collaborated with me and my staff in the social work of the wings, were transferred. One became Governor of another prison and the Principal officer went to promotion in the 'Main'.

Statistics showed that over a third of the men sent to the hostel were failures either while they were on parole or because shortly after discharge they committed crimes which involved further imprisonment. For the period of eighteen months from January 20, 1961, to July 13, 1962, of the 55 men accommodated in the hostel, the Warden reported 16 failures. For the entire period, since its inception in 1959, there had been, by July 13, 1962, 31 failures out of a total of 103 men. This included 7 out of 22 Dartmoor men, but the Wandsworth candidates had not fared any better: with 24 known failures to date out of a total of 91 men. Those were not figures about which to be smug. Yet the idea was sound and also practical common sense. It was obvious, as I have said that the fault lay in selection.

I myself was puzzled when I looked at the records and social histories of the men on those 'special' wings. To me, far from comprising the 'cream' of the recidivists, they seemed to include a considerable number of incorrigible alcoholics, who while in the 'Main' had been rejected by the Warden of the hostel for alcoholics, with whom I had established a close professional casework liaison. There were also several psychopaths, at least two formerly certified mental patients and a more than high percentage of 'confidence' men, glib of tongue, swift of charm and repartee, and full of ideas which, if not strictly dishonest, were at least morally dubious. These men seemed to everyone except the new Assistant Governor and Principal officer to be running the wings to their liking. Investigation enlightened me.

The pilot 'scheme' full of enthusiasm but with only a smattering of psychology and social-work acquired from reading and hearsay, and with an incredible ignorance of the explosive material that was being handled under no trained supervision, had been 'operating' for two years before I entered the wings. The pattern was already set rigid.

The selection board for the wings consisted solely of the Assistant Governor in his first recidivist prison and a Principal officer who had consistently and openly stated that a woman's place was in the home, not working with prisoners. He did not apparently consider how I, as a widow with two young sons, was to support myself and them. These two, accepted men recommended to them by the Wing officers of the 'Main'.

Most of the officers honestly tried to select suitable material, but they were given no guidance as to what was wanted. Others, hostile to the staff on the rehabilitation wings and glad of the opportunity to rid themselves of the trouble-makers and difficult types, recommended a motley crew. The two men selecting prisoners for the rehabilitation wings had neither the experience nor the desire to see what was happening.

The Wing officers, as I found in my own work, were a very reliable and important source of knowledge of the men in their charge. If the Assistant Governor and Principal Officer to the rehabilitation wings had won their allegiance and support—which they never did—the subsequent percentage of failures in the hostel scheme might have been considerably smaller.

It was saddening to see what should have been a useful project producing decent citizens so badly handled and en-trusted to 'confidence men' among the prisoners. The idea of letting prisoners run their affairs was a good one, imported from the United States where, as in Canada, it had been in operation for over twenty years. Also American was the idea of encouraging them to help in the community. The difference was that across the Atlantic such prisoners were very carefully chosen and had always skilled guidance behind them. The rates of success were therefore higher. After all, the only true test is whether the selected men commit no further offences. The men of Wandsworth mostly failed in this.

Yet this depressing picture had its amusing side too. Many of the 'con' men's claims, uttered with all the likable charm which is part of their stock-in-trade, were quite entertaining. The 'con' men were refreshing in their opinions, provided one did not take them too seriously. A number of them, after group discussions and talks by outsiders, jumped on to a new 'bandwaggon' of false pretences, calling themselves sociologists, psychologists and social workers. Those who knew of our existence in the prison contacted us to verify the men's claims. Others must have been disappointed as their protégés faced the courts yet again.

However, perhaps the men do less harm in social-work

rôles than in posing at the Dorchester or Hilton as majors, colonels, admirals, wing commanders, wealthy business tycoons, inventors, engineers and company directors (often sporting hyphenated names). These suck dry unsuspecting contacts met in those vineyards of wealth. No one regards a sociologist or social worker as being wealthy or well-paid!

Most of these men return to prison. One such who posed as psycho-sociologist (whatever that is) kept out of trouble for less than three months. This was the usual pattern with 'confidence' men, probably the most difficult of all to help to live a normal, honest life.

PART II

PART III

Introduction

This section of the book was one of the most difficult to write. How does one talk about other people's views without making one's own seem prejudiced? I have therefore tried over a period of time to acquire an impersonal outlook on theories put forward by many well-meaning persons, some prominent scholars and some the victims of their own crimes or those of their protégés.

I did a good deal of analysis into my own motives for wanting to write about those ideas, which caused me varying degrees of anxiety. I read and listened to everything I could on matters of prison reform, all of which interested me, while others alarmed me. Some of those theorists expressed my own views; others lived in cloud-cuckoo land. I have always tried not to shirk unpleasant tasks, thus, although I found it difficult sometimes to disagree with suggestions put forward in good faith by those prompted by the same impulses as drove me into the fields of nursing and social work, yet I felt they ought to be examined more closely and discussed.

Among other things I came to the conclusion that a great deal of nonsense is talked and written about 'objectivity' and the value of not having a subjective viewpoint. Only a computer is truly objective and unemotional, and who wants to be a computer? A personal outlook, which is yet not mawkishly sentimental, has its value also. As I hope to show, even the research scientists cannot rid themselves of the human failing (if it be a fault) of a personal outlook and of occasionally riding their own hobby horses at the expense of strict accuracy.

I also made a close study of terms in common usage in order to clarify my own ideas, and in the next chapter I incorporate some of those terms in the hope that this will be of help to the reader. It will also show how mistaken views have arisen through the wrong use of words.

* * * *

I have tried to avoid the pitfall of making too sweeping generalisations about reforms. I have also tried to keep to ideas which I have read and heard expressed. Even in this small orbit there is plenty of room for healthy doubts.

Most of this section may seem at first destructive. Yet, having always held that destructive criticism is useless without constructive suggestions, I offer later, wherever possible, practical alternatives.

As Baroness Wootton, that brilliant sociologist, states:[1]

'Valid, scientific proof moreover, means proof which can be empirically substantiated. Criticism of somebody else's theory is therefore not merely a matter of intellectual acuity: the most effective criticism of all is to show that a theory does not square with the facts.'

This then is the real purpose of this section.

What are the commonly discussed themes in discussions on the rehabilitation of the offender? They are:

1) After-care. Should it be professional or voluntary?

2) The rôle of the Prison officer.

3) The employment of the prisoner.

4) The value of research and the research worker in criminology.

5) Probation officers and parole.

Each of these and some others theories will be reviewed in the succeeding chapters.

[1] *Socrates, Science and Social Problems.* (New Society No. 1, October 4, 1962.) Barbara, Baroness Wootton of Abinger, former Professor of Social Studies, University of London.

Chapter VII

WHAT ARE WE TALKING ABOUT?

It may seem at first sight unnecessary to define certain words now in common usage. Yet the community's growing interest in social problems, particularly since the introduction of the welfare state, makes this important. Whether we are discussing the care of the aged or the rehabilitation of the physically disabled, mentally handicapped or the criminal, we should all know just what we mean when we talk about welfare or social work. Familiarity with words, if it does not exactly breed contempt, does tend to cloud and distort their meaning.

Dictionaries, according to the personal interest of their compilers, give interesting shades of difference to definitions, but a study of various lexicons and encyclopaedias clarified for me my impressions of certain categories of social work. These definitions, sometimes startling in their bluntness, jolted me out of any complacency I might have had. I had not known the precise meaning of terms that I, like everyone else, had been using loosely for years.

The *Encyclopaedia Britannica* defines 'criminology' as 'the study of the causation, correction and prevention of criminal behaviour. It is not a clearly distinct and integrated science but rather one that collects the contributions of diverse specialists who study crime and related phenomena.

'It is applied therefore to certain sociologists, psychiatrists, psychologists, lawyers, police officials, prison administrators, parole and probation officers and others who specialize in some aspects of criminology.'

The same encyclopaedia in defining 'Social service' states:

'Three generally accepted methods are now identified in Social service.

i) The first is social casework which aims through understanding the individual in his total situation to help him make the maximum use of the established institutions.

'ii) The second is social group work which seeks through an understanding of the behaviour of individuals in a group setting to help them utilize their fullest capacities for their own welfare and for the welfare of the group as a whole.

iii) The third is community organization, which attempts to help groups of individuals or groups of agencies so to work together that their combined efforts will be conducive to the social welfare of the whole community . . . .

'As Social service becomes a significant field of professional activity in which both men and women are employed, the nature, length and educational level of preparation are increasingly important. In both Britain and the U.S.A. university sponsorships of programmes of professional preparation and liberal arts studies as desirable pre-professional preparation are generally recognised. The programme of professional study itself combines theory of the practice of social service methods, concurrent with or followed by field instruction within social agencies and knowledge of the history, structure and administration of social welfare programmes . . . .

'Professional training for the field of Social service in the 1950s however was moving towards a common base which recognised the process of 'helping' as something which requires actual practice in the use of theory essential for this purpose.'

'Social welfare' as distinct from social work is lucidly described by the *Encyclopaedia Britannica*.

'Social welfare is considered as including the attempts made by governments and voluntary organizations to help families and individuals by maintaining incomes at an acceptable level, by providing medical care and public health services, by furthering adequate housing and community development, by providing services to facilitate social adjustment and by furnishing facilities for recreation. In addition, social welfare includes legislation and facilities designed to protect those special groups considered to be the responsibility of the community.'

Chapter VIII

VOLUNTARY
OR PROFESSIONAL AFTER-CARE?

Social work in Britain has tended to be carried out by three groups of people.

a) Professionally trained social workers who may work for either a statutory or voluntary organization.

b) Amateurs (full or part-time welfare workers, sometimes salaried) who may be attached either to a voluntary society or to a statutory body.

c) Individuals who have come to be known as 'do-gooders', rarely holding any social-work appointment or salary and without practical or academic experience in this field.

In many instances, the first two interweave with, and complement, each other. The practical experience acquired over the years by (b) is valuable, and if they work in co-operation with (a), they may have a function almost indistinguishable from that of the professional *in certain fields*. This qualification of function is important because, although the voluntary worker can be, and is, used effectively in many of the simpler tasks, particularly those of supplying material needs, he is excluded, through lack of experience and training, from establishing a deeper case relationship, which is necessary for effective social work. (See *Encyclopaedia Britannica* definitions, in the previous chapter).

The third types are sometimes well-meaning, but, because of their inexperience, ambitions and the insecurity of their position, often resentful of a) and b). They would often be better named 'do-badders'. They can and do, commit terrible blunders when unguided or unwilling to be guided. Often also, different workers give contradictory advice. This makes a confused, worried and scared man more distressed if his desire for help is genuine, and makes his insecurity and dependence worse if he is a scrounger.

In any social-work province, such meddling may be harmful; but in prison or after-care work it may well be disastrous to both man and community. When, however, the 'do-gooders' are willing to accept supervision and guidance, and perhaps training, they can form a useful reserve line.

Numerous sociologists and committees have urged the need for professional training in social work as the social system is growing daily more complex. The Younghusband Report emphasises this.[1]

'In our view, the essential case for training is that a body of knowledge now exists which individual workers cannot acquire by experience alone, and that social work practice now rests upon a systematic method and principles of work for which individual workers need training.'

It is being more and more understood that it is necessary to handle this huge task efficiently. We must have an extensive knowledge of man's nature, of psychology and of specialized social case-work techniques if we are to learn what makes some individuals into criminals while others remain law-abiding. Only when we have found out a little about those matters, can we select certain men as having likely prospects for rehabilitation.

The professional social worker is, therefore, as the encyclopaedias affirm, an expert. He is specially qualified by study and practice, and his knowledge makes him authoritative. Yet the Younghusband definition is still not wide enough. It lacks warmth. It is a clinical description. It takes no account of the social worker's own personality and ability.

Some social workers, fortunately few, are coldly scientific and analytical. They tend to grow too familiar with their subject academically, and to adopt an impersonal, rather callous, attitude to the live material of their studies—human

[1] *Report of the Working Party on Social Workers in the Local Authority Health and Welfare Services.* (H.M.S.O. 1959).

beings. Their minds are active, but their understanding becomes as a pillar of salt. These are not the best types for practical social work. They often find their niche in social research.

Their weakness is that they sometimes tend to think, and are encouraged to think, that they and their work are more important than practical social rehabilitation. As John Madge says,[2] there are two reasons for this

'It is arguable that those who pin their faith too exclusively on the Inverse Deductive Method are in reality reflecting a certain confusion in their own aims. There are two reasons why this should be so: 1) the almost universal instruction that knowledge is in some way superior to activity; this is bound to encourage the belief that the search for truths and generalisations is in itself a sufficient aim. 2) The other reason is that social scientists—or at least respectable ones—have traditionally been shuttered off from contact with their raw material.'

Others, and they are in the majority, go into social work in the same spirit as those who enter the Church, teaching nursing or medicine, namely, to follow a vocation. Salary and status are not the principal incentives to such persons. They wish to employ a talent that they feel they have been given, and have developed, to diminish a little the unhappiness that they see all round them.

'Voluntary worker' is a confusing term which covers two types of personnel. There are those who work for voluntary agencies as opposed to statutory authorities. They may be trained social workers and receive salaries—for example, Secretaries of Guilds or Councils of Social Service. Then there are those working under qualified supervision, who may be paid or unpaid—for example, workers in Citizens' Advice Bureaux. The unpaid is the only real 'voluntary' worker, but he has no responsibility.

Britain has a long and proud history of voluntary social welfare, and very inspiring reading it makes. From voluntary

[2] *The Tools of Social Science,* John Madge. (Longmans).

efforts have grown many of the benefits of the Welfare State. Without such noble and selfless humanitarianism, Britain would still be in the Dark Ages. The blind, the deaf and dumb, the cripple, the disabled, the spastic child would throng our streets as helpless beggars. The alcoholic would be lying in a drunken stupor in the gutter. The aged would have no warmth, perhaps no roof and no-one to comfort them in their growing weakness. The helpless child would still be exploited in the home and in industry, a mass of bruises, a cowering, great-eyed, under-nourished reproach to humanity. The needy would still be shuffling round dirty and depressing workhouses. The insane would still be soiling the straw on the floors of Bedlam; the sick would be powerless in the hands of loutish and uninterested, often cruel, women from the lowest walks of life. The prisoner would still be herded with others, chained and manacled in evil-smelling holes. His only employment would be on the treadmill, and he would be illiterate, diseased, neglected and ferocious—a half-starved wolf.

The Church too, of all denominations including the Jewish, has its orphanages, schools and homes for the destitute, the addict, the unmarried mother and the discharged prisoner. It keeps an ever-open door for the needy and distressed, and it has lightened many grave social problems.

Some humane industrialists have given millions to improve the social, as well as working, conditions of their employees. Meanwhile universities have founded centres in communities surrounding them, and give generously of their time and money to better life in their localities.

The Services have a long history of care for the disabled, the homeless, the veteran, the widow and orphan. Some of the care is now statutory, but it originated in voluntary organisations who have provided funds through flag days, poppy days and other projects. Through them have come homes for veterans and their families, convalescent homes, orphanages, schools, even factories for the disabled.

Even animals have not been forgotten in this flood of magnanimity and goodwill. It is through voluntary effort and the fighting indignation of many good people, some now famous, others unknown, that most of the social legislation in this country has appeared on the statute books.

This massive influence coming from all that is best in mankind has been, and, I hope, always will be, a considerable force—a power to be reckoned with and respected. For from our free responses have sprung most of the good motives, the ideals, the capacity for love and sacrifice which differentiates man from the animals.

Whether voluntary workers are trained or untrained, full-time or part-time, they form a solid background to the welfare state, which has only too often the impersonality of a robot, the inelasticity of a programmed computer. Whatever their shortcomings—and they are only human after all, and so fallible and vulnerable—without them the welfare state would be a very poor thing in every sense of the word and the highly-qualified social worker would be working in a vacuum.

The voluntary agency and worker have considerable advantages over the statutory body. They can experiment with new schemes and new ideas and they have an enviable independence. They are not staff of statutory authorities, and they do not have to submit their ideals, their plans for the betterment of humanity, to Government departments. Their plans are not rejected on the grounds that 'they will cost too much, and we must watch the taxpayers' (or ratepayers') money.' No authority says, 'No! The Minister will not like it. He would be asked embarrassing questions in the House or by the Press.'

Yet this powerful weapon of the voluntary agencies can be, and sometimes is, subject to abuse. Just because they are not answerable to anyone except their own committees (if any) and perhaps to those whom they are helping, the voluntary societies have provided an umbrella for a number of unofficial organisations which often duplicate the admirable work already being done.

Most, fortunately, can do no harm, but others are highly dangerous. Sooner or later the genuine voluntary agency has to protest against the bogus one, and if helpless has to call in the statutory authority. Societies and self-styled Institutes, with often self-appointed and untrained 'directors', 'superintendents' or 'wardens', have periodically sprung up, proclaiming that they were offering services to the community which were needed and unavailable from any other source. The public swallow these lies, through ignorance of the societies offering genuine help which these agencies are imitating, like weeds, the real flowers, or from desperation and their need for such services.

The public should be on their guard against such charlatans. They need to acquire the suspicious mind of the professional social worker, who never takes anything on chance, but checks to find if claims are *bona fide*.

Some of these bogus 'do-gooders' cover themselves by admitting proudly and blatantly that they are unqualified to offer the services they promise. But, they say, as no one else is offering such services, or fit to offer them, they are here to be the salvation of all who need them. They claim that the established agencies are no good or non-existent (which is often untrue).

Thus have arisen at various times the unofficial nursery schools, whose sole motive was profit-making, with children in dirty and unhygienic conditions and no trained staff. So have come the 'homes' for unmarried mothers—homes which, when checked by the authorities, were found to be the bases for illegal operations, prostitution and white-slave traffic. So have arisen the unofficial nursing homes and hostels run by untrained staff, and unofficial after-care societies, which may use this valuable service as a cover for less worthy purposes. This sort of 'after-care' was described in a radio broadcast entitled 'Crime and the Police', on August 23, 1963. I took verbatim notes at the time.

It was the tale of a bank robber speaking from Dartmoor, and the commentator introduced the story with the remark: 'This tale would be tragic if it weren't so funny!'

The robber described how he had been drawn to a man on his working party who, he thought, was on 'the social register'. The robber admitted that he was a 'con' man, who could approach a number of rich people outside the prison. He told the 'social register' individual of his plan, which was to interest his rich contacts, when he was discharged, in forming a 'welfare organisation' for prisoners, who would force reforms on the government.

The robber got the 'social register' type and the rich men interested. He claimed that they collected £20,000 from the contacts towards the organisation. Unfortunately the 'social register' type got on so well with the rich men that he considered the robber expendable, and went ahead without him. The robber confessed that he had suggested forming a 'welfare' society as a front, because thus lots and lots of criminals would go through their hands, and they would be able to select the cream for planning and carrying out a big job. The robber claimed that the 'welfare' organisation was in existence, but without himself. 'What they're doing now, I don't know'.

Whether this tale was fantasy or not, it points to the danger of encouraging unofficial societies without adequate supervision. The story has never been refuted; and from personal experience in this and other countries I know that such societies for all sorts of purposes do spring up. Whether or not the original motive is worthy, the founders soon become the tools and victims of those they are trying to help.

If such 'do-gooders' are sincere, they can be, and usually are, encouraged to join officially recognized ventures, whether statutory or voluntary. If not, they are usually exposed in time. So they fizzle out, but not without doing considerable damage, not only to their victims but to the public image of social service generally.

*　　*　　*　　*

Several myths about social work have grown up over the years and need to be faced and challenged. Far too much gossip and too many ill-founded statements based on prejudice have created barriers which need not exist.

The first myth concerns the importance and value of being

an amateur rather than a professional. This legend has developed from two sides. There is snob value in the amateur status in sport as opposed to the professional. Amateurs are extolled for entering sport for the love of the game. They usually have private means, whereas the professional goes into the game for money. The profit motive is regarded as baser. And yet often a man who enters a sport for financial reasons is prompted by the same love of the game as the amateur flaunts.

There is also a 'Lady Bountiful' pose, a carry-over from the days of patronage and charity. Much social and welfare work in Britain still suffers from the tradition of this well-meaning lady. Social work still tends not to be regarded as a vocation, a profession which demands rigorous training, discipline and experience over a long period.

Today, a halting attempt is made by some amateurs to 'do social work' because it has become fashionable. It is a way of being accepted by the 'establishment', of gaining publicity for themselves. Married women 'take it up', as though social work were a piece of plain knitting to while away an idle hour. Their intelligence, it is claimed, needs to busy itself with more than the kitchen sink. Also, by showing this philanthropy, they will assist their husbands in their political or business careers. Near-religious maniacs, themselves unbalanced personalities, offer 'help' as a means to gain the souls of their victims.

Such motives are not sufficiently high for social work, and the quality of the work so given is correspondingly poor. To the really tolerant social worker, colour, religion and politics are immaterial.

Some members of the House of Lords, during the debate on the Younghusband Report, wondered whether there was a genuine distinction between professionally-qualified social workers and those engaged in social welfare with only the qualifications of good sense and experience. While they conceded that some form of training was necessary, they thought there was a danger of placing too much emphasis on it because of the current liking for professionalism. The suggestion appeared to be that more emphasis should be placed on administrative and organisational ability and less on the study of human motivation and behaviour.

However—as other members realised and pointed out, though not in so many words—without reasonable understanding of human motivation, it is extremely difficult to help people effectively and economically. Also those very disciplines acquired through university training improve and develop any administrative and organising talent. The practical, trained social worker is far removed from the cartoon fantasy of the dreamy, absent-minded professor of philosophy.

To say that an amateur social worker provides *ipso facto* better help to the community than a professional does is presumptuous nonsense. One does not turn out a Christian Dior model on a home sewing machine. The model's deceptive simplicity has taken years of special skill and training, with expert cutters in a cutting room. Nor does the claim that one is a French dressmaker, when one is not even a tailor, make such a dress. It will be made 'of such stuff as dreams are made on' and disillusionment, bitterness at no improvement in the individual's plight or community 'helped' will result.

What the House of Lords and others have failed to realize is that medicine passed from barbers to qualified doctors, and nursing to women willing to train. Personnel trained in public-health knowledge was seen to be necessary if plagues, infection and mortality were to be reduced. Now the community has begun to realize the trial-and-error methods of amateurs are not adequate to deal with increasingly complex social matters such as housing, child care, mental health, geriatrics and criminal violence. Whether we like it or not, the days of the amateur dispensing charity, common sense and pearls of doubtful wisdom are numbered.

There is increasing anxiety about serious social problems and a feeling that physicians and surgeons are needed for the sick community. Instead of well-meaning ministering angels, who can only stroke the head, pat the restless hand and administer the temporarily cooling drink, workers with more drastic, therapeutic knowledge are, it is felt, required. The patient is obviously becoming sicker, in spite of care, sympathy and sentimentality. 'The sick society' is a commonplace expression. And just as one would not trust one's sick life-partner to the remedies of a lay person, no matter how kind, so the final responsibility for treatment of the sick community should be in the hands of the specialist.

In spite of this, however, the word 'professional' for a social worker still tends to be regarded as a dirty or derisory term. Those who regard it so are sometimes ignorant of what is meant and sometimes envious. Another myth is that only from the voluntary worker will the client receive warmth, sympathy, understanding, love. The professional, it is said, is so cold and objective that he is of no use to people in distress. He has not got the voluntary worker's big warm, sentimental heart and the desire to help. What presumption this is! The amateur has no monopoly of sympathy.

In fact, it is just because the trained social worker has this deep desire to help other people with their problems and to alleviate social distress that he has taken the trouble, often at great self-sacrifice, to acquire the necessary techniques. He has achieved expertise to give useful advice and to help a man to an appreciation of his own capacities. Whether individuals avail themselves of this expertise is not the true concern of the social worker. He just makes himself available to anybody who wants him.

A third argument which has no scientific basis is danger-ously like a sop to the less capable. Examinations and the ability to pass them do not necessarily make a good pro-fessional person, it is said. This may or may not be true. What is certain is that examinations are the only means of testing a person's capacity in studies and disciplines. They are a guarantee that the examinee was at least interested in his subject; possibly also had an inherited flair for a particular profession, whether engineering, medicine or social work. Meanwhile, lack of written proof of ability is no guarantee that one has anything to offer, no matter what protestations may be made about interest in certain fields.

The answer to those who pooh-pooh examinations as a guarantee of efficiency is to ask them: 'Would you entrust yourself to a Channel tunnel built by amateurs, or your child, whose skull is fractured in a car accident, to a barber as in the old days?' Those questions are ludicrous. Yet people are willing to entrust prisoners and their families to unskilled persons, either through indifference and shortsightedness or because of this cult in Britain amounting almost to worship of the amateur status.

A fourth misrepresentation is that social workers are no good at their job because they do not provide houses for people who come to them (even though the applicants have not been on any housing list!), or £20 a week National Assistance, and so on.

These ridiculous suggestions I have heard made to groups of prisoners as if such benefits were their 'rights', and the accusation was levelled against social workers that they were keeping the men from obtaining them. Yet I never heard that anyone else was able to perform those miracles. Idle appeals like these to the selfish side of men foster discontent and resentment against authority, and, though later the men find that these accusations are false, the damage is done.

A fifth myth is that people who have been in close contact with prisoners for years are better equipped to understand them than any social worker. The prison officer, the prison visitor, even the ex-prisoner are all put forward as more capable candidates for social work. If that were so, why has the problem of recidivism not long ago been solved? Why is crime still on the increase? One might as well say that a nursing orderly is fit to perform a lobectomy, either because he has had tuberculosis or has been nursing tubercular patients for years, or has seen the operation performed, or has read it up in a book, or—more relevantly to prison social work —has had lectures on other illnesses.

'A little learning' is indeed a dangerous thing. This argument therefore is specious.

The social worker would be the last to claim that he has found a cure for crime; but at least he is fully aware of the gargantuan task ahead of him and has equipped himself with tools and experience which may alleviate this social ailment.

Closely allied to this fifth argument is one proffered by ex-prisoners, usually by those with records of false pretences.

'So many prison reformers know everything about prison except what it feels like to be inside. That knowledge is the most essential part of a reformer's equipment.'[3]

It is a false doctrine that prisoners and recidivists, especially confidence men, know better than the rest of us how to cure crime. To them and their supporters I should say: 'Physician, heal thyself.' One does not have to have tuberculosis or cancer in order to be a good medical officer, nurse or surgeon. If those men, often—regrettably consulted as experts and interviewed by press, radio, television and politicians, know so much about the rehabilitation of the offender, how is it that they have never applied their ideas to their own lives? I do not say that a hardened criminal may not become a reformed character; if he cannot we are all wasting our time. What I maintain is that he cannot suddenly, by virtue of his experience, blossom into a sociologist or criminologist. He may be a prison reformer in the sense that he points out the need for improving material conditions, but he will not be a reformer of other people.

*　　*　　*　　*

Let us now turn to the three types of workers mentioned at the beginning of this chapter—the professional social worker, the voluntary worker, and the untrained, unsupervised worker. Let us see how they apply themselves to that most difficult of all forms of welfare, the rehabilitation of the offender, comprising in-care and after-care.

The professional treatment of the offender and after-care of the discharged prisoner are the infants of the social services; in fact, the infants are scarcely born. The reason for this late parturition is obvious. For centuries man has accepted— and many still accept—the doctrine of retribution in dealing with offenders against society. An eye for an eye and a tooth for a

[3] *Five Years for Fraud.* Anon. (Sampson Low, 1936).

tooth—in many instances, a whole mouthful of teeth—has been the attitude. The emotions of fear, anger and hatred have been more powerful counter-agents to penal reform and curative treatment than to reform in any other field.

Civilised persons do not find it hard to be moved by emotions of pity, love and even indignation and a sense of guilt at the fate of the sick. They feel similar pity for the orphaned, widowed, aged indigent, mentally ill, the crippled and otherwise incapacitated. Suggest, however, that the criminal is as much in need of this pity and there is either a horrified raising of the hands or an indifferent shrug of the shoulders.

Yet in spite of this hostility or indifference there has appeared an undercurrent of growing disapproval of retribution unaccompanied by any hope of reform. The demand has increased for better and more professional work on the reclamation of the wrong-doer.

This undercurrent has been swelling ever since the recommendations of the Gladstone Committee in 1895. This recommended that:

'For the future reformation and deterrence should be treated as primary and concurrent objects and that prison treatment should be efficiently designed to maintain, stimulate or awaken the higher susceptibilities of prisoners and turn them out of prison better men and women both physically and morally than when they came in.'

I have already quoted the Maxwell Report which recommended the appointment of trained social workers in prisons. All prisons now have them, though not in nearly adequate enough numbers to do satisfactory case-work on all who could benefit.

The Morrison-Butler Report[4] emphasized the necessity for the prison social worker.

'The proper handling of a prisoner's family and social rela-

[4] *Prisons and Borstals* (4th edition). Page 36 para. 53, H.M.S.O. 1960.

tions may well be of first importance both in helping his adaptation to prison life and preparing him for the future. While these are the general concern of the staff, particularly of the Chaplains and Assistant Governors, they are sufficiently important to require specialised handling. At most local prisons, therefore, there are qualified and experienced social workers known as Prison Welfare Officers employed by N.A.D.P.A.S.'[5]

Another aspect was emphasised by J. Spencer.[6]

'The social worker, both in the fields of group work and in that of casework, is no longer concerned only with the task of alleviating material distress, but is engaged also in the more difficult job of helping the individual to adapt himself to the problems of the world in which he lives.'

In practice the criminological social worker, whether probation officer or prison social worker, has a triple rôle. First, he, or it may be she, (though for the purpose of simplicity in writing, I shall use the male term), is concerned with the material welfare of his cases. With a number of prisoners this is the only rôle he is called on to play. In this function he is often confused with the lay welfare officer, but in fact his training and knowledge of the numerous sources of help available, and the ability and authority to contact the right one distinguish him. He is, as it were, a professional liaison officer between the 'client' and the agency best able to cope with the problem.

Baroness Wootton[7] expressed this admirably.

'This middleman function is in itself so expert a service as to qualify for professional status in its own right.'

[5] Prison Welfare Officers since January 1966, have been probation officers under the combined probation and parole service.
[6] 'The Place of the Social Workers in the Prisons'. *Howard Journal*, 1951. Spencer.
[7] *Social Science & Social Pathology*. Op. cit.

Allied to this middleman rôle is the building up by the social worker of a team of able and willing helpers and colleagues inside and outside the prison, so that a man may be referred to them for specialised treatment.

Secondly, as pointed out previously, the prison social worker is a professional caseworker with knowledge and experience of a man's nature and needs. Thirdly he acts as a consultant to other bodies, and gives advice or information on particular social problems. In the probation service the other people are usually judges or magistrates. In prisons they may be members of the Home Office, the prison staff such as the Governor, the Senior medical officer, the chaplain or psychologist.

Most of the voluntary societies and workers (some employed by statutory authorities such as the Ministry of Labour and National Assistance Board[8]) welcomed the arrival of the social worker in the prisons, saying that this had long been needed to expand the task of rehabilitation. The Church Army and the Salvation Army, who already had representatives in the prisons, became among our staunchest allies in the work of after-care.

The two religious armies were vital to the social worker. They traced missing relatives from whom men had been parted often for many years. They helped, whenever approached, with living accommodation for the prisoner about to be discharged 'N.F.A.' (with no fixed abode or address).

Some people, relying on reports from discharged prisoners criticise these hostels. How many critics, however, could as a labour of love, endure night after night to admit the dregs of humanity and to clear up morning after morning the dirt, vomit, and wet and soiled bedlinen left by these men? Many of them are dirtier than animals in their habits, and windows have to be opened each morning to let out the stench. I describe in the next section a prisoner's night in such a hostel. It is not the 'armies' or the workers who provide unsuitable accommodation; it is the 'lodgers'. It is up to the men themselves to improve their ways to help those wonderful, self-

[8] Now incorporated into the Ministry of Social Security.

sacrificing people, who are Christians in every sense of the word.

More specialised hostels, such as Norman House, St. Luke's House and the Rowton Houses, are also a great support to London prison social workers in assisting with this problem of the homeless. The W.R.V.S., who have formed a prison welfare section, are invaluable to the resident prison social worker for supplying reports on home visits to the men's families. The majority of prisoners are not local, but come from all parts, some from Scotland, many from Ireland, some even from the West Indies.

The Discharged Prisoners' Aid Societies, possibly through fear and insecurity, were the most difficult to persuade of a prison social worker's use. Many never accepted that they were part of a team. These societies had been the victims of much criticism from prisoners, and of adverse reports, however tactfully worded. Books had discussed their inability to move with the times and to employ trained social workers for after-care. They could hardly be blamed if they showed resentment of the resident social workers who had taken their place.

In some prisons no compromise was possible, and prison social workers, some ex-probation officers, left the service in disappointment. Others, myself included, felt vexed when the societies' after-care officers showed, by their reports of interviews with the men we sent to them, that they had never read our case-histories. Or they refused to act upon the detailed histories prepared, with recommendations, by the prison social worker—often after months of study of a man.

The D.P.A.s had therefore nobody but themselves to blame if more and more of those case-histories went to trained social workers outside, such as probation officers. These showed, by conferring with us, that they were genuinely thinking of the prisoners' welfare and future.

The D.P.A. officers did useful work, however, and were probably happiest in visiting the homes of the prisoners. In this, along with the W.R.V.S., they contributed towards a man's preparation for his discharge.

The third class, the unskilled amateurs, in a number of cases misread, if they troubled to read it at all, the Maxwell Report. They bypassed the social workers, who were responsible for the welfare and after-care plans of each prisoner, and either contacted the prisoners direct, by letter or visit, or discussed them with Governors, Assistant Governors or chaplains. This was what they had done when the D.P.A. visitor had been coming daily to the prison. This, of course, led to duplication of advice and suggestions—to the confusion of some prisoners and the delight of others, who loved to 'mix it', as the prison jargon has it. A certain amount of dangling bananas as bait also caused some prisoners to drift into their hands.

One non-Christian religious organisation appeared to be gaining a remarkable number of 'converts' from Church of England or 'no denomination' prisoners. The chaplain and I discovered that each 'convert' was offered £10 on release from prison if he belonged to this 'church'!

Many of those Associate and 'after-care' societies misinterpreted the Maxwell Report about not only the prison social worker's position but their own rôle. They did not realise that they were supposed to be helping the social workers and the D.P.A. after-care officers by acting as friends to the ex-prisoners, not setting themselves up as pseudo-social workers to these bitter and bewildered men. Fortunately, in time, after we had made contact with their sponsors, many altered their ideas and consulted the prison social workers to ensure that a man whom they wished to interview was not already being looked after. Most learned through the Governors that to avoid duplication they should first contact the social worker.

It is often said in vindication of amateurs that they possess common sense, which more than makes up for lack of expertise. Here are a few instances of 'common sense'. Sometimes the mistakes made by amateurs are not without humour.

A prison visitor, a good and kindly man, once told me at a conference of a humbling experience. He had taken an interest in a prisoner, and had visited him twice weekly. On the man's discharge, he invited him to his home for supper.

Afterwards, while the visitor's wife was washing up in the kitchen, he suggested that the released man, who was sitting in the living-room, might like to give thanks to God for his release and to ask for strength to go straight in the future. The ex-prisoner willingly agreed. Some time was spent in prayer, both visitor and his guest kneeling in reverence while the visitor prayed aloud. A further short talk ensued. Then their guest said politely that he must go. He bade his hosts goodbye, thanking them for all their kindness, and assuring his former prison visitor of his desire to live a decent, honest life.

The prison visitor retired to bed, happy that he had done something really worthwhile. He had brought a man to God and made a better citizen out of this thief. Only when undressing did he discover that, while he was interceding for his guest in prayer, the pickpocket had skilfully relieved him of his wallet of notes and gold fob watch which had belonged to his grandfather. His expression was rueful as he said to me: 'I just don't know how the dickens he did it or why! I had got him a job and he had plenty of money. Of course, he never turned up for the job.'

This I think, though touchingly human in its gentle foolishness, illustrates the difference between sympathy and understanding.

Every human being is capable of sympathy. Possibly even the Gestapo had twinges of it. In social work and, in particular, prison social work, this is just not sufficient. One must also have an understanding of the human mind and behaviour.

I know of a social worker appointed to a large prison where one of the unofficial schemes had begun, who had the frustrating experience, during the initial months of appointment of having to soothe irate prisoners because a do-gooder insisted on making unofficial home visits to their wives. On three occasions the visitor had persuaded the prisoners' wives that their husbands were completely worthless and useless as providers for the home. On this person's advice the wives had instituted divorce proceedings.

All this visitor's arguments may have been right, but to interfere between a man and his wife is surely no part of another individual's duties. The visitor called it his method of 'rehabilitating the offender'! Yet the men concerned, bitter at having lost their wives and families through meddling, would surely be the least likely to be reclaimed. With no homes to return to, they would be filled with hatred and hostility on their discharge. Yet their rehabilitation was boldly claimed and never challenged by the authorities.

Another agitated man had to be interviewed by a prison social worker before he 'broke up the place' as the prison officer said. The officer had hastily sent for the social worker. The man, though a recidivist, was 'a decent bloke', according to the Principal officer, and he did not wish to put him on report for punishment. 'There's obviously something needling him. He's just returned to his cell after a visit from his wife.'

The social worker, thinking the matter sounded urgent, hurried over to the wing. A surly, reluctant prisoner was brought before her, and sat unwillingly on a chair opposite.

There was a few seconds' polite conversation to thaw the atmosphere. Then the man's trouble boiled over, and his tale poured out.

The prisoner, as appeared from his record and social case-history from the Welfare department, was weak rather than wicked. He had committed several thefts for various reasons. For a number of them, one would have thought, he might have been put on probation as there were extenuating circumstances; but he had never been given this chance. He was quiet, well-spoken and polite. His marriage was emotionally fairly stable, and there were very few such in the prison. His wife had always stuck by him, receiving him back after each sentence was completed. There were two young children. They had lived in a series of furnished rooms.

During his present sentence the man, whom we may call Charles, though that is not his name, had been referred to this do-gooder instead of to the official Welfare department. He had expressed anxiety about his wife and family, and wondered how they would manage this time, as his sentence was the longest he had ever received. They had recently moved into rooms which were rather more expensive than formerly, but they were all they could find which would accept two children.

The self-styled social worker had volunteered to visit the wife, and was gratefully given the address by Charles.

Before he saw the wife, the man had approached the landlady, and told her indignantly that the rent was too high. How did she expect poor Mrs X to pay it when her husband was in prison?

That evening, the landlady's husband went upstairs to Mrs X and told her that she and the children would have to go. This was a respectable house, and they weren't having any gaol-birds around. Mrs X, in tears, reported this to her husband the next day, when she visited the prison.

The social worker tried to sort out the mess, but the landlord was adamant. As the couple had moved from area to area, they had lost their original place on a council-house waiting list. Regrettably, nothing could be done for Mrs X except to put her into Accommodation Part III with her children or take the children away temporarily and give them into the care of the Children's Officer. The first unhappy alternative seemed the lesser of two evils, and was all that could be done by the statutory authorities.

One of the worst examples of irresponsibility under the guise of common-sense, sympathy and 'effective rehabilitation' concerned a man who was due for discharge in six weeks' time. One afternoon he was on the prison social worker's list for a pre-release interview.

During his imprisonment Tony (as we shall call him) had made few applications for help with social and domestic difficulties. He was described by a social worker, who knew him and had dealt with him on a previous occasion, as being of a rather retiring nature. He did not appear physically very strong, but was pale, thin, and below average height. He was 38 years old, but had no skill or trade and no fixed address. His previous convictions had been for theft, loitering with intent, robbery, robbery with violence and assault.

Not too likely a prospect for rehabilitation as a 'special case', thought the social worker Mr S. as he read the case

E

history. However, as Tony's length of sentence required that he should be seen about detailed discharge plans, Mr S. asked him to come into the office.

It was only the second or third time that Mr S. had seen him, as he had been in another wing. During the conversation Mr S., who was naturally watching Tony's expression, realized that something was wrong. There was a certain look about the pupils of the eyes, a glitter of the iris, a diffuseness and slurring of speech.

He asked Tony if he had any plans for his release. Tony replied slowly that he had been seen by Mr Y. (an Associate of a voluntary society). Keeping down his irritation that once more the Welfare department had had its responsibilities taken over by an outsider, Mr S. asked for further details. It appeared that this Mr Y. was a clerk who was interested in both prison and hospital welfare. Eager to help both Tony and a hospital, he thought it would be a good idea for Tony to become a hospital porter, and used his influence with the hospital authorities to have them accept his protégé. When Mr S. asked Tony if this was what he really wanted to do, Tony replied: 'I don't know.'

At the end of the afternoon, Mr S. was still anxious about Tony's discharge arrangements. He was the authorised person to deal with all such arrangements, but these had not been discussed with him. He would have curbed his natural annoyance and asked Mr Y. to come and talk over the plans he had made for Tony, but something more was tugging at his mind, and he went across to the Prison Records office. No sign was found of Tony's record. Other work kept Mr S. from further search, but he asked the prison officer if he would kindly trace the record for him. Next morning Tony's record was in the Welfare office. An Assistant Governor had had it in his filing cabinet, after seeing Mr Y. and encouraging him to go ahead with his plans for Tony.

What Mr S. read sent him hurrying across to the Assistant Governor. On his way along the empty wing, he saw Tony sitting on a bench outside the Centre Principal officer's office, hunched in a state of apathetic misery. Mr S. smiled and called out brightly, 'Good morning, Tony.'

Tony's reply was surprising. 'They're all talking about me, you see.'

Thinking that some pressure was being put on Tony by other prisoners, and that he was about to report it to the Centre Principal officer, Mr S. paused and asked 'Who are talking about you, Tony?'

'All those b———s of screws, there. Don't you see them? Can't you hear them whispering? They're talking about me, I tell you.'

Mr S. felt his spine crawl. The wing was empty and silent, except for the Centre Principal Officer's telephone, which startled them by ringing.

Mr S. tried to smile and said: 'Don't worry, Tony. I'll speak to them and tell them not to talk about you.'

Tony shook his head disbelievingly with a strained look on his face.

Mr S. had had his hunch of the previous afternoon confirmed by the prison record and Tony's present behaviour. He went, a greatly worried man, to see the Assistant Governor.

He explained the discharge arrangements. The Assistant Governor said he knew that Mr Y. had fixed Tony up with a hospital job and he thought it was a good thing, for the prison social workers could not be expected to find jobs for every prisoner on discharge. Mr S. pointed out that this was one of the Welfare officers' most important responsibilities, whether they did it individually, through the Ministry of Labour, through Associates or prison visitors or visiting employers, or by the man writing himself for jobs. The Assistant Governor brushed this aside, and still insisted that Mr Y., who was a kind, nice man, had done a good piece of social work.

Mr S. suggested that Mr Y's. personality was irrelevant to the business and asked the Assistant Governor if he had read the prison record, which was, of course, unavailable to an outsider such as Mr Y. He also asked if the Assistant Governor would like to come and see Tony, now on the bench outside, and repeated his recent conversation with the man.

The Assistant Governor admitted that he had read the prison record. Mr S. then asked if he thought it was a good idea to recommend Tony as a hospital porter. He said 'Yes'.

It is unpleasant to sound critical of the administrative staff. Mr S. felt uncomfortable but determined. 'Well I don't, Mr A.,' he replied with some heat. 'Would you be willing to accept responsibility if a twice-certified schizophrenic-paranoid went berserk in a self-operating lift taking a desperately ill patient to the theatre or a serious heart-case for an X-ray?'

The Assistant Governor's only reply was a tolerant smile of resignation at this stupid 'professional,' who was jealous of Mr Y. and did not wish him to have the chance of doing good to a prisoner.

Mr S. continued: 'Well, fortunately for you, you wouldn't have to take the rap, but I should, and while I'm willing to stand or fall by my own mistakes I won't risk mistakes by an intruder, who holds no position and has no access to records. He, too, would, of course, be absolved. Certainly, as the person responsible for this man's discharge arrangements I shall not recommend him for employment in his present condition. Furthermore, if you won't notify the Senior medical officer and the Senior psychologist about Tony's mental condition, I shall.'

Though his own work was piling up, Mr S. visited the senior Medical Officer and the senior Psychologist to report poor Tony's condition and to ask if they would see him as soon as possible. Then the Welfare department could make the proper recommendation for his discharge. This they agreed to do.

Within forty-eight hours, the man's mental state had become so disturbed that there was no further talk about finding him a job. For the third time in his prison history, he had again to be certified. Mr S. telephoned the hospital matron, who was horrified at the risk the hospital had run.

The last words on this theme may be left to the Advisory

Council on the Treatment of Offenders[9] and to the Young-husband Report[10] from which it quotes:

'There are certain dangers attached to selecting persons to work with prisoners and we wish to stress the importance of careful selection, perhaps involving some period of probationary service.

'As to training, it is necessary to stress that this is not work for inexperienced amateurs. It requires a warm heart but also a clear head, compassion combined with insight, lack of illusion, and preparedness for disappointment. Most after-care auxiliaries will find their good intentions more effectively translated into rewarding achievement if they can have some training and can work under the guidance of professional social workers. The point is well made in a different context by the Younghusband Report:

'If voluntary workers are asked to give regular time, and to take appropriate responsibility, there then exists an obligation to equip them to do their job competently. Training is essential if voluntary workers are to give their services knowledgeably and acceptably, and training can help them to feel an integral part of the service. It is particularly important if they are to recognise when the situation requires a professionally trained worker or a different service.'

---

[9] *The Organisation of After-Care.* Report of Advisory Council on the Treatment of Offenders. H.M.S.O. 1963.
[10] Op. cit. paragraph 1059.

Chapter IX

THE PRISON OFFICER

By the world outside prison walls, by the Press and public alike, the prison officer is regarded, as a 'warder' and often contemptuously called one. He is a turnkey, a 'screw' in prison jargon, someone of inferior intelligence and ability. He is fitted only to lock and unlock doors for criminals, and he has a loutish, sometimes cruel outlook on those in his custody.

Just how accurate is this picture? How up to date? It is, I think, high time that a clearer, more realistic look should be taken at the modern prison officer and the rôle he plays in prison life. Let us study him under three aspects—as a man, an officer and a social worker.

The prison officer as a man

The officer, like the prisoner, is not some different species, apart from mankind as one often feels. If I may paraphrase Shylock's speech:

'Hath not a prison officer eyes? Hath not a prison officer hands, organs, dimensions, senses, affections, passions? Fed with the same food, hurt with the same weapons, subject to the same diseases, healed by the same means, warmed and cooled by the same winter and summer as a Christian is? If you prick us, do we not bleed? If you tickle us, do we not laugh? If you poison us, do we not die?'

I worked daily, and often nightly, with prison officers at Wandsworth. I ate with them and joined in their social activities for over two years. I also met prison officers at Wakefield. I should have been very stupid and unobservant if I had not got to know the typical prison officer—if there is such a man—very well.

I found that these men with whom I had to work in harness had a great many social and economic problems which represented a substantial and complex task for their own two welfare officers at Head Office in Whitehall. In some instances they were as difficult as those of the prisoners. In addition, they had to accept long hours of duty; to serve what was virtually a life-sentence and to accept compulsory sex-control, as many in the large local prisons were separated from their wives. They ran daily risk of attack, perhaps death, and endured great anxiety as to what would happen to their wives and children if they were hurt.

If prison officers were sick or injured in attacks by prisoners, I was usually informed by the Gate officer or their fellow-officers. I used to feel that it was as much part of my job to give comfort and encouragement to those often discouraged men as to the prisoners themselves. In my spare time I would pay social visits to their homes if I possibly could, or at least send a message of goodwill. My staff and I got into the habit of sending 'Get Well' cards as a little gesture of appreciation of the help we received from officers when on duty.

A great source of discontent was their transfers to other prisons or from others to Wandsworth, even though such transfers were a condition of employment. In either case they had not only to adjust to new surroundings, staff and prisoners, but to accept that, because of shortage of living-quarters, they might be separated from their families for an unknown period.

If officers were bachelors (and there were very few of those), things were not so bad. The majority were, however, married men with families, and disliked having to live apart from their wives. They stayed in the bachelor quarters as lonely grass-widowers, remaining on extra duty because nights were so tedious. They could only go to the 'pictures', to the 'local' or the Officers' Club with other officers who could talk about nothing but 'shop'. The loneliness of a large metropolis struck just as hardly at those men as the youngest undergraduate or boy or girl away from home for the first time in their bed-sitters.

Why more prison officers' marriages did not come adrift was a miracle to me and a testimonial to their patience as men and women.

The loneliness was emphasised and further aggravated by the fact that, although they were supposed to be off duty for one week-end in four, officers had sometimes to forgo that pleasure. When they should have gone to visit their families in Manchester or Liverpool or wherever they were, the officers had to stay on duty because of shortage of staff in the prison. Some officers might be sick; some on leave, others on escort duty to other prisons which entailed a night away. Or some-times—most frustrating of all—the prison was 'on guard,' expecting an eruption of violence or an attempted break-out.

There was strong resentment that prisoners who had broken the law in serious ways should be listened to with respect by prominent people outside prison, and that their word should be taken as authoritative, and never checked for falsehoods. One officer, a Chief for thirty-two years, protested vigorously in print against accusations of sadism in prison officers. He said that such complaints were usually made by prisoners who deliberately provoked prison officers, and that it was as much as the officer's job would be worth to start an attack. The prison officer, he wrote, 'is always on the defensive; so that if, as I saw for myself on several occasions in Wandsworth, a prisoner attacks him, he is entitled to defend himself.'

I knew every sick and injured prisoner in the hospitals, inside and outside Wandsworth prison, and the causes of their injuries, and in over two years I did not once see a prisoner injured by officers. One violent maniac, who with his long nails had almost gouged out a Principal Officer's eye (one of the kindest of officers at that), had to be forcibly restrained in the padded cell. Yet not even there could there have been concealment of officer-inflicted injuries—from me or from anyone else.

Several officers I knew had been attacked by prisoners, but I came across only one instance of what might remotely be called sadism by a ruthlessly ambitious officer. Because some prisoners would not 'toe the line' and accept him as their 'friend and adviser,' he had his own way of punishing them for daring to reject his view of himself as a social worker—which of course he was not. He never, however, went to the length of physical violence.

Some prison officers—very few, I am pleased to admit—were resentful that so much help was given to prisoners with housing and other matters. I was asked by one very disgruntled officer why I did not assist prison officers to get houses when they retired? He pointed out, with some justice, that the prison officer, unless he becomes a Chief, is in a very insecure housing position when he leaves the service. As long as he is in service he obtains some living accommodation, usually satisfactory, but, because of his transfers, he is never eligible to be put on a council housing list.

There was resentment also at the long wait for promotion, when men apparently less able became Assistant Governors, Class II.

The Prison Officer as an Officer

In his book on prisons, Hugh Klare[1] makes certain important comments which I can personally bear out.

Giving a historical picture of the rôle of the prison officer, he remarks:

'Taking the short view, regarded as a job of work to be done here and now, it meant long periods of boredom interspersed with occasional sharp bursts of danger. It implied being locked behind prison walls more or less for the rest of your working life. It brought comparatively little public approbation, and comparatively much criticism-triggered off by ex-prisoners and penal reformers on the one hand, and die-hard reactionaries on the other. Above all, it meant living with criminals.'

Unfortunately this rôle and this general impression which the public so often obtains, is by no means a matter of past

1 *Anatomy of Prison*, by Hugh J. Klare. (Hutchinson 1960).

history. To the lay public who are never given the opportunity of working in or even seeing the inside of a large English Victorian prison, the words 'prison officers' conjure up to many, a Dickensian picture of brutal louts, semi-literate, open to bribes from prisoners and prisoners' friends alike, cursing at their charges non-stop and knocking them about. The modern prison officer is far from this image though, as in every occupation, there are a few black sheep.

As for Hugh Klare's remark about being 'locked behind prison walls more or less for the rest of your working life', many a prison officer in the Centre at Wandsworth, especially those of senior rank, has remarked to me that the prisoners were in some instances luckier than he, because the formers' sentences would come to an end, whereas the officer is confined to a life sentence, or at least to one until he retires.

I have already tried to illustrate my experience of the prison officer both as a custodian and as a friendly and interested co-operator with me and my department in our work, though I feel no words are adequate to do them justice. I found the majority of the officers truly among my staunchest allies and supporters in my difficult and novel situation—where one might have expected hostility.

I like to feel that two reasons were involved in my being able to learn what the modern prison officer is really like.

In Wandsworth, I found that only when my department developed, and proved to have some meaning and to be doing something constructive, did the more intelligent officers display their real views and personalities. Any newcomer in such an establishment is very much aware, unless he is over-confident, of being on trial. It is a barrier which, I am glad to think we surmounted.

Secondly, as social workers it was part of our job, a very important part, to show neither prejudice nor favouritism, among either prisoners or staff. The first week's cadet's words would be listened to with the same respect and courtesy as those perhaps more mature words of Chief or Governor.

I myself learned from friendly discussions with officers who had had ten to twenty years' experience of recidivists things about criminals which might have taken me a similar time to pick up. My staff and I profited from their wisdom and kindliness both to us and to the prisoners in their charge.

As Hugh Klare so wisely remarks:

'Most human beings have a need to be appreciated, to feel that they matter for their own sake, as individuals. Prison officers are no exception to this rule, and in their situation it is not surprising that they feel somewhat frustrated.'

Of course he was in this instance referring to a strongly worded Prison Officers' Association publication of a prize article on the status of the prison officer in the new steps in reform. They could also however apply to the prison officer and the social worker. It is, I consider one of the important functions of the prison social worker to take the prison officer along with him in the efforts at rehabilitation of the offender.

The prison officer could so easily have resented us, not just as newcomers, but because our presence in the prison represented a threat—an alignment with the prisoners whose status it was considered was being raised by considering them worthy of social reclamation, against the officers whose duty it was to keep the prisoners in order.

Yet from almost the first day, I tried to make it clear that we hoped the prison officers would participate in such efforts at rehabilitation.

Prison officers from Chiefs downwards were daily in and out of my office to give or to receive advice of prisoners' problems. They also invited me out for drinks, which I politely declined. I found none of them with any fear of ridicule from their colleagues when they came up to interview or be interviewed; they had only a growing interest in our work. Of course, not all of them agreed with our function or presence, at least at first, and I was ragged, often unmercifully. My sense of fun and genuine liking for the officers, however, helped me always to raise a laugh, so that later on, a dis-believing officer would admit: 'Well, there may be something in it, Mrs Trotter, but rather you than me!'

I found many prison officers with a genuine interest in our work and a desire to be involved which I should have liked to encourage, but my recommendation of having selected officers, two at a time to work with us in our department fell on deaf ears or rather blind eyes, for the suggestion was a written one in February 1961. It did not however prevent me from hearing and seeing at first hand, the many kindnesses most prison officers, especially the Principal officers in charge of wings, paid to the prisoners in their charge. Many a prisoner would have been put on a charge to the Governor and punished for some act of indiscipline if it had not been for those officers' experience, almost intuition that something was troubling a man, which a prison social worker might be able to resolve. Such officers often and often used to come up to my office asking if I or one of my colleagues would see a man in the privacy of my office, if the officer brought him along. Naturally, we never refused.

I therefore agree with Hugh Klare when he writes:
'Meanwhile, they are entitled to sympathy and respect from the public, and, above all, from penal reformers. In fact, if penal reformers take it upon themselves to advocate changes which make greater demands upon the prison service, they incur a considerable moral obligation towards the members of that service. For outsiders to press for reforms and then condemn those who might have to carry them out as reactionary because they do not always receive such suggestions with marked relish, is not only thoughtless but unfair.'

Prisoners are not always the most reliable source of information, and, though many receive notoriety by cheap denigrations of their guards, others praise the work they do. It is refreshing to read in a reliable newspaper a prisoner's letter which endorses the views of so many of us who operate daily with the officers.[2]

'Sir,—As one who, as recently as last month, completed a five year prison sentence, may I say a brief word about prison

[2] *The Daily Telegraph*. Letters to the Editor. (November 27th, 1965).

officers, who as a class have recently come in for so much unjustified denigration?

'During the whole of my sentence, which I spent at Wormwood Scrubs, I had nothing but admiration for these men. As an ex-officer I consider myself a reasonably good judge of men and during my sentence—for the greater part of which I was a "leader" and as such had the virtual run of the prison—I came to know practically every officer in the establishment.

'I never once in all that time saw any act of brutality or violence of any nature by an officer upon an inmate. This despite provocation, on occasions, which I would not myself have tolerated.

'I did see tremendous kindness and helpfulness shown by the great majority of officers to those in their charge.

'Realising, as they did, that loss of freedom is the great punishment (and it is!) they gave hope and encouragement without stint.

'Within the strict prison regulations they advised and assisted and helped tremendously in the rehabilitation of all who needed it.

'I know numerous cases of officers giving up their time, unpaid, so that prisoners could enjoy some extra recreation or games.————Our prison officers do the most distasteful job in the world, and they do it as gentlemen.

'Do not hesitate to append my name to this letter. It may bring comfort to many whose loved ones are in prison.'

Though this letter is on the fulsome side at times, it is sincere and gives as good a testimonial of the prison officer as I have read. If he were the uncouth, illiterate boor sometimes depicted, there would never have been room for the idea of using him in another rôle; that of social worker.

The prison officers' main duties will always be primarily custodial. Yet the service provides a reservoir of help in the battle against crime. This I deal with in the next section. This reserve might be drained if these men (and women) are not encouraged to think of themselves in their job with respect and to be publicly depicted and acknowledged as worthy of such; not, as frequently, as though they were not much better than the former custodians of Auschwitz or Belsen. It is time the ordinary citizen grasped that their welfare, property, perhaps lives, rest greatly in the hands of those officers too often decried by those who have an axe to grind or who go by hearsay statements from unreliable sources.

For the prison officer, if pricked, *does* bleed like all of us, sometimes literally by physical assault; but also psychologically, and such haemorrhaging could have more serious effects on him. Because, in spite of the protection of the Prison Officers' Association, the prison officer is still bound to silence by the Official Secrets Act.

Having given the views of a professional social worker, the secretary of a great prison reform society and an ex-prisoner, perhaps it is only fair that the last word should be left to a highly experienced prison officer, champion of his colleagues and of many prisoners.

Mr Harley Cronin, M.B.E., in his autobiographical book,[3] makes use of a Biblical simile to point out that though the prison officer and his career is now largely protected from the 'Upper Millstone', as he calls the hierarchy of ranks and administrative bodies above him:

'The threat from the Nether Millstone—from below, if indeed that is the relation between officer and prisoner in these days —is still, as it always has been, ever-present. By that I mean the constant danger from wild accusations of brutality towards prisoners or other misbehaviour on the part of the prison staff. Such accusations, though usually based on the bare say-so of the dregs of the criminal world, have too often been received, in the past by the officer's superiors, and still today by press and public, in a spirit very much in conflict with the Common Law principle that a man is innocent until found guilty. In the case of the prison officer, the too common tendency has been to lay the burden of proof of his innocence, against the

[3] Harley Cronin, M.B.E. (Former General Secretary of the Prison Officers' Association): *The Screw Turns*. (John Long, London, 1967) page 76.

word of some thug or other of his associates, squarely on the shoulders of the officer himself.'

Mr Cronin then goes on to cite some examples during his office as a full-time Secretary of the P.O.A. He directs a strong word of reproach against certain M.P.s and others who seem willing to take the side of the prisoner on insufficient evidence against the prison officer. After telling the truth about an alleged assault on a prisoner, describing the results of the official enquiry he writes:

'Little or no publicity was given in the press to the exoneration of the prison officers against whom the allegations were made.'[4]

He directs a final reproach at persons who ought to listen with as much respect to the words of prison officers as they do to prisoners.

'We do not expect all our Members of Parliament to be statesmen of genius, but surely, in politics of all professions, they should at least have acquired sufficient knowledge of the world, and even of the criminal world, to make some of them less ready than they have proved themselves to believe the worst of any prison officer or official, on what is often the unsupported word of a crook or crooks.'[5]

I have experienced an instance of the outlook against which Mr Cronin protests. At a conference I was attending I grew exasperated when one of the speakers, an ex-prisoner, told hair-raising stories of the behaviour of prison officers to an audience consisting largely of lay, voluntary workers.

At question time I rose to defend prison officers by describing the incident on page 136 of this book. Up jumped a man in the audience to tell the conference his version of the story, implying unjustifiably that the injured Principal Officer was the instigator of the assault and deserved all he got. He made no mention of the prisoner being certified insane on occasions both before and after the attack (he claimed to be Jesus Christ!).

[4] Op. cit. page 82, para. 3.
[5] Op. cit. page 87, para. 3.

Not wishing to turn the argument into a free-for-all I silenced my critic by asking if he had ever worked in or visited Wandsworth or any other prison, especially at the time of the incident. I must admit my words dripped acid courtesy. The man had to confess he had not. Then I asked the source of his information. He had to acknowledge to me and to the audience that he had learned it from another ex-prisoner who had come from Wandsworth to the office of his voluntary society, set up to help prisoners, and run by amateurs! The "do-gooder" sat down, still defiantly unrepentant and convinced that I was only another of those hostile "insiders" who have to whitewash what goes on inside prisons. How little did he realize that if I had found officers as vicious as often described I should have fought to have such abuses stopped as ardently as any of the amateurs.

The Prison Officer as a Social Worker

In a letter in 1964, Lord Stonham, then President of the Prison Reform Council, House of Lords, wrote in refutation of statements made by the chairman of the Prison Officers' Association: [6]

'What astonishes me about Mr Castell is that he made no mention of the passage in my speech where, after referring to certain necessary changes, I said there would be an "ample supply of officers who, no longer burdened with having to spend half the day locking doors and counting heads, would have time to be social workers."

' "The prison officer is the only person who has real contact with the prisoner. He sees him at work, in his cell and at recreation. Among such officers there is a large, and as yet untapped, resource of experience and knowledge. They, and not outside experts, are the logical people to be concerned with rehabilitation and training, both inside and outside the prison."

' "They should be given the chance to make it their job

[6] *Daily Telegraph*. Letters to the Editor. (November 18th, 1964).

to see a man's wife when he enters prison—keep him in touch with his family and help to raise his morale and self-respect and gear his whole prison training to the job and the life he will go to on release."

'In this I anticipated almost word for word the recommendations which Mr Castell has now sent to the Home Secretary on behalf of his Association. If this means that I am displaying ignorance it is an ignorance I am happy to share with him. Yours faithfully, Stonham.'

Using this letter which expresses a view that is still common, let us analyse the recommendations it makes. Then I will discuss other factors which must be taken into account before the prison officer can be regarded as a social worker. About these factors I have seen nothing written.

'. . . Would have time to be social workers.' This phrase is reminiscent of the one I mentioned earlier about the married women with time on their hands who 'take it up' like a piece of plain knitting, to gain an interest and because their intelligence merits it. More, much more, than mere time is needed to make a social worker.

'The prison officer is the only person who has real contact with the prisoner.' What about the chaplains, the resident social workers, now probation officers, the assistant governors, the prison visitors? Or is Lord Stonham unaware that they exist or of what their work with the prisoners involves? Daily physical contact is no substitute for a deeper case-relationship. Because of disciplinary rules, the strained attitude of the prisoner to the prison officers, and pressure of disciplinary work, physical contact is all that the prison officer has to offer in most instances.

Or has Lord Stonham thought about those mentioned as the 'outside experts'? I heard that term used of my department only in the wings where the prison officers had been consistently imbued with hostility against us. Those men, dissatisfied with their position as prison officers, were under the mistaken impression that social work was an easy task which any fool could do. When we were appointed they felt insecure and envious and obstructed us in every possible way. Sneeringly they called us 'professional outsiders' to the prisoners in their charge, and they claimed, greatly to the annoyance of many of the men, that only they, the officers, could help them with their social and domestic problems.

'They should be given the chance to make it their job to see a man's wife when he enters prison.' This, even if the prison officer had the experience and ability to answer the wives' questions satisfactorily, would surely lead to duplication and contradictory advice, such as we experienced with other amateurs. This advice, because of the amateurs' lack of knowledge and techniques, is more often inaccurate and distressing than helpful unless it is carefully supervised by the 'outside experts,' whom Lord Stonham brushes aside as unnecessary.

In this he and others who suggest that prison officers, like probation officers and social workers, should have the post of 'guide, counsellor and friend' are riding an egalitarian hobby-horse. This is unrealistic and a contradiction of all the more intelligent and enlightened views of recent years about the task of social work.

Even if such a suggestion were accepted, it would come up against a number of difficulties.

The prison officers could not be the social workers because there are already well-established and efficient professional social workers.

Most prison officers have no desire to become social workers. The more intelligent of them realise that, like the Church and Medicine, social work is a vocation. Many pointed out to us their limitations, and remarked that with their present knowledge they could not deal with more than the simplest of welfare applications.

Prison officers from Chiefs downwards from more than one prison have informed me that the idea of making them social workers would not work. They would be neither fish nor flesh nor good red herring. They (and they after all are the people who would have to operate, not the theorists) just do not feel that they could claim to be a man's friend and adviser one day and then perhaps, the next day, have him removed to punishment block for some breach of prison discipline. At present the professional social worker is rightly isolated from the disciplinarian function, which is the prison officer's first responsibility. If prison officers are unhappy in fulfilling this important duty, and are envious of the social worker's immunity, they should be honest and not remain prison officers.

Would the prison officer as he is at present be able to command the confidence of the prisoners? Prisoners themselves said that they would seldom divulge any of their anxieties to 'screws' if there were social workers or chaplains around. Some officers have won the respect of their charges, not as social workers but as 'decent chaps'. If, through being untrained, and a few lectures in social studies do not constitute adequate training, they made a mess of a man's affairs, they would lose the respect they at present hold.

Nor did the men like the idea of prison officers visiting their wives. They felt this was a job for social workers.

Prison officers, with whom I discussed these matters on a number of occasions, also saw the risks involved in becoming too closely implicated in such matters. An officer might find himself being blackmailed by a prisoner who accused him of going to bed with the prisoner's wife. We ought to face reality, as most of the officers have done, and accept that some prisoners are quite ruthless and unscrupulous and would resort to just such measures. It is a danger not unknown to all male visitors to prisoners' families—even probation officers. The prison officer is more vulnerable.

Tied as they were to trade-union regulations, how would prison officers get round the fact that a good social worker, like the chaplain or the medical officer takes no thought for the hours he devotes to his job? Prison officers themselves were not slow to note that, though the prison social workers arrived before 9 a.m., with one shift of officers, many were still working until almost 9 p.m. with the night shift of officers. They had no hours off in between except for meals, and not always for those, and had no pay for overtime. Nor was there enough opportunity to take time off in lieu with such shortage of staff. To many officers it was a puzzle that such men as the prisoners could command such an unstinting labour of love. Some of the prisoners could understand and used this in their staunch efforts to fight any hostility against us, which at least showed appreciation which we had not even expected from anyone. I treasure letters from such men, though none of us worked to receive praise or thanks. The truth was that we just loved our work. To me it was a great wrench to give up the happiest work I had ever done.

Few officers agreed that they would be willing to give up their uniform allowance, shoe allowance, travel warrants, free housing and other privileges. None of these is granted to, nor indeed expected by, the social workers. Or would the theorists suggest that the officers both had their cake and helped themselves to another in the form of a social worker's salary? What then, would the parliamentarians say in justification to the taxpayer?

Finally, can the theorists guarantee that outside professional bodies and persons would accept the prison officer, as he is at present, as a colleague to whom confidential matters could be safely divulged?

A number of less efficient officers think with envy that all that social workers do is to contact those the officers regard as V.I.P.s such as Principal probation officers. They feel they could do that just as well. But could they? Human nature being what it is, even in this increasingly egalitarian society, as long as there are trained social workers or chaplains or a Governor in charge of the affairs of prisoners, outside workers on this level will want to discuss their plans for the prisoner with one of them. An authoritative colleague is needed for contact, though the outside authorities might be interested to hear the views of the Wing Officer.

One has to be realistic and accept that the social worker must be able to talk on equal terms with such men and women and to show that he knows what he is talking about. Otherwise any approach will be met with polite regrets or a frigid snub. Indeed social workers are used to those.

It is suggested that prison officers should see wives to give them social-work advice, but when, then, are the officers to find time, amid their custodial duties, to keep records, as social workers do, of those visits for future reference? This is very confidential work which requires skill and integrity of a high order. Further, if the wives had problems, would the officers know what to do about them or what contacts to make? What also about professional casework and secretarial staff to type out and maintain records, correspondence and reports?

Apart from these external factors, there are others which are intrinsic to a good social worker. They also would have to be assessed. Three principal emotions are looked for in a social worker; love of people, an understanding compassion and unselfishness.

If prison officers have those qualities, and some have them, those are the men (or women) I should wish to select. Those who wish to 'take it up' because it raises their status and self-esteem have a completely selfish motive and they will be failures. Let such advocates of officers' as social workers, ask themselves: Is prison rehabilitation for the benefit of the prisoner and the community or to keep some discontented officers happy? As a social worker I know what *my* answer would be.

A careful check ought to be made of all recommendations, and the motives behind them, dealing with alteration of the prison officer's status to that of professional caseworker. There may be some officers intellectually and emotionally capable of becoming prison social workers, and these should be encouraged to undertake at least the minimum training for the probation service under which prison social workers serve. They should take their chance in competition with all other social workers wishing to enter this service. At least one prison officer did just that, and rose to a senior administrative position in the prison social-work service.

I cannot reiterate too often that, if there is to be any hope of reclamation of offenders, particularly recidivists, nothing but the highest motivation and greatest possible experience in other fields as well as prison work is good enough. For this is the most difficult of all social work.

Apart from those who may leave the prison-officer service to become social workers or probation officers, the more enlightened prison officers can play an important and interesting rôle. This I recommended in 1961.

I visualized then that there might be a corps of welfare assistants, carefully selected from officers of the right personality. They would receive at least part of their training in the prisons by a course of lectures by prison administrative staff, and these would describe the workings of each department, medical, psychological, teaching, and the welfare department. (I still have a course of carefully prepared lectures which were never given, although they were prepared at officers' requests.) The 'rehabilitation scheme' stood in the way of these recommendations; therefore the Governor at the time refused permission. I also recommended that officers in couples should be seconded to work as welfare assistants in the welfare department under the supervision and guidance of the Senior prison welfare officers (as we then were).

By this scheme I should have been applying to the prison social-work service one of the recommendations of the Young-husband Report. I wish the Home Office could have accepted this. When I was interviewed by members of the Advisory Council on the Treatment of Offenders, I suggested that this Report might be applied to prison social work. Medical social workers in many hospitals now have welfare assistants to do many of the routine duties which formerly took up so much of the almoners' time, and I visualized that prison officers might assist in the social rehabilitation of the offender by doing practical welfare work. More complicated cases calling for detailed casework would still have been the responsibility of the fully-trained social worker.

I am still of the opinion that many officers would find satisfaction in this rôle, yet they would not have the strain which full social work would put on them.

Chapter X

EMPLOYMENT IN PRISONS

Apart from the question of capital punishment, probably no topic of prison reform has roused so much discussion, or produced so many reports and theories, as that of the employment of offenders.

Most advocates recommend this active form of rehabilitation for two reasons. It is economically good in that it saves the taxpayer's money, and it keeps a man from degenerating. Both these motives are to be commended. The trouble is that they have not always worked out in practice in Britain, particularly in the big local prisons where the largest percentage of the prison population is housed.

The theorists who advocate employment of prisoners do not give guidance as to how and by whom the administration is to be carried out. Some criticise what is not done and suggest what ought to be done without being fully aware of the reasons why certain types of work are not available. The problems of employing men in the prisons of England and Wales are staggering in their complexity. I do not think anyone not employed in the prison service can grasp just how complicated they are.

Because of the lack of master switches—such as I saw in Canada—which open cells in a matter of seconds, it takes several hours just to lock and unlock doors several times a day. There is also the checking of numbers as the men file past, to make sure there have been no escapes. Also there are not enough staff trained as supervisors or instructors, even if they could be spared from custodial duties. The poor quality of labour available creates a difficulty, again particularly in local prisons. With most of the inmates serving short sentences, the working population is transient. The type of work has also to be limited to jobs which require a minimum of skill and training. As many of the offenders are physically and mentally capable only of this type of labour, this is not such a problem as it seems, and, on the whole, prison administration has risen to the need admirably. There are no fewer than 56 forms of employment available.[1] Nor is vocational training omitted.[2]

However, there are still three difficulties which face the administrator trying to organise work inside prisons to save the taxpayer's money. Overcrowded, over-built prisons lack space. Materials to provide the work, because of the floating populations, have to be purchased in small quantities rather than bulk. This is obviously uneconomic.

The trade unions outside may be hostile to prison work for profit. In the days of high unemployment, it may have been necessary to bar a man from union membership because he had a prison record. Until recently, with full employment and the country crying out for increased production, it has been an anachronism.

The Advisory Council on the Employment of Prisoners in its report[3] touches upon the problem.

'We are very conscious of the grave deficiencies in the employment of prisoners in local prisons, and other things being equal, it would clearly be right to improve them first. There are, however, serious obstacles—gross overcrowding, old, unsuitable buildings, a shortage of prison officers—to make rapid progress in local prisons, and while it is clearly necessary to make great efforts to remove these obstacles as soon as possible, we do not think that improvements in central and regional prisons should be delayed until local prisons are ready for a substantial advance.'

Thus, while admitting the necessity in local prisons, they brush the needs of the majority of prisoners under the carpet, making a virtue of expediency.

[1] C.f. Appendix 2.
[2] C.f. Appendix 2.
[3] *The Organisation of Work for Prisoners.* Report of the Advisory Council on the Employment of Prisoners. H.M.S.O. 1964, p. 45.

Later, as though repenting of their laissez-faire recommend-ation, for local prisons they suggest:[4] 'At the same time early practical steps should be taken to improve employment in local prisons.' But they omit to say how.

Nor does the report give any assistance to prison administra-tors on how to deal with the problem of the poor quality of their labour force. This could lead to extravagant waste of materials and tools. How, for instance, would one handle a large group of men who have a life-long history of failure at almost every human endeavour? This begins with truancy from school, so that a considerable number of them cannot read or write, and cannot therefore understand the simplest written instructions. Their unhappy marriages are sometimes broken up. They cannot hold down the simplest of jobs for any length of time. Many have an alcoholic history. Would employment in even the most efficient workshop such as the Advisory Council describes as ideal, achieve the rehabilitation of such men?

This carefully prepared report under the chairmanship of Sir Wilfred Anson MBE does make certain recommendations, which, if they could be carried out, might perhaps alleviate this constant problem facing prison administrators and re-formers. The sting is that there seems no way under the present conditions by which they could be achieved.

Much of the wording of the report has a familiar ring. It is no reproach to the hardworking Council that, almost word for word, certain paragraphs contain suggestions made by an earlier report.[5] This came from the Departmental Committee on the Employment of Prisoners under the chairmanship of Major Isidore Salmon.

This committee had listened in 1931-32 to evidence given by members of the Howard League for Penal Reform, among others. This first report, like the latest in 1964, recommended a complete reorganisation of the administrative system, in-cluding the appointment of a manager and an Industrial Com-

[4] Ditto. p. 49.
[5] Report of the Departmental Committee on the Employment of Prisoners. Chairman, Major I. Salmon, 1933. H.M.S.O.

missioner. It went even further and stated that a prisoner should work a full day's stint and have deductions made from his full-time earnings for the maintenance of his family and for his own board in the prison. To date, this is done only in the prison hostels.

What happened to those recommendations prepared, no doubt, at great expense of time and money? Why, thirty-three years later, is it necessary to have another committee making similar suggestions with the same apologies and excuses about the difficulties of applying them, particularly in local prisons?

Will it be another thirty-three years before the suggestions are implemented? Is it because the recommendations are just no good or because they are impracticable?

A little study of some of the proposals might shed light on this. The motives of both committees are beyond reproach by any sociologist or criminologist. They were expressed best in the report of the Prison Commissioners for 1923.

'It is not to make prisons pleasant but to construct a system of training such as will fit the prisoner to re-enter the world as a citizen. To this end the first requisite is greater activity of mind and body and the creation of habits of sustained industry.'

In 1934 the first Director of Industries and Stores was appointed as a result of the 1933 Committee's recommendation. This committee also proposed that each workshop should be in the hands of a manager, who would appoint the teaching staff.

Thirty-three years later, the 1964 Report remarks in paragraph 23 that.

'Of all the different prison industries, only a very few, e.g. printing and weaving, are under the control of specialist supervisors. However adequate this may have been in the past, it is difficult to believe that the major industries, such as woodworking, can be expanded and brought up to a high pitch of efficiency unless there is in charge of each a manager with extensive experience in that industry.'

The 1959 Prisons and Borstals Report is more explicit.

'Supervision of the workshops, 250 in number, is exercised through a headquarters staff of travelling Supervisors and 23 Industrial Managers at the prisons and of the farms and gardens through the Supervisor of Farms and Gardens.

With such a headquarters staff headed by the Director of Industries, why then should it be necessary for the suggestion in paragraph 27 of the 1964 Report?

'As we see it, however, there is a very big task of industrial development which must be performed if prison industries are to be made much more efficient. We suggest that a man with wide experience of management in really progressive industry is needed to take charge of the necessary development. The extent of his responsibilities and his position in the headquarters organisation are matters requiring very careful consideration.'

Would this not be a duplication of the Director's functions?

*   *   *   *

What then can be done, particularly in the closed prisons, may ask the distraught reformers? It is easy to say the penal reforms ought to be organised in this way or that. The authorities usually already know all this. What they want are suggestions and practical methods not already in operation.

If one is to be frank, what is needed is a complete and drastic change of outlook on this whole problem. This is simpler than piling bureaucracy on bureaucracy, and more practical as well as less expensive. Changes might include the severe cutting down of numbers in local prisons by excluding certain types of offenders, such as drunks and alcoholics, serving sentences of only a few days or weeks. The local prisons should not be regarded as doss-houses where inconvenient citizens are put out of society's way for greater or lesser terms. The psychopaths and psychiatric patients should be isolated either at Grendon Hall or in prison hospitals. More violent, dangerous and recalcitrant recidivists should be segregated in special prisons.

There should be an extension of the hostel scheme and a parole system about which I shall write later. Industry should be encouraged to set up auxiliary factories, inside prisons, as in Canada.

Quite candidly I feel that Britain is not yet prepared emotionally for such drastic moves nor is there the staff. However, this does not mean that such moves are not long overdue. Compared with most civilised countries we are still behind in penal reform. To the objection that all this will cost a lot, the answer is that it will cost more not to try to put some of these suggestions into effect.

Chapter XI

THE VALUE OF RESEARCH
IN CRIMINOLOGY

Introduction

There are special frustrating and formidable obstacles which research workers, Advisory Committees and Royal Commissions have to face in the fields of sociology and criminology. By the time their research is completed and their recommendations published, these may be outdated because the circumstances have altered. Or, unknown to them, their suggestions may be already in operation. Or they may offer no practical solution to the problems.

Yet this does not explain the doubts held by many experts and others concerning the value of research. Such critical comments as are made are usually dismissed by research workers as 'emotional hostility' to the idea of change or as a guilty need by the critics to justify themselves. A certain amount of emotionalism is, of course, involved, but is the answer as simple as that? Or is there something inherently at fault with present research in these branches of human studies?

There is an element of truth in the cynical saying: 'Those who can, write; those who cannot, become critics.' I have a sneaking suspicion that some persons offers are motivated, perhaps unconsciously, to do research in sociology or criminology because their interests lie in theory, and because they are not very good at practical relationships with people.

There is more than a grain of truth, too, in P. H. Cook's[1] statement:

[1] 'Methods of Field Research'. P. H. Cook, *Australian Journal of Psychology*. 3(2)90 (1951).

'There may be an uneasy recognition of the existence of major problems, indeed problems closely related to the subject of the research, but considerable anxiety associated with the task of tackling them. The advent of the research worker is hailed as providing an apparently painless way out of this conflict; executive authority may be under pressure to do something about problems which can no longer be avoided; it accepts research therefore in the hope that this will postpone indefinitely the need for action. Research then may be used as a neurotic escape from the need of facing up to problems.'

This playing for time may also be the underlying motive for the setting up of Advisory Committees and Royal Commissions.

An authoritative comment on this whole question is given by A. W. Peterson, former Chairman of the Prison Commission.[2]

'Research is a laborious process and may cause inconvenience and extra work for the staff of establishments. But it is an essential stage in the development of more effective treatment, if this is to be based not on abstract theory but on practical experience.'

Though Mr Peterson does not underline the last two words, they are most important to the personnel of the establishments involved in daily dealings with offenders. Enthusiastic researchers, cocooned often in a cloak of ideals and wishful thinking, tend sometimes to ignore this; but like a bride, settling down after the romantic honeymoon to the serious business of marriage, the worker in the penal establishment puts away his dreams and ideals with a sigh, and gets down to the prosaic, unromantic practicalities with the material to hand. Workers engaged in day-to-day activities await such reports with hope and interest. They are usually disappointed and often irritated by important omissions or

[2] 'The Next Decade' by A. W. Peterson. (*Prison Service Journal*, No. 4, January 1962).

twisting of facts to suit the theories of the researchers. The reports also seldom give them any information that they did not already know.

The unpalatable fact is that social research in those departments of human activity is a necessary evil. As R. L. Morrison puts it:[3]

'Very briefly, the general background situation as regards research in penal institutions can be regarded as one in which many people in the field, both specialists and laymen, recognise the need for research, want to do it themselves but have little scope for this, partly because the pressures of practical routine work prevent them and partly because the authorities have been slow to accept the idea of either pure or applied research as an essential and integral part of any institutional treatment system which aspires to be efficient.'

Mr Morrison goes on to say that he, with a group of other prison psychologists, recognises that there is a place for all sorts of research in the world of criminology, but they have reservations.

'At the best however, we regard "outside" research by universities or other research workers with mixed feelings. We realize that some of these investigators may bring to their task, skills and knowledge which we ourselves lack: we also know that most of them are seriously deficient in specialised knowledge of prison conditions. In their most extreme form, these deficiencies not only vitiate the research results of such workers but also result in distorted accounts of prison work. As regards the latter, we are particularly concerned with the unfortunate repercussions which such work will have, and has in fact had in some circumstances on the work of prison psychologists and especially on our relations with colleagues and inmates.'

With these views and others expressed in this article, Mr Morrison rightly associates other personnel.

[3] *Research in Penal Institutions,* by R. L. Morrison. Same ref. as 2, p. 44.

'It seems likely that such feelings are not peculiar to psychologists in prisons but are shared to a greater or lesser degree by others—doctors, Assistant Governors, social workers and so on.'

Research, then, and those engaged in it should be looked at cautiously and an attempt made to see if their claims square with the facts. Too often the results of research are regarded as infallible, and the authorities and others accept researchers' allegations, criticisms and suggestions as though they were some sort of divine truth. How has this attitude arisen?

Possibly it has come from two sources. There is a genuine desire to remedy evils in the social and prison system. This ennobling motive has prompted the practical and realistic recommendations, throughout the years, of the Howard League for Penal Reform. It was, and is, the motive which has driven all great prison reformers, such as John Howard, Elizabeth Fry and Alexander Paterson, to agitate for improvements in the treatment of prisoners.

Apart however, from this motive which is beyond reproach, there has been, and regrettably still is, an outlook which considers knowledge for knowledge's sake more important than its practical application.

Baroness Wootton,[4] has a comment on the application of scientific method to social questions.

'There can be no doubt that the influence of what is called the Socratic method in the arts faculties of our universities has been enormous; and it is in these faculties that perhaps regrettably social problems are chiefly studied. The essence of the Socratic method lies in the emphasis it lays upon discussion and generally critical discussion at that. Its virtue is supposed to be that it should teach people to think for themselves. No doubt it does . . . In sociology, economics and psychology alike, elaborate theoretical systems have been built on amazingly narrow substrata of fact.'

[4] 'Socrates, Science and Social Problems' by Lady Wootton. (Article in *New Society*, No. 1, October 4, 1962).

The value of research in criminology

Advisory Committees and Royal Commissions

Thousands of pounds are spent yearly on Committees and research workers who have to go to the people who are doing the practical work to find out what is being done and to hear their views on suggested improvements. Reports are published incorporating those interviews. Would it not cost less and be as effective to ask the staff directly for facts, instead of calling in lay persons, however well qualified in other fields, and paying them grants?

I agree with Lady Wootton, in her remarks in the article already cited, that among obsolescent instruments 'is the traditional procedure of Royal commissioners or similar committees of enquiry.

'Typically a Royal Commission proceeds by taking evidence from, and asking questions of, persons who are supposed to be knowledgeable in the particular field under review. This practice is apt to produce a rich crop of opinions but a pitifully small yield of fact. E.g. the Wolfenden Report produced evidence from such respectable persons as the Rt. Hon. Viscount Hailsham Q.C. and the Lord Chief Justice of England and from such bodies as the British Social Biology Council, but seems to have made no investigation into the lives and problems of the persons most directly affected by the laws on those subjects.'

John Madge[5] expresses a similar view.

'During the past century there has been a spate of Royal Commissions and Parliamentary Committees, covering a vast range of subjects. They have gathered an enormous store of evidence from the most eminent of public figures. For a long time great prestige has been attached to them and great changes have followed their reports and yet, when we examine the basis of their authoritative conclusions, we find that seldom have they been able to do more than record a cross-

[5] Op. cit.

F.

section of authoritative opinions of the day. They have crystallised and adjudicated between the currents of opinion of their time, but these have seldom been able to adduce important new facts in support of these opinions.

'The Webbs were entirely disillusioned as to the value of such Commissions (S&B Webb 1932—*Methods of Social Study* p.142). "Of all recognised sources of information the oral evidence given in the course of these enquiries has proved to be the least profitable—reading and analysing the interminable questions and answers—Still more, for the money spent over them—the yield of solid fact is absurdly small." (The two Royal Commissions with which the Webbs were most closely connected were the Royal Commission on Labour, 1892-4, and the Royal Commission of the Poor Law, 1905-9.)

'Most professional social investigators would today probably tend to a similar view. The truth is that we are no longer overwhelmed by an unsupported array of opinions, however impressive, unless—as is sometimes the case in medicine e.g.—no alternative basis for decision can be found.'

Statistics

Throughout the years, in working and in preparing papers, I have naturally had to study and to submit statistics. I find them interesting, but, again, I have had to resist the temptation to accept what they appeared to be saying as infallible. Too often I found, as with reports, that by the time they were published they were already *démodés*. Even an annual figure, released to the Press of the number of convicted offenders in prisons and Borstals, is outdated by the time the annual report is published. Some of the men included will have been discharged; other new offenders will have been admitted. Nor do such figures give the more worthwhile information, such as the number of new offenders and of recidivists.

Provided that statistics are used to illustrate and emphasise a theory or to point an average, their use is legitimate. Yet the trend too often is to make sweeping generalisations from them and to commit the logical fallacy of arguing from the particular premise to the universal.

'That we should reject the official criminal statistics as evidence of criminal trends is hard doctrine because it means that we must be content to confess ourselves quite ignorant as to whether our population is becoming more or less addicted to crime. Nevertheless such ignorance has to be admitted. The most that can be said is that the figures show two or three features which are so marked and persistent as to give reasonable grounds for regarding them as likely indications of the relative frequency of different kinds of crime and different types of criminal.

'The first of these features is the overwhelming predominance of the offences committed by motorists: the typical criminal of today is not the thief or the thug but the motorist .... Motorists thus constitute over 48% of all those convicted of any criminal charge in any court.'[6]

Lady Wootton was cautioning us against taking such statistics at their face value as being the total information necessary and thus giving them too much importance.

To illustrate her point, with which anyone dealing with social problems will agree, she continues;

'A long, long way behind the motorist and a long way also behind the thieves and housebreakers, come those who are convicted of indictable sexual offences. These numbered 408 in 1955; smaller still, is the number of those who are found guilty of crimes of violence. Violent crime looms large in the press; but whether or not it is (as is widely believed) becoming more frequent, it is happily still rare. To anyone familiar with the intensity of the hatreds which lie smouldering in many a family circle (as revealed e.g. in matrimonial or similar proceedings in the courts) it is the absence of physical

[6] *Social Science and Social Pathology—Conclusions (Practical)*, by Baroness Wootton. (George Allen & Unwin Ltd.)

violence, rather than its occasional happening, which remains a standing miracle."[7]

Another factor which statistics do not reveal is the submerged part of the iceberg of crime. Police and authorities are only too well aware that the number of criminals caught and sentenced by no means represents all the crime which is committed in the country. Some criminals are known to the police, but conviction cannot be obtained for lack of evidence and witnesses. Others (and there is no knowledge how many) are never discovered.

Statistics have, however, a historic value in that they can be used to plot out a graph of the rise and fall of crime or success and failure of treatment. For example, here is a graph of the courses entered and examinations passed in the City and Guilds examinations since 1950 in the Borstals of England and Wales.

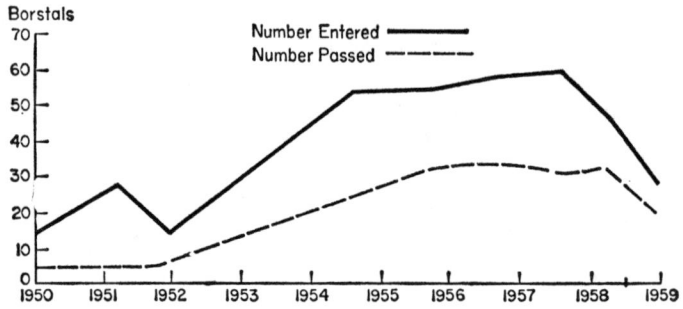

Howard Jones[8] in his book gives some interesting and useful tables showing the percentages, in different age groups over the years, of persons found guilty of indictable offences and, in more detail, of those found guilty of certain offences.

[7] Op. Cit.
[8] *Crime in a Changing Society*. Howard Jones, Chapter II, Penguin Books, 1965.

TABLE I
Percentages in different age groups found guilty of indictable offences.

	Under 14	14 and under 17	17 and under 21	21 and under 30	30 and over
1953	19.4	13.9	10.8	21.4	34.5
1962	15.6	16.8	17.3	22.7	27.5

'Crime is, it seems, increasing faster among our young people than among the older age groups. The adults' share of the total crime problem is gradually shrinking.

'The other major tendency has been for the amount of violent crime to increase more rapidly than such offences as simple stealing or false pretences. The statistics suggest that this new-found destructiveness is also mainly a teenage trend.'

TABLE II
Percentages in different age groups of total found guilty of certain offences.

	Under 14		14 and under 17		17 and under 21		21 and under 30		30 and over	
	1938	1962	1938	1962	1938	1962	1938	1962	1938	1962
Serious damage	37.4	29.5	15.4	22.2	13.5	19.5	15.4	16.0	18.3	12.8
Personal violence	2.3	3.0	5.0	11.9	10.3	27.5	32.2	33.3	50.2	24.3
Sex	5.1	4.0	15.3	15.2	15.3	17.3	20.6	21.9	43.7	41.6
Robbery	11.8	10.2	7.9	12.5	28.4	29.7	41.7	37.2	10.2	10.4
Breaking and entering	37.1	22.1	25.5	23.7	12.8	20.3	14.7	22.3	9.9	11.6
Fraud and false pretences	0.9	1.8	3.3	3.1	6.5	8.7	26.0	27.8	63.3	58.6
Receiving	9.6	13.7	9.2	16.9	10.0	13.5	26.7	22.7	44.5	33.2
Larceny	19.4	16.2	15.8	15.9	15.8	15.9	21.1	21.3	27.9	30.7

Research Workers

By studying outside views by researchers, Advisory Committees etc., those whose appointments involve first-hand knowledge of offenders and their relatives may gain fresh insight. Their own absorption with work, usually under great pressure, may leave them little time to stand back and regard it objectively.

On the other hand, the research worker, particularly if his home base is elsewhere with only periodic incursions into courts or prisons, is also at risk. Though statistically he may interview a large number of offenders, unless adequately protected either by being a former member of court or prison staff or by constant consultation with the workers into whose domain he is researching, he may be misled by the views he hears expressed by others he interviews.

When researchers stick to their own subjects, in which they are probably brilliant, they may produce reliable and worthwhile contributions both to their special body of knowledge and to knowledge in general. It is when they move away from their own fields that the trouble sometimes starts.

When I want accurate information about prisons I prefer to read books written by prison Governors and prison chaplains. When I wish to gain further knowledge of the criminal and how he is handled, I prefer to read works by judges, J.P.s, magistrates and probation officers.

Though few of these men and women may have undertaken academic research they are more expert in their subjects than any outsider coming in to 'study conditions'. They have been busy dealing with the problems and the men about whom the researchers can only write.

I know of no other science, except perhaps education, where those not directly trained in the subject are given permission to go ahead and tell the personnel involved how they ought to be doing their jobs.

Some researchers are loath to accept that their work should be 'vetted' by those into whose work they are researching. They wax indignant at the very suggestion, instead of welcoming it. They claim that, because they are expert in an acedemic discipline or have practical knowledge of some other sociological field, it is insulting to suggest that this does not *de facto* make them an authority in another in which they have never worked. This shows not only a lack of humility, but is not even common sense. Fortunately such an attitude is rare. However, I entirely endorse R. L. Morrison's[9] recommendations about research in his article.

'We would suggest that prison psychologists, either as a group or through their Chief, should be consulted on the necessity and advisability of any piece of "outside research" at the earliest possible point, i.e. when any particular scheme is being planned or projected and before official permission is given. We feel that, in all cases, our views should be sought on whether any project agreed as necessary should be undertaken by outside workers alone or in real partnership with prison psychologists, or whether prison teams could best conduct such work themselves . . . We are however concerned that such outside research might be regarded as completely adequate by itself, that research be left at that without any recognition of the need to supplement it by other approaches, which, as far as the Prison Service is concerned, we should regard as more realistic and likely to prove more fruitful in any case.

'We consider that research done within the prison field by prison personnel in contact with offenders and experienced in the understanding of their attitudes and behaviour is a really urgent necessity.'

One would think such a suggestion unnecessary, and the handling of research by those engaged in the work, as in the exact sciences, self-evident. Yet in the domain of criminology the sad fact is that this is not so, which may be why not so much progress is being made as could be.

[9] *Prison Service Journal* No. 4, Jan. 1962.

Chapter XII

DEVELOPING CASEWORK
IN PRISON

Misconceptions are side-effects in the growth of any new career. Prison welfare or social work has been no exception. Even now, under the aegis of the probation service, there is still considerable misunderstanding of the role of the prison social worker.

The unanimous desire for professional standards of social work in prisons displayed in official reports, particularly in the most recent, those of the Morison Committee[1] and the Advisory Committee on the Treatment of Offenders[2], show a keen awareness of this need, but also of the difficulties involved in achieving it. Their words deserve support and respect. So too do the workers of all grades engaged in this challenging task of rehabilitating the offender. It will help towards understanding if we consider the situation during the early developing years of casework in the prisons of England and Wales.

Voluntary workers, some prison staff, certain social agencies, even prisoners at first believed that prison social workers concerned themselves solely with the discharge plans for all men a month or less before their release. The suggestion has often been made that prison welfare should start from the day a man is admitted, while in fact social workers in prisons have always done this. Others claimed that prison social workers concerned themselves solely with the men, doing little or nothing for or with wives and depend-

[1] The Departmental Committee on the Probation Service (usually called MC in footnotes in Home Office Reports for convenient brevity)—appointed in May 1959, under the chairmanship of Mr. (later Sir) Ronald Morison Q.C. Main Report, published March, 1962. H.M.S.O.
[2] Usually called ACTO in Reports, for convenient brevity.

ents. A reading of excerpts from the Maxwell Report, the Advisory Council on the Treatment of Offenders Report on the Organisation of After-Care and other official Reports might have enlightened those outside critics. This matter will be dealt with later.

The impression given to such critics by prisoners and their dependents that little was done for them by official prison sources, or that there was a complete lack of liaison between prison social workers and others outside, did not have the support of the Report of the Commissioners of Prisons for 1961:

'Governors and Chaplains without exception, have been impressed by the valuable contribution which is being made by prison welfare officers in this important (welfare) field of prison work, and by the way in which they have co-operated with all those concerned with training and treatment as members of the prison staff team.'

The entire success of potential rehabilitation of offenders and of recidivists in particular, depended and still depends on the highly varied and skilled tri-partite framework set up or enlarged upon by prison social workers after appointment, which I have already described on pages 56-60 and 124-5. Even with substantial help from prison staff and from statutory and voluntary agencies, prison social workers had and still have colossal case-loads which hamper success and frustrate the workers. The problem of present prisoners' rehabilitation in Britain is gargantuan and too many adverse factors, such as the hostility of the general uninitiated public and the fears of some trade unions, militate against it. I doubt, (and hope I shall be permitted some healthy scepticism, not as destructive criticism, but to make the reader face facts), if the problem will be solved merely by the recent integration of the social workers' service with the probation service. The ratio of trained social workers to offenders needing help and willing to benefit is too small. It is piling Pelion on Ossa to expect the probation service to carry out effectively, without vastly more increased personnel than even the two recent

Reports recommended, both preventive probation and curative treatment in prison and after-care.

N.A.D.P.A.S., giving evidence to the sub-committee of the Advisory Committee on the Treatment of Offenders, 1961, wrote in their Memorandum: [3]

'45. Recent critics have made the charge that the majority of ex-prisoners have a lack of confidence in the Movement's power to rehabilitate them. But ex-prisoners express a similar lack of confidence in the Courts to give them a fair hearing; in the Prison System to reform them; and in Society to give them their due. The minority who can accept these things are those whom the Movement is most able to help, and who are least anxious to give publicity to their experiences. Our 'freelance' friends are able to be selective in their choice of clients. The maligned 'D.P.A.' must accept all comers and do their best.

5th September, 1961.'

This may therefore be an opportune place to describe what was done, and by whom, in a developing service in those early days, which exercised some influence on future Committees' recommendations, and in more general terms than those of Wandsworth described in Section I.

The following Table from the 1961-2 Report of N.A.D.P.A.S. gives a wider picture of prison social work than that depicted on pages 55-60 of this book for the same year. It shows the growing volume of work applied to all prisons in England and Wales. It gives monthly average figures of applications from prisoners; interviews by prison social workers; external enquiries by them; interviews with visiting dependents; prisoners referred by the social workers for after-care.

---

[3] Report of the National Association of Discharged Prisoners' Aid Societies 1961-62, Appendix 2—page 33 (Sect. 45).

Developing casework in prison

Appendix 5[4]

Prisons	Population (all categories) at 26th December 1961	Population (excluding untried) at 26th December 1961	Discharge after sentence	Transfers to other prisons (excluding untried)	Welfare applications to P.W.O. from prisoners	P.W.O's interviews with prisoners	External enquiries by P.W.O. (letter)	P.W.O.'s interviews with visiting dependents	Prisoners referred by P.W.O. for after-care
	Monthly Averages								
	1	2	3	4	5	6	7	8	9
Appleton Thorn	78	78	13	3	—	—	—	—	—
Ashwell	291	291	73	10	107	287	276	3	3
Askham Grange	63	63	6	2	—	—	—	—	—
Bedford	221	194	36	39	—	—	—	—	—
Bela River	228	228	55	7	54	212	97	1	13
Birmingham	740	598	130	228	232	505	240	14	10
Bristol	397	362	89	32	—	84	147	16	—
Brixton	591	331	260	28	—	—	—	—	—
Canterbury	304	268	40	69	—	205	123	9	1
Cardiff	432	412	152	42	185	430	158	13	3
Dorchester	202	177	41	18	—	—	—	—	—
Drake Hall	253	253	162	20	47	180	36	1	1
Durham	990	912	193	403	139	275	146	3	8
Eastchurch	438	438	70	22	130	254	165	5	4
Exeter	493	460	103	26	86	114	118	1	11
Ford	255	255	31	6	—	—	—	—	—
Gloucester	264	253	47	37	55	94	44	2	3
Holloway (L)	301	281	94	26	—	—	—	—	—
Lancaster	204	204	15	3	28	87	77	1	11
Leeds	961	769	145	395	—	—	—	—	—
Leicester	325	290	54	78	112	161	80	7	—
Leyhill	393	393	25	7	4	19	24	—	8
Lincoln	589	535	120	41	87	84	100	1	15
Liverpool	1419	1291	204	196	252	—	277	7	8
Maidstone	405	405	32	8	117	75	111	2	10
Manchester	1526	1337	291	171	—	—	278	27	17
Moor Court	25	25	5	1	—	—	—	—	—
Norwich	279	255	43	20	48	255	145	3	—
Oxford	235	192	30	63	—	—	—	—	20
Pentonville	1225	1225	303	100	—	—	—	—	14
Preston	585	585	126	26	490	423	203	3	14
Spring Hill	134	134	33	7	—	—	—	—	—
Stafford	938	938	178	58	159	157	163	2	13
Sudbury	319	319	26	7	37	75	55	1	14
Swansea	292	274	53	30	—	—	—	—	—
Thorp Arch	232	232	42	7	—	—	—	—	7
The Verne	298	298	17	12	34	60	38	—	7
Wakefield	602	602	23	15	—	—	—	—	—
Wandsworth	1626	1626	182	235	267	459	249	12	46
Winchester	573	544	30	36	—	—	—	—	—
Wormwood Scrubs	1120	1120	59	276	201	229	182	6	30

Caution: Due to administrative difficulties in a developing service complete accuracy in the above figures cannot be claimed. They are presented as an indication of work undertaken. Where reliable returns for an adequate period are not available they have been omitted.
Notes: (only those referring to columns directly applicable to social work are given here).
Column 7 represents written enquiries made by the department on behalf of prisoners to dependents, prospective employers, welfare agencies etc.
Column 9 represents prisoners discharged who have agreed to accept continuing guidance and friendship (as distinct from routine job, clothing, accommodation, and N.A.B. arrangements) from an after-care agency.

[4] Op. cit. Page 40.

The Report gave notes on six colums of this table connected with the social work being done in the prisons at
that time, but omitted explanation of two of the most important on which case-histories were principally compiled,
doubtless considering their headings self-explanatory. As
however it is in the area of those columns that confusion has
sometimes arisen, I consider a brief analysis of them might
be useful.

Column 5 of the N.A.D.P.A.S. table lists welfare applications *at the request* of prisoners. These were dealt with sep-
arately from pre-discharge interviews, included in *Column* 6.
The latter were not counted as 'welfare' interviews. The
former dealt solely with prisoners' economic, domestic/
marital and emotional needs.

Unfortunately the table, the only one of its kind, lists
figures for a mere twenty-two out of the forty-one prisons
in the relevant Monthly Averages columns at the time of its
compilation. It is a pity that many large prisons had to be
excluded.

As their populations show, they would probably have been
able to submit comparably large figures of casework per
month.

I do not know why N.A.D.P.A.S. chose to give average
monthly figures of social work instead of average annual
ones; but even on this basis, the figures handled by a very
small number of social workers (forty-three in the twenty-
two prisons) is surprisingly high.

This may be better illustrated by giving totals for the
seven relevant social work columns for those twenty-two
prisons:

	Monthly Averages						
Column	3	4	5	6	7	8	9
Average Total	3,641	2,412	2,571	4,722	3,532	140	270
Tentative Total (Annual)	43,692	28,944	30,852	56,664	42,384	1,680	3,240

More than double each of those figures would give a fairly
accurate assessment of the social work done by sixty-five

social workers then in post in all the prisons listed, together with four at N.A.D.P.A.S. headquarters.

Columns 6 and 7 do not mean that 56,664 individual men applied for interviews or that 42,384 separate men were interviewed by the social workers. Casework varied on men. In some cases, only routine discharge arrangements were made; in others quite extensive social problems were dealt with throughout the entire length of men's terms of imprisonment; in still others, such as alcoholics, very full and comprehensive life-histories were taken.

Those tables may however give in some measure an answer to those critics mentioned by N.A.D.P.A.S. to the A.C.T.O. sub-committee.

Some social agencies reported a lack of referrals from prison social workers. This apparent lack lay in the Maxwell Report to which I have made reference throughout this book. It was the foundation stone on which the prison welfare service was based, the charter as it were of both the prison social workers and the after-care officers of the local Discharged Prisoners' Aid Societies.[5]

The two relevant clauses are summarised on p.33, Clause 3, para. 154.

'That the Welfare Officers of the Aid Societies, when released by the appointment of Prison Welfare Officers from their present responsibilities for welfare work inside the prison, should act as the field-workers and "after-care" agents of their Societies, to make such enquiries as are necessary during sentence and carry out the plans approved by their Society after considering such recommendations as Prison Welfare Officers may make. (Paras 115-116).

Clause 3 para. 116 in this context embodies the following sentences:

'To enable the Prison Welfare Officer to help prisoners to deal with the many problems which beset persons whose lives have been suddenly interrupted by a prison sentence, it

[5]With the discontinuation of the Discharged Prisoners' Aid Societies and with their function now handed over to the Probation and After-Care Service during 1966, this procedure is now discontinued.

will often be necessary for someone to visit a prisoner's home or to make enquiries by interviewing persons outside the prison. To enable the Prison Welfare Officer to prepare adequate case histories and submit to the Aid Societies considered plans for the future of particular prisoners, it will often be necessary for enquiries to be made in this quarter and that.'

The first obligatory outside contacts the prison social workers extensively used for prisoners and their families, therefore, were the then existing D.P.A.s. These agencies paid home visits, details of which were attached to prison social workers' confidential case-histories. Details and recommendations for each man's discharge had also to be sent to these bodies, that is, 100 per cent referral. The probation service were possibly the social workers' next greatest source of personal contact and referral—hence the logical amalgamation of two professional services. Next came direct and daily contact by personal interviews and correspondence with other professional colleagues in hospitals, public health and Children's officers' departments.

A few excerpts from reports of several prison social workers recorded in the N.A.D.P.A.S. Reports for 1960-1 and 1961-2 give an indication of their work. For lack of space here these have regrettably to be curtailed.

1960-61. N.A.D.P.A.S. Report.
H.M. Prison, Preston. (Pages 24-7 Appendix 3.)

8. *Notable incidents:*— (ii) Reconciliation effected after interviews at prison between young inmate and his wife who was about to commence divorce proceedings. Employment arranged (skilled bricklayer) in another part of the country to enable them to escape mother-in-law trouble.

13. *Appreciation of Help from Associated Organisations:*— Our warmest thanks are due to the Probation Service and to the W.V.S. for their help unstintingly given in many directions . . .

(Author's comment: the welfare officers of Preston prison

also reported their appreciation of help and co-operation from the prison staff, prison visitors and the D.P.A. officer.)

N.A.D.P.A.S. Head Office Metropolitan Family Caseworker. (Pages 30-31). Most of the families we have helped have been introduced to us by Prison Welfare Officers to whom prisoner husbands have confided their problems. A number have been referred by other Social Work agencies, the National Assistance Board or the Police, and one or two have found our address in the telephone directory. Some wives come to see us at our office but most are visited in their own homes.

In a number of cases the husbands have been first offenders so that their wives have had no experience of what help they could draw on, and so feel utterly alone to cope as best they can. At the other end of the scale is a minority who know the ropes only too well and to whom the husbands' imprisonment means the addition of just another agency from which 'a bit of extra' can be cadged . . .

As a last word, quite apart from all these tangible problems, a great variety of intangible ones build up in the minds of those lonely and heavily burdened wives. The opportunity to talk freely and frankly to somebody who 'knows all about it' is a relief which often enables them to face anew the tragic consequences of a partner's transgressions. On our part it is an integral contribution to the after-care picture.

1961-62 N.A.D.P.A.S. Report

H.M. Prison, Drake Hall

Hire Purchase. Several letters have been written to Hire Purchase firms making for an extension in which to meet their demands. None of my requests was refused, but the Hire Purchase firms seemed rather pleased to accept a nominal payment. Four letters were written to the Electric and Gas Companies asking for an extension of time before either of the two were cut off, and in all cases success was achieved, a pre-payment meter was fixed much to the satisfaction of all concerned.

H.M. Prison, Birmingham

Relatives:—Accommodation in the prison for Welfare Officers to meet prisoners' wives and families is still very limited. In spite of this, however, we have endeavoured to maintain our policy of open visits for reconciliation, domestic and other purposes. We have found these extremely valuable and they only help to confirm the view that outside contact, where possible and practicable, with the family as a whole calls for serious consideration.

The Maxwell Report recommendations about the rôle of the prison social workers were later supplemented from a source which defines their duties as being of two kinds:

'They are concerned with *all* the social and domestic problems of prisoners during their sentences and with planning their future on release.' (*Prisons and Borstals, England & Wales. H.M.S.O. 1962. Para. 11.*)

Certain agencies seemed to be unaware that they were in a number of instances (there is no knowing how many) duplicating the work already being done by the prison social workers.

In the N.A.D.P.A.S. 1961-2 Report, the Prison Welfare officers of H.M. Prison Pentonville write:

'We have found the W.V.S. an invaluable friend, reliable and generous and willing to try anything. We have relied much also on Health Visitors for home visits and on many others less frequently. We are thankful to all of them and troubled by the haphazard arrangements which often lead to duplication of visits. It is our experience (and in common sense to be expected) that the home circumstances of our inmates are almost invariably well known to at least one responsible authority, whether Health Visitor, Probation Officer, F.W.A. or F.S.U. worker etc., and the visit of enquiry usually duplicates work already done by others. Apart from the annoyance caused by such overlapping there is a great waste of time and money involved.'

As professional workers themselves, a number of them

former probation officers, prison social workers made their own referrals and contacted directly those workers who already knew the families as the Pentonville staff describe and as I have done on pages 124-5. There was, for instance, no need to ask another agency to approach an N.A.B. or housing area manager or a hire-purchase firm about payments' relief. We dealt daily with these and similar problems. What was the purpose of the Maxwell Report (para. 99) recommending the appointment of professionally-trained social workers to assist the men with their problems and with rehabilitation, if they only referred those problems to other agencies to do the work they were trained to do?

Some agencies appeared unaware of the recommendations of the Advisory Council's Report on the Treatment of Offenders which gives weight to the arguments of prison social workers. This states on page 23 (para. 89):

'Lack of co-ordination such as leads to contact being made by an outside agency by more than one staff member. Such duplication can best be avoided if the social worker in prison normally deals with all casework communication with outside agencies; and he should know of any contact made with them by other members of the team.'

This is emphasized on page 62 (para. 217 [3]) of the Report:

'The social worker in the prison should be the normal channel of communication in social casework matters with the various outside agencies.'

Another criticism levelled at the prison social workers, from agencies rarely used by them, was that the former gave insufficient information. The reason for this apparent lack is the almost Hippocratic outlook adopted by trained caseworkers.

Prison social workers are very careful when giving confidential information about men in prison. There are too many unqualified 'do-gooders', not always attached to professional agencies, who may not have the professional reticence about information given in confidence, even with the men's consent. With such, prison social workers shut up like clams and gave the minimum of information, especially in the formative years of the service. When however, they are dealing with authorised persons, many of whom come with the men's wives to meet them in supervised welfare visits, they receive no such complaints; just the reverse.

Well-meaning persons and agencies therefore, who are approached by or on behalf of prisoners or ex-prisoners and their families, should be cautious and would be well-advised to check first with the official prison social worker as recommended by all the official reports, before embarking on any form of help in case it is either unsuitable for the individual involved or is already being given. The self-narrated experience of the prison visitor described on page 127 is also an example of the impulsive, sentimental heart ruling the cautious head, where persons can find themselves embarking into waters which may become too deep for them. If however they do, they can always contact the prison social worker involved in the case.

Since those 'teething' years an important change has come about.

If the Maxwell Report was the foundation stone on which the prison welfare service was laid, the two more recent and far-reaching Reports referred to at the beginning of this chapter[6] have built an edifice which makes the status and responsibilities of the prison social worker quite clear.

Carrying out the Morison Committee's recommendation[7] that 'the Home Office should publish periodically a report on the work of the service, bringing out the extent of its own activity', the Home Office produced the first in 1966.[8]

This Report treats at great and interesting lengths many of the Morison and ACTO Committee's suggestions, principally on the probation service. We are however here only concerned with the effect of those recommendations on the

[6] Page 168.
[7] MC para. 183.
[8] Report on the Work of the Probation and After-Care Department 1962 to 1965— Cmnd. 3107—H.M.S.O. October 1966.

prison welfare service.[9] These are dealt with in the sections *The Prison Welfare Service* and *Tasks for Voluntary Effort*.[10]

These concern themselves with many of ACTO's suggestions, including in the prison welfare section the following:[11]

'Development of the prison welfare service and its extensions to all prisons was a vital part of the Council's plan for providing an effective scheme of after-care, and they concluded that it would no longer be appropriate for the prison social worker to be the agent of a voluntary society. They were concerned to ensure on the one hand that social work should become an integral part of the life and work of the prison (and in particular that it should involve fully the prison officers), and on the other that the prison social worker should possess the same qualities and skills as the probation officers with whom he must achieve full understanding and co-operation if the help they jointly and severally offered to prisoners was to be both acceptable and effective.'

This last sentence about the qualities and skills of the prison social workers is a strange comment in view of the statements in Chapter II of the Home Office Report. The Morison Committee, the Advisory Council for Probation and After-Care (appointed February 1965), the Home Office itself, all are cited as expressing their various anxieties about how the essential expansion of the probation and after-care service could take place with staff shortages, entry by untrained persons, an insufficient proportion of highly qualified men and women (including a reasonable proportion of good graduates), excessive case-loads, wastage of officers with university qualifications, representing about eight per cent of the total number with such qualifications in 1964, and the Home Office's own realisation of the need to accept the Morison Committee's conclusion 'that it would be unrealistic to name a date after which appointment of untrained persons

[9] In spite of ACTO's preference for the more enlightening term, the Home Office Report clings to the former terminology. It must therefore be continued wherever this Report is cited.

[10] Cmnd. 3107—paras. 100-107, pages 35-38, paras. 115-124. pages 41-45.

[11] Cmnd. 3107— para. 100— quoting ACTO Chap. 4.

to the service should be forbidden'.[12] These are the same problems which beset N.A.D.P.A.S. with *their* staffing of prison welfare departments; though as page 85 of this book shows, the percentage of university-trained prison welfare officers in post in 1961 was over fifty per cent.

In any case, co-opting the prison welfare officers into the probation service was the obvious answer to some of those problems and to a unified service for the rehabilitation of the offender.

On 1st January 1966[13] 'each probation committee became the employer of every welfare officer already in post at any prison in its area and these officers assumed the position of seconded probation officers.'

The Report then describes the work to be done by those officers inside the prison; work already done by them for years, as shown in this book.

Nothing could have been sadder if those voluntary bodies which had for so long proved their worth in the developing years of prison social work had been ignored in the new plans. It would also have been a fatal error. The system would have collapsed through over-work.

Fortunately, as the Report shows in its section on *Tasks for Voluntary effort*, ACTO recognised the important part begun by, and still to be played by, voluntary effort.[14]

It lists the agencies I have described already on pages 56-60 and 124-5, as being an essential and integral part of the tri-partite welfare service now carried over into the Probation and After-Care Service.

If Chapter II of this Home Office Report and a few other sections might create despondency in the heart of anyone reading them who cared about the future of rehabilitation of offenders, for an official Report it somehow also manages to exude a spirit of enthusiasm and determination to succeed against overwhelming odds. It describes the persistent efforts

[12] Cmnd. 3107—Chapter II, paras. 37, (MC paras. 267-270, 275 & 276): 40 (MC para. 276): and para. 42 (MC para 284)
[13] Cmnd. 3107—para. 102.
[14] Cmnd. 3107. paras 115, 116, 120, 121, 123.

of all, from Advisory bodies, universities, the Home Office staff down to individual officers, to raise the professional standard of this most difficult of social work. They have not yet quite succeeded but such determination should appeal to those willing to join such challenging work. At least most people will now be able to grasp what the prison social workers have been saying for years, that this task calls for the highest of skills and motivation. This will not deter right types.

I should like to conclude this chapter by saying that while there can be no doubt that the prison social workers will benefit by their improved recognition and the support of the probation service, these social workers have also much to offer the older service; the use of Associates, hostels for dis- charged prisoners etc. and, perhaps most valuable of all, with no disrespect to outside agencies, the close liaisons built up carefully over many years, with their accompanying invaluable privileges, between prison welfare departments and prison staff of all ranks; privileges and friendly co-operation not formerly so accessible to the probation service.

About the ability of the combined service to undertake parole duties as well, I have more reservations with which I shall deal next.

Chapter XIII

WHAT IS INVOLVED IN PAROLE?

Nuttall's and Chambers dictionaries both describe parole as being a promise given by word of mouth, a word of honour.

It is this definition of parole which makes the public doubtful. Frankly, they do not consider a prisoner capable of keeping his word of honour, and there is some justification for this doubt.

Webster gives a more detailed definition: 'The law permitting convicts to be released on parole during good behaviour before the expiration of their terms'.

Parole for offenders before their sentence is completed tends to be regarded in much the same way as probation was on *its* introduction—as a 'let-off', a further confirmation of the view that crime really pays. In actual fact, full social reclamation, especially for a recidivist, is a very painful, often dangerous, rebirth with many complications. The process requires sympathy and understanding from the community as well as the skill and experience of prison staff and social workers.

This whole question of parole is controversial, and has many aspects which require cautious study. Yet probably no other method of rehabilitation offers better prospects to the ex-prisoner or to the community. George G. Killinger, former Chairman of the United States Board of Parole, wrote:[1]

'An adequate parole system is our best protection to society. In the interests of protecting society, as well as attempting to guide such prisoners back to law-abiding social adjustments, it is particularly important to recognize the desirability of

---

[1] *The Functions and Responsibilities of Parole Boards*, George G. Killinger—Advances in Understanding the Offender—1950 Yearbook of National Probation and Parole Association. Ed. Marjorie Bell (American Public).

releasing under special conditions even the most serious offenders. It is true that there are many dangerous criminals in our penetentiaries who should not be released at all, but under existing laws there is nothing that can prevent them from coming out of prison at the expiration of their sentences, and at that time without supervision or further control.

'Undoubtedly, some offenders will never develop into law-abiding citizens, no matter how carefully they are selected, supervised and guided after release. However, it is a much safer policy to maintain some control through parole supervision than to release them completely free at the prison gates.

'One of the most important phases of the whole rehabilitative process is proper and intelligent parole supervision. Supervision *is* parole.'

Parole works. I have seen the results in Ontario. Whereas prisons achieve little or nothing in the way of reformation of a man's character, parole gives him self-respect and awareness of being trusted by the community. He gradually rises to that trust and to society's approval of him, and makes an effort to become a worthy citizen. This is surely good psychology as well as good sense.

Those responsible for granting and for managing the parole also feel more relf-respect than they would if they were dealing solely with men in prison, in unnatural surroundings.

Howard Association and Parole

The idea of releasing men and women from prison on parole is not new in Britain. As early as 1904 many reform societies were anxious about the problem of habitual drunkards. The secretary of the existing Howard Association, Edward Grubb, made a tour of the U.S.A. He reported back on the importance of the indeterminate sentence combined with parole on licence.

The Howard Association, as a result of Grubb's recommendations, proposed as new objectives in the policy:

a) general powers of release on licence after a proportion of a man's sentence was served, those powers to be exercised by the Prison Commissioners through a parole board.

b) the appointment of local parole committee together with parole officers.

The reason for the failure to establish such worth-while objectives, even supported by Bills and Acts such as the Habitual Drunkards Act, was the simple one that nobody knew how to cure an alcoholic.

By 1908 the Howard Association was advising indeterminate sentences with parole, for other offenders, when the authorities felt the offenders would benefit from it. The Howard Association was supported in this by the Penal Reform League.

Yet neither society was able to convince the Government, although Part II of the Prevention of Crime Bill included the proposals of an absolute indeterminate sentence and release entirely at the discretion of the authorities.

Now, nearly thirty years later, the idea of parole is once more percolating through to those authorities which are trying to do something about the crises of increasing crime (some actually increasing; some such as motoring offences, created by new laws) and to alleviate the gross overcrowding of prisons.

The Government White Paper, *The Adult Offender*[2] proposes that 'the Home Secretary should be empowered to release on licence any prisoner who has served at least one-third of his sentence or twelve months, whichever is the longer. Release on licence would be limited to those who were likely to respond to generous treatment and who were not regarded as a risk to the public. The licence would run until the date on which the prisoner would otherwise have been released; that is to say, the date on which, having earned his one-third good conduct remission, he would have been released.'

[2] *The Adult Offender.* H.M.S.O. 1965.

Why has it taken so long?

Why has it taken so long to accept what has proved effective in other countries for decades? Are British criminals worse and more incorrigible than those in Canada, America, Denmark or Sweden? Are there more of them? The answer is: No. So what has caused the delay?

One cause may be the traditional rôle of British justice and prisons in the eyes of the public. To Mr. Average Citizen the courts and prisons should be retributive. Successive governments have been afraid to go against the tide of popular opinion as to how the offender should be handled.

Another reason is that in this country there is a good deal of woolly thinking as to what parole is and involves. This is largely because the advocates of parole have had little or no experience of its application, beyond a few visits as outsiders to countries where it is established. Ministers studying suggestions have tended to dismiss them as Utopian ideals.

Britain is not yet ready to accept the idea of an effective parole. Thus the Home Office cannot find enough trained personnel. The 'watch dog' idea of a parole officer's duties just does not appeal to those who would make the best parole officers, namely social workers such as probation officers and prison social workers. It is to be hoped that the Home Office will not settle for less than fully trained social workers of the right personality. Otherwise parole will be repudiated by the public as prisoners commit further crimes, scoffing at release on licence with supervision by persons unable to help them to lead decent lives.

Staff, though trained, should not be overloaded with cases, as their training will be undermined with vast numbers. Individual attention and supervision are necessary if parole is to be effective.

Parole here is untried, unproven. Modern prisons are also essential but delayed. New and better buildings are needed for education and health, and it is easier for a government to win approval, for extra expenditure on schools, universities and hospitals, together with the necessary staff to man them, than it is to prove an urgent case for building prisons on modern lines.

Yet, although initially expensive, enlightened rehabilitation would in time actually save the taxpayer money, and would also satisfy the growing demand that the criminal should make restitution to his victims.

What is involved in parole?

Dictionary definitions do not go beyond their limited function, which is to define. They do not discuss techniques.

It is not always realised by those who recommend that the probation service should embrace after-care that the two functions are not the same and, in some instances, may be conflicting. The poor probation officer, asked to act in both rôles, might well feel schizophrenic.

Apart from the sheer impracticability of combining both important aspects of rehabilitation, there is a vital distinction between probation and parole which is most easily described in medical terms.

Probation of offenders is primarily intended to arrest the growth of their criminal tendencies. It is like *preventive* medicine. Parole, on the other hand, deals with those who have already developed a serious ailment, which in many instances has not yielded to any form of treatment. The majority have not even had treatment but have been left to rot. Parole is *curative* medicine.

The two types of 'patients' reflect two very different attitudes of mind, requiring a different approach. In one, there is a certain amount of trepidation, latent hope, relief and a determination not to require further treatment. In the other, there is little or no trepidation, only cynical doubt, a hard shell of indifference and a despairing awareness that the ailment is chronic, probably incurable; or else there is an unrealistic denial of guilt; a feeling that the patient is as healthy as everyone else. Other people, say prisoners have a 'down' on them and are hypocrites, and just as bad as they.

Other people were the cause of them becoming criminals in the first place. They do not need treatment. Neither of those attitudes can be changed by an untrained amateur.

Because of this difference in outlook, each group stands a better chance of recovery if treated by different social workers. Specialist staffs should concentrate on those whose ailments most interest them. It is this realisation of the difference between preventive and curative therapy of the offender which makes other countries choose to have two types of social workers. Some deal with offenders in the courts; the others handle the more intractible and formidable rehabilitation of the offenders from prisons.

Practical Difficulties of Combined Probation and Parole

I have had experience of both forms of 'treatment', and I foresee the utter unpracticality of loading this great burden of after-care, with all the new techniques which would be involved, on an already overworked body of dedicated workers. At present, the prison social workers have caseloads of nearly 500 men each; sometimes over 1000 in large local prisons.

Not all of these, of course would be granted parole. Even so, probation officers would find it intolerable to take on, in addition to all their court duties, reports to magistrates and their own casework, an additional heavy burden of after-care of discharged prisoners.

If the probation officer's health and brain are not to crack under the strain, he will have to take some of his duties more lightly. The prisoner on parole, who does not enlist the probation officer's first loyalty or interest, would suffer. His so-called 'rehabilitation' would, I suspect, have to be inevitably limited to a monthly letter from him to his parole officer, reporting his whereabouts and jobs which might be non-existent. Very little personal contact or patient and friendly talks over his problems would take place, and there would be few home visits. This combined rôle usually comes from theorists, few themselves social workers, who have ridden hard the hobby-horse of the same social worker 'following through.' This is one of the the theories I analyse in more detail in Chapter XIII. To many professional social workers and to many clients, the importance of this is exaggerated out of all proportion. Clients do not need or want such molly-coddling. Provided they have at one time only one social worker to whom to turn for advice and help, most applicants are able quickly to accept a change of face and personality. This has been my experience in nearly twenty-six years of social work. Human beings, even in deep distress, are much more adaptable than many sentimental theorists believe. It is the duplication, sometimes contradiction, of advice by multiple counsellors on the same problem at the same time which does the harm and which trained social workers dislike.

Besides, most social workers quickly realise that no one is indispensable, and they hand over their 'cases' to the worker who comes next in the development of a man's rehabilitation. This will be a social worker who, the first one is aware, is better qualified for this next stage and can give more time to assisting the man.

Possessiveness grates on the spirit of the truly dedicated social worker, who is solely concerned with the client's final recovery to a useful life in the community. If, to achieve this aim, the social worker has to hand over a case-history to a colleague in a different though affiliated field, the question of retaining the case never arises in his mind. There may be a forgivable desire to cling, caused by interest in the man's problems, but he has to resist this when he has the other person's welfare at heart.

Unless this fallacy of 'following through' is exposed, all the bright hopes of parole succeeding in this country will be doomed to fade through strain.

Parole Recommendations

There is still considerable suspicion in Britain of the indeterminate sentence. To many it spells the entry of the police state. Shades of persons kept indefinitely in the Tower of London or debtors' prisons or Bedlam haunt them.

Yet, if they are honestly looking at a prisoner's reclamation as a form of social medicine, a means to social healing, they will surely think of him as a patient. We do not tell a physician: 'We are sending this man to you. We do not know what is wrong with him, but you have ten days (or three months or two years) to cure him'. We refer the man and leave it to the doctor to decide when it will be safe to let him leave hospital for convalescence. If complications or relapses occur during treatment, we leave the decision of the extra time required again to the doctor. There is no question of the doctor being compelled to discharge a very sick man after a length of time which may have been spent only in diagnosis, not treatment.

There is thus much to be said for the use of the indeterminate sentence, but only when it is known that proper treatment towards recovery will be given. As such treatment is still elementary in British prisons and in many, not available, there is strong reason for withholding its application to offenders before the courts. There is not much use—in fact there might be appalling harm—in referring a man to a prison where he would receive no help and no treatment to conquer his weakness, especially if he could obtain help outside the prison walls.

Parole can work though less efficiently with a definite sentence, which is the method recommended in the White Paper *The Adult Offender.*[3] However, certain conditions must be applied. There must be:
a) Initial observation as to whether an offender would benefit from training and parole and would be a good risk socially.
b) A period of training involving working in contact with the outside world, but under the surveillance of the prison staff: in other words, an extension of the hostel schemes, which are at present limited to pitifully small numbers not always carefully selected.

Therapy for carefully chosen candidates should also include

[3] Op. cit.

pre-parole discussions with social agencies in the community and training in good citizenship, of a practical as well as a theoretical nature, such as we carried out in Canada. In Canada and in the United States, prisoners while still under sentence, have for many decades done valuable voluntary work in and for their communities. In England and Wales there are still only a very few wary experiments in various towns and in a few prisons.

This whole idea of reorientating the offender to his social surroundings needs to be part of a national scheme, with the communities themselves taking an active part. They should encourage the prisoner to feel that he is not an outcast, but an indispensable and useful member of society.

Parole on licence should last for a sufficient time to ensure that the offender has re-learned (or perhaps learned for the first time) to walk. Sentenced prisoners are just as much individuals as hospital out-patients. Therapy for a similar offence may take a longer or shorter time according to the individual's character, psychological nature and willpower. After a leg amputation, one man may learn to walk with his new, artificial limb in a matter of weeks, while another may take months, even years. If a man is released from parole before he has learned to do without his 'crutches' or 'nurse' and to stand on his own, he may well relapse into crime.

Parole should in no sense be a 'let-off'. The offender must realise that it is still a form of discipline ordered by the court. At first the official discipline is externally applied by a parole board, and later comes self-discipline, with the parole officer standing by to assist in his client's rehabilitation.

In the licence order there should be a strong deterrent clause to discourage lapses into old ways. In Ontario, for example, a man serving a sentence of three years may be released on parole at the end of one year to serve the balance of his sentence, less time off for good behaviour. He may be on parole for a year or for eighteen months. If, during that time, he commits another crime or breaks the terms of his parole, he is liable, on being convicted of the new offence, to a heavy punishment. He may have not only to serve this new sentence (which tends to be the maximum as he is on parole) but to complete the rest of his original sentence (two years), plus another, one third of the original sentence (one year), for breach of parole. He may therefore find himself faced with an unconditional term of further imprisonment of five and a half years, in addition to the original year already served, just when he was tasting the 'sweets of freedom'. We found this a powerful deterrent, though of course lapses occurred sometimes.

It is to be hoped that, when parole is adopted here, that the authorities will not neglect the value of this 'bite'. Men on parole have to learn that it is not only treatment but a trust and a privilege, and must not be abused or spoiled for others who may appreciate the opportunities it affords.

A candidate for parole ought to appear before a board consisting of persons who have known and worked with him throughout his term of training and of those into whose care he is to go. It should consist only of those trained in asking relevant questions which will not terrify or discourage him or arouse his resentment. Thus much of the nervousness and hostility caused by the bungling of amateur board members will be eliminated.

Chapter XIV

OTHER THEORIES

We have studied theories about prison officers, voluntary and professional workers, prison employment, prisoners' families and parole. Now let us look briefly at some other aspects of the criminological world.

Causes of Crime

As I propose to write in the next section about some of the causes of crime, I shall deal here only shortly with some of the favourite theories. One of the most frequently mentioned is 'the broken home'. As Lady Wootton[1] shows, this may be a too easy diagnosis.

'Encouraging also is the tendency to focus attention upon persistent offenders as distinct from the whole body of convicted persons. On the face of it, one might well guess that it would be with the persistent offenders that significant peculiarities would most likely be found; though, even so, one must not forget the possibility that his peculiarities may be due at least as much to what has been done to him as to what he himself has done. Occasional convictions may well be explained by a host of more or less accidental circumstances, but the chances of those accidents recurring repeatedly in the life of the same individual (especially when he is by definition forewarned) must surely be more formidable. It is therefore somewhat surprising to find that in several cases the few hypotheses which emerge in tolerably respectable shape from the study of heterogeneous groups of offenders actually

[1] *Social Science and Social Pathology,* by Barbara Wootton. (Allen & Unwin 1964).

threaten to collapse when tested against the records of the recidivists. Notably this is true of that old favourite, the broken home. Thus Healy and Bronner (1926) found to their surprise hardly any difference in the incidence of broken homes as between those who did and those who did not persist in delinquency. As we have seen, the Gluecks also, in their study of 'Juvenile Delinquents Grown Up,' have recorded that the same proportion of their subjects who subsequently reformed and of those who "continued to recidivate" had "enjoyed the affectionate regard of their mothers" and that the "two groups further resemble each other in being to an equal extent the products of homes which had been broken"; while the Mannheim and Wilkins enquiry (1955) found that "although more boys entered Borstal from broken homes than would be expected if the Borstal entry was drawn equally from complete or broken homes, those from broken homes, after Borstal training, did not appear to be worse risks than those from complete homes." Indeed, "no factors in home background afforded a useful prognosis before Borstal, so long as there was a home background of some kind." '

All that can therefore be said as a result of those and other investigations is that the broken home may have some effect, but it is not a cause of crime.

In this book, which I recommend to the reader, Lady Wootton lists and studies thirteen other theories on crime. These are as follows: 1) The delinquent comes from a large family; 2) Criminality is in the family, that is, hereditary; 3) Club membership decreases likelihood of delinquency; 4) Decline in religious belief is a cause; 5) Poor employability and employment record accompany crime; 6) Social status affects crime; 7) Poverty is a cause; 8) Mothers employed outside the home cause crime; 9) Truancy from school is a cause; 10) The broken home causes crime; 11) Poor physical health is a cause; 12) Poor educational achievement accompanies crime; 13) Recidivism starts with younger age groups.

Lady Wootton summarises as follows her careful investigations of those theories on which research was done on both sides of the Atlantic by prominent sociologists and criminologists.

'All in all therefore, this collection of studies though chosen for its comparative methodological merit, produces only the most meagre and dubiously supported generalisations.

'On the whole, it seems that offenders come from relatively large families. Not infrequently (according to some investigators very frequently) other members of the delinquents' (variously defined) families have also been in trouble with the law. Offenders are unlikely to be regular churchgoers, but the evidence as to whether club membership discourages delinquency is widely 'contradictory'. If they are of age to be employed, they are likely to be classified as "poor" rather than as "good" workers. Most of them seem to come from the lower social classes, but again the evidence as to the extent to which they can be described as exceptionally poor is conflicting. Nor is there any clear indication that their delinquency is associated with the employment of their mothers outside the home. Their health is probably no worse than that of other people, but many of them have earned poor reputations at school, though these may well be prejudiced by their teachers' knowledge of their delinquencies. In their school days, they are quite likely to have truanted from school and perhaps an unusually large proportion of them come from homes in which at some (frequently unspecified) time both parents were not, for whatever reason, living together; yet even on those points, the findings of some enquiries are negative. Beyond this, we cannot go.'

The Criminal is Not Responsible

'The poor criminal is mentally sick, even mad. He is not responsible for his actions.'

Only the psychopath grasps at this excuse for his actions, because it is part of his character never to face up to himself. This theory takes no cognizance of free will, which is a human being's heritage. Prison staff (with the exception of some psychologists) are either amused or irritated by this mawkish attitude to the criminal. Offenders themselves resent such a slur, often bitterly. They would much rather be thought bad than mad. I found this applied to prisoners of both sexes.

This view, once predominant in the United States and now largely rejected there, would not only make a mockery of law and justice, but would make casework more difficult. The prisoner and social worker would have first to disentangle themselves from the former's resentment at being thought 'not right in the head'. Further, if the offender is not responsible for his actions, how can he be encouraged to rehabilitate himself?

Character of Criminal

'The criminal is wicked while we are good'.

This pharisaic outlook makes certain organisations detested by prisoners. I should have liked sometimes to put up, across the gates of prisons, the words, 'Judge not, that ye be not judged.'

After a great deal of casework on an alcoholic, a skilled worker who expressed a genuine desire to undergo treatment, I had recommended him for an alcoholics' hostel. The warden, a fine social worker, had a job ready for him. All Paddy, as we shall call him, required for this job were some overalls. I had assured the man that I would request a board to provide those, but that he would have to appear before the members to confirm the request. Paddy was sincerely determined to make an effort (most of his offences had been committed under the influence of drink), and was grateful for the opportunity of help, not hitherto available to him.

Smilingly, I fetched Paddy, a huge, tough Irishman, into the room where the members sat. All had read the case-paper and knew Paddy's character and hopes for the future. Instead of encouraging him, as the warden of the hostel and I had been doing for weeks, the chairman chose to give a long, sanctimonious homily on the evils of drink and how it had led poor Paddy into wickedness. Normally, the chairman was a pleasant and kindly person.

I sat, becoming more and more angry at myself as I saw Paddy's distress and felt months of good casework being undone, all because I had brought this alcoholic before the board. I had had no opportunity to talk to Mr X. before the meeting began, but I felt that did not excuse me. I expected Paddy to believe that I had brought him into the room on false pretences. The Secretary of the board was fidgeting beside me, and muttering that this was a disgrace, and what did Mr X. think he was playing at?

The chaplain and prison psychologist were looking displeased; but Mr X. went blithely on, sure that he was doing a good job of saving a soul and that everybody was approving his speech. The tension kept building up.

I should have understood perfectly if this hulk of Irish had risen and punched the chairman's nose. To the horror of us all, Paddy, who had been so smiling and politely grateful at the beginning of the meeting, suddenly put his head in his hands, and burst into tears.

I pushed back my chair and went round the table to Paddy, without so much as an 'Excuse me'. I placed my arm round his shoulders, murmuring apologies and saying: 'Come away, Paddy. Come away. Oh, I'm so sorry! I did not know it would be like this.'

Paddy and I left the room. The chairman stopped in mid-sentence. The secretary, to show his disapproval, also left the meeting just as Paddy and I reached the door.

I took the unconventional step of conducting Paddy to the Chief's office to recover, and asked the Chief if it would be possible for Paddy to have a cup of tea. (Nothing stronger was allowed in prison, and it would not have done in his case anyhow!) I reassured Paddy that neither the warden nor I condemned him, just the contrary. Whatever his past life might have been, it was with his future that we were concerned. Fortunately, Paddy, like the Chief, a big, jovial man, and myself, had a sense of humour, and after a little, thanks principally to Chief, we were all laughing at ourselves for taking the incident so seriously.

Only then did I return grim-faced to the meeting, determined that never again should any of our 'special cases' be subjected to such amateurish bungling. I am pleased to report that Paddy was not discouraged, and two years later was still sober and still out of prison, the longest spell outside—except for his childhood—in his 40-odd years.

Ourselves and the Criminal

'We are no better than the criminals.' This is a fairly recent argument put forward, I suspect, by people, who think that, by saying this, they will encourage the offender to consider them as friends. I was taken aback to hear a well-known M.P., invited to talk to a large group of prisoners, say with a laugh: 'We are no better than you. We just haven't been caught!' This, of course, raised a cheap laugh, but at what a cost to dignity and sincerity!

I myself could not help wondering what his constituents would have thought if they had heard him. Yet this man, and others who have made similar self-accusations, underestimate the prisoners and do not win any favour by these advances. The men themselves, after such remarks, consistently said to me:

'Who does ———— think he is? He isn't kissing babies for votes in here.'

After a senior member of the staff had made the same insincere confession, they were quite indignant. 'What a ———— nerve! We want someone better than ourselves to look up to as an example. It's not much encouragement, is it, Mrs Trotter, to be told by those we should respect, that they are crooks at heart? And if it was a lie, then what's his purpose? How can *he* claim to be the one to rehabilitate us? Who's he kidding?'

In fact, the only prisoners who seemed to approve of such remarks, and to use them constantly as an excuse for their own actions were the 'con' men (confidence tricksters). I have even heard one such being interviewed on television and bragging of his achievements in the world of fraud, claiming that he was no worse than his audience who defrauded the Income Tax people, did not pay their bus fares and so on. Yet he had just been boasting of having robbed tycoons and others of thousands of pounds!

Another speaker in Wandsworth, peppering his entire talk with prison jargon of 'slap and tickle', 'porridge' etc., had the audience, myself included, convulsed with laughter. The subject-matter of his talk was good and of use for the prisoners' future. Yet there was adverse criticism afterwards because of his manner. All he had hoped to achieve was obliterated by this mock 'I'm a buddy of yours. I can talk your language' attitude.

A number of the men talked to me after he had gone. Said one: 'I have never used such words in my life, Mrs. Trotter. I may be a prisoner and a bad man, but I don't like to be patronised.'

This prisoner too, remarked on the visitor's insincerity. I tried hard to convince him that the speaker was not the rough diamond he appeared and was genuinely interested in helping prisoners. I did not succeed. Again came the comment from others that they did not want speakers who descended to their level or lower. They wanted people whom they could respect.

Even so responsible a writer as Howard Jones writes: [2]

'Some of us may attempt to deny our implication with the criminal problem by blaming it all upon the residents of the delinquency areas. "Them", the disreputable slum dwellers or the spendthift residents of council houses. Another, even commoner way of putting ourselves in the right is to say that "crime is in the blood". Somebody we know gets into trouble and at once people remember that his father was in trouble with the police when he was a boy or that there was a cousin who went bankrupt, an aunt who was divorced or a grand-father who got merrily drunk from time to time.

[2] *Crime in a Changing Society,* Howard Jones. (Penguin Books 1965).

'Evidence of this kind is so flimsy that we could obviously only be brought to believe it if our own emotions and needs were strongly involved. Reason will be given for suggesting that they are; it is our very similarity to the criminal which we are trying to deny by portraying his as essentially someone from another world or at least another family.'

Does this sound familiar? We resemble criminals indeed, but not in the sense that Jones and others suggest. If those who use this specious argument would only realize how prisoners really feel and think, they would drop what is, after all, only hypocrisy.

Visits and Letters to Prisoners

This is a sore point among prisoners and their relatives, and a number of writers, without weighing all the facts, have taken the sentimental viewpoint and recommended that restrictions should go.

This sounds very worthy and helpful in saving a man from becoming institutionalised by keeping him in touch with his family, so that the home is not split up. As a social worker, I should like to support such a suggestion, but, having operated in more than one prison, I just do not see how this freedom could be arranged.

It tends to be forgotten in a maze of impotent rage and sentimentality in the public, that the first duty of the prison staff in the prison is to safeguard security and to prevent escapes. One means to ensure these is by the censorship of all letters going to and from the prisoners. At Wandsworth, six officers sat in an office, for at least three hours every morning, checking every word written. The officers were not only useful; they were necessary. For sometimes a man would write an atrocious, vilifying letter to his wife. This, if he had been allowed to send it, would most probably have broken up an already shaky marriage and lost him a home to go to on his discharge. Such a letter was sent back to the man to be rewritten.

Sometimes too, a letter to a prisoner brought bad news. Such a letter would be handed to the Governor or, through him, to the Senior prison social worker. He would give it to the man in the privacy of an office with a sympathetic person present, rather than in a three-bunked cell. Thus if the prisoner wanted help or even compassionate leave, he was able to apply at once.

Another officer was the 'postman' for the prison, and spent a considerable part of each day collecting, stamping and posting letters for this huge organisation. If daily letters were allowed, the control would soon become impossible.

If the advocates of such reforms had seen as many of the letters inside prison as the staff have, they would realise the necessity for careful censorship, even as a means to rehabilitation, and might not be so sentimental about adopting the 'poor prisoner's' point of view. A similar administrative and security difficulty arises over visits which would have to be supervised by officers to ensure that weapons and/or means of escape are not being handed over or wives attacked by suspicious husbands.

Fines and restitution

'More offenders should be fined instead of being imprisoned, and restitution to their victims ought to be made by them.'

Both those suggestions are good in theory. The only difficulty is their application. With offenders, capable of holding down a good and steady job, either or both, might and possibly ought to be followed.

The trouble is that the majority of offenders, especially recidivists, seem at present unable to hold down any kind of job, well-paid or otherwise. As many of them and their relatives depend on National Assistance between terms of imprisonment, it would be robbing Peter to pay Paul to take for fines and restitution money provided by the ratepayer and taxpayer. How also would money from such a source be collected? In Canada and in Scotland there is 'garnisheeing of wages' by Court Order, and fines and restitution are taken off at source, like P.A.Y.E., before the man receives his pay packet. This money is then sent to the court. If, however, a man is not working, there is little use in recommending such methods.

Home Visits

'The prison social worker (formerly prison welfare officer) should do home visits outside the prison.'

This is one suggestion frequently rolled off the tongue or the pen by non-professional social workers, because it sounds at first logical and full of commonsense—the idol of the lay person.

The idea that prison rehabilitation (or in-care as it would be called in medical social work) and after-care should be a continuous process handled by the same social worker, requires cautious study. Logic is a science, while common-sense, though sometimes good, is based more on intuition than on the careful checking of the validity of arguments. The social worker is much more sceptical than the zealous lay person who lets emotion carry him away. Nothing is taken for granted in the social worker's eyes; every idea is looked at from all possible angles to see whether it could be worked and whether, even if it could be worked, it is necessary.

Is it true or necessary that the same person should handle the case from initial reception to full rehabilitation in society? The arguments in favour are very plausible, and appear at first glance to be eminently sensible. After all, if the prisoner has to spend time building up a relationship of trust and confidence with more than one person, this may delay his final rehabilitation. Yet, is this necessarily so?

When a patient goes to hospital, he first visits 'outpatients' or 'casualty' for observation and some preliminary treatment. He is then admitted to a surgical ward for operation. Post-operative complications of a medical nature may require further examinations and either transfer to a medical ward or the calling in of a medical specialist. On his discharge, he may be referred for continued treatment by his general practitioner and health visitor or District nurse.

Would those who recommend the same social worker all through for the prisoner suggest that the sister who first takes a patient's social particulars and reassures him in 'Outpatients' or 'Casualty' should therefore, to avoid tension, be transferred to his ward? Should she be in every ward where every patient coming to her department is received? Should she also. on each patient's discharge, continue to see him at home and do the visits and treatment of the health visitor and district nurse? This sounds ludicrous, does it not? Yet this is comparable to what some reformers suggest.

Even such a learned body as the Advisory Council on After-Care produces, as an argument for joining after-care to the probation service, the fact that then a man on discharge could be referred back to his probation officer, with whom he is already familiar. What if he is going to a different area, as is highly possible on discharge? What if as is still more likely in local prisons, he has never been given the opportunity of probation always Borstal and later prison sentences?

One D.P.A. Society gave evidence to the Advisory Council. They also make the recommendation that the prison social worker should make the home visits. In fact they went further, stating: 'We recommend that the prison welfare officer and after-care officer should be merged into one. We see the new welfare officer working both inside and outside the prisons.'

It is a fact that, a great number of prisoners, especially in local prisons from which the majority in this country are discharged, are not local residents. How, therefore, could the prison social worker visit the families while the men were 'inside'; and befriend each man on his discharge, with further home visits for as long as these were needed?

Apart from the chaotic administrative difficulties involved, such ideas are just not feasible, even on the grounds of commonsense. When a man is, for example, in prison in Wandsworth or Pentonville, and his family in Glasgow or Manchester, would any sensible person recommend that the prison social worker should take time off from his already overburdened casework inside the prison to visit such a family? There is, of course, a simpler method of dealing with such a situation, particularly with the recidivist and his family, who are probably well-known to several social agencies in his home town.

It appears that those eager people who make such recommendations just do not realize, as Lady Wootton does, what a closely-woven web of intercommunication exists between the professional social worker inside and the social worker, voluntary or statutory, outside, and how important it is to avoid duplication of visits. Thus, even if a man's family resides in the prison area, say London, an experienced prison social worker almost automatically does one of two things. He starts a correspondence with the wife, and offers to see her when she visits her husband. Or, if the prisoner is in distress because he has left his family in dire need, the prison social worker, like the medical social worker, first assures him that he will attend to the problem. Then, returning to the office, he contacts the requisite social agency, if the matter is of sufficient urgency. It may be the Council of Social Service, Family Welfare Association or Co-ordinating Committee if material help is required. Or if one of the children is on probation, it may be the probation officer already known to the family. Or, if the family is likely to be broken up, he will contact the Childrens' Officer of the area. He will then dictate a letter, going into more detail, to support the telephone call, local or long-distance. If he is very busy he may only write the letter, dispensing with the telephone.

On receiving a report from the agency contacted, and such reports are very punctually received, often within the next day or so, we will then tell the man the result. This will have taken much less time than if the suggestion that the prison social worker should drop his own work and visit the home had been followed.

Officers' Dress

'Prison Officers should wear civilian dress.'

I have never heard this suggestion approved by the majority of officers or by any prisoner. Only those officers already discontented with their rôle, fortunately few, and envious of what they thought was the superior status of the Governor and his staff and the social workers, might prefer civilian dress. They muttered sometimes that, if they were out of those so-and-so uniforms, they would show they were as good as the staff which wore it. 'Let us wear lounge suits', they grumble to outsiders. 'Then we'll make better social workers than the Assistant Governors or prison welfare officers or chaplains, and everybody will treat us with the respect they get'.

What such malcontents and their supporters do not see is that respect has to be earned, and this is a particularly difficult task with hardened, cynical prisoners and from outside, professional people. It is not clothing which makes prisoners look up to staff but hard work and personality. I never found a good hard-working prison officer, with a sympathetic personality, who was less respected by the prisoners than staff in civilian clothing.

Here is an extract from a letter from a prison officer in reply to an article written by Mrs Pauline Morris in the *Prison Service Journal*, Number 6, January 1963.

' . . . . . After reading her article on "Staff Problems" I was left with the impression that it is not welfare officers we are short of [the P.O. Association have only two at headquarters] but medical officers, holding the Diploma in Psychiatric Medicine (for the staff, of course—and "exclusively for them"). Her description of prison officers labels us a bunch of paranoids. . . .

' . . . . . As for confidence—if we were short of this we would never have joined. What man without confidence would throw away steady employment (as many do) to take the Wakefield "gamble".[3] Let me hasten to add that it wasn't the choice for

[3] Refers to Wakefield College where prison staff are trained.

most of us "the local nick"[4] or the Labour Exchange. Perhaps however, we reported for interview and medical whilst suffering from an illusion of grandeur.

'Yes, we have pride. We are proud of our "relics of paramilitarism".[5] We know that it helps us to maintain some dignity and above all, some discipline. Would our wayward motorist respond to a "bowler hatted" traffic policeman waving an umbrella? I have spoken to inmates (yes, I can do this without speaking out of the corner of my mouth) and the inevitable reply when asked their opinion of civilians in prison is one of complete contempt. One of their most derogatory expressions is "he's only a 'civvy'." This of course does not include the Governor or medical staff [or, the author of this book hopes, the social workers!], but I have known officers of these ranks suggest that it would sometimes be beneficial for the superior grades to go in uniform. However, pride is a symptom of paranoia—so our psychologists will take note! . . .

' . . . . . In our quieter moments, we have peculiar fancies. One of our fantasies is that prisons are hospitals, and that our charges are patients, we of course are the nursing staff. We regard our superior grades as doctors and doctors in training. We believe that the treatment meted out to our patients is at present correct and that, although they may become ill again, at least they derive some benefit from it. The system is running smoothly. Then from outside the hospital some general practitioner (who alas! unlike our true-life medical counterparts, never did his training in the hospital) tells us how to do our job. We then become angry and our paranoia becomes apparent.

'If Pauline Morris has assessed us correctly then there can be no doubt we are truly in need of psychological workers for the staff.'[6]

The pride in doing a good and important job and in a

[4] Jargon for the local prison.
[5] 'Staff Problems' by Pauline Morris (*Prison Service Journal No. 6, January 1963, Vol. II*).
[6] p. 43, column 1—R. F. Bunker (*Prison Service Journal No. 7, April 1963, Vol. II*).

uniform shows clearly through the humour of this letter. I too have often heard the derogatory expression 'Only a civvy' used by prisoners with a curl of the lip for 'do-gooders' and other would-be reformers.

Both sides have also remarked to me on the link which service medals make. Occasionally a prison officer will receive a man on his landing who asks about his experiences and his service and then, turns out to have been in the same regiment, perhaps even to have gone through the same campaigns. This breaks down the barrier of hostility and makes the handling of that particular prisoner no trouble. The prisoner has in fact been known to spread around the wing the comment: 'What a good chap our old screw So-and-So is.' Thus the handling of over 100 men on his landing may become a 'piece of cake' for that officer. This has happened to more than one officer in Wandsworth and I expect in other prisons.

If the officer had been in 'civvies', the prisoners would have shown their latent, sometimes obvious, hostility, unless he had divulged his service record to the right prisoner—which he was unlikely to do. The sight of a uniform, especially with war ribbons, rouses respect, however grudging, in most prisoners, no matter what may be said by outsiders to the contrary. I myself have seen and heard so much evidence of this.

Besides, the wearing of a uniform is beneficial to the officer. It boosts his morale, often much in need of encouragement in face of public criticism and offenders' hostility to the prison régime. It helps him economically, in that he does not have to wear out his civilian clothes. As a woman, I may add perhaps a comment on appearance. The uniform gave the older men a certain dignity; even took years off their ages. I was surprised, on meeting some of them socially, how much older they appeared in civilian clothes! As age is sometimes taken by prisoners as synonymous with weakness and unfitness, the uniform may save the officers from dangerous situations.

PART THREE

So far in this book we have touched only lightly on the principal subjects—the men themselves; and more heavily, perhaps depressingly so, on theories and ideals. We must now take a closer look at crime, the criminals themselves and the work done with them. We must study possible causes of crime and from an academic as well as a practical point of view observe whether it is possible to diminish it. This of course would also diminish attendant anxieties in the community and the men's families and acquaintances. Having examined many ideas and theories about the social rehabilitation of the offender, let us try to assemble something more constructive.

In the first place, rehabilitation, as I pointed out earlier, is by no means as simple a task as many of these authors and authorities would have us believe. There is no easy road nor any short cut to this most difficult form of social work. The infant science of criminology, unless we are careful, may become smothered by confused, badly thought-out ideas and a plethora of technical and pseudo-professional language.

We need now to look at the prisoner as a man. What is he as an individual? What is he as a criminal? Are we treating symptoms rather than causes in our handling of crime? How do we help a man to rehabilitate himself? What talents and agencies are required?

There is throughout all social studies and all social work one common factor. Simply expressed, it is man and the study of man. In studying man in his entirety, whether deviant or normal (if there is a normal), those schools of philosophy which have insisted that the *via media* which takes into account the three aspects of man's nature—(i) physical material and socio-economic); (ii) mental (thoughts, reason and emotions); and (iii) spiritual, (a moral outlook on life being the threshold to this side of man) may yet provide a nearer solution to the problems of mankind, than has yet been attained.

In the original draft of this section I included chapters on psychology, ethics, metaphysics and logic and their bearing on studies of the offender. Although all four of these disciplines are essential for a social worker's training, his 'tools of the trade' to assist him in his difficult task of understanding other human beings and their problems, I felt that perhaps such studies were too academic for this book and of more interest to me than to the general reader.

If however, there are readers interested in those subjects, I refer them to the Bibliography, which contains the titles of books which I found invaluable in my researches and in social work.

In this introduction I felt I ought, however, to discuss briefly, the application of psychology to the offender. Some people think that this, together with psychiatric findings tend to absolve the individual from all responsibility for his actions. This is not so. For, as we have the same impulses, feelings, consciousness and unconsciousness, we should also, on that premise, all be social criminals. Whatever faults we may commit on ourselves or even in our family circles, the majority of us do not do such violence to society as brings us into conflict with the rules made by the community.

Something more than psychological factors must therefore account for this difference. Without going into the deeper waters of ethics and moral philosophy, I shall mention here some of the more frequent ethical problems which confront the social worker.

Most prison social workers and probation officers, if they are frank with themselves, feel that, by concentrating on the material and mental needs of their charges, they are by-passing the spiritual aspect of a man's character, which requires treatment and support as much as either of the others. Why then this concentration on only two sides of a man's nature?

I think the answer lies in Christ's own query: 'If a son shall ask bread of any of you that is a father will he give him a stone?' It is less than useless to tell a starving, emotionally depressed man that he is putting the most important part of his nature in peril. First, you must feed and comfort him; convince him that you are his friend, and then you can begin when he is ready, to discuss with him the deeper issues in his future development.

The first two are so overwhelming in their demands and urgency; the third such a terrifying responsibility that most sociologists and many psychologists shrink from even admitting equally imperative, spiritual claims. Some deny the existence of a spirit, stating that if you give a man sufficient material benefits and perhaps encourage him to assist others less fortunate than himself, he will be perfectly integrated, happy and contented. This may well have been one of the psychological causes why the doctrine of Universal Hedonism held such sway over moral thought for nearly two centuries, the 18th and 19th. There has been a dangerous revival of this in the 1950s and '60s with the growth of the affluent society about which I shall have more to say later.

Moral philosophers have argued about this third side of man's being for centuries. We, if we really wish to help a criminal to reform, dare not shirk the responsibility of looking at some of the views about the spiritual part of man's personality.

Investigation into the nature of ethics, good and evil, means and ends, guilt and punishment may help us to a more complete form of treatment and cure. We all know that wealth and material possessions in the law-abiding citizen do not automatically bring happiness. We know too, that those communities where wealth and property are 'shared', and more or less equally divided, seethe inwardly with unhappiness and frustration and require a strong police government to maintain those views. We also know that there is some mysterious factor 'x' in human nature which can produce physical illness irrespective of material or mental conditions, or which can make a selfish, ruthless criminal throw away his life to rescue a child he sees in danger. The psychologists call it the unconscious; they are not concerned with moral judgements.

The moralists probing deeper, name it conscience, an awareness of guilt.

If then happiness is not to be found for the individual in the possession of material wealth or in mental balance where can it be sought?

There has been crime since Cain first murdered Abel and Jacob obtained Esau's lot by false pretences. It would therefore be only the most unreal presumption to suppose that we can ever completely solve this problem of crime with the flimsy weapons at our disposal. Where then can the worker point the way to happiness to offenders? It lies in self-respect, in self-discipline, in an inner glow of confidence that what one is doing is right in every way; what McDougall calls joy— a combination of complex emotions, a higher pleasure. These are ethical qualities.

We are dealing with something dynamic, not a row of figures in a statistical report or with an individual on the psychiatrist's couch. Everyone, even criminals are anxious to have some relief, some cure for the pain and suffering, physical, mental and emotional, sometimes moral, which crime causes.

Why should there be this basic need in humanity for moral standards? Is it just wishful thinking? Have we really any free will and choice in our actions? The behaviourist schools following Freud deny this.

If I were an atheist, this universal prevalence, even in primitive tribes, this unknown factor 'x' we are trying to isolate, would make me pause in my doubts about there being no more to a man than a physical organism, a number of impulses, emotion and a series of electrical impulses.

Eugene Heimler expresses this doubt in his book[1]. 'But I also know that the very desire in me to have a God is a proof of his existence. Can you understand this? If you were raised like Tarzan, away from all human influence, with no words to teach you, would you not know sexual desire when your body was ready for it? Would not your desire indicate that somewhere woman must exist? It is the same with God. My

[1] *A Link in the Chain.*

wish for God is my knowledge of him.'

Ethics and related subjects still survive all criticism, all attempts by Freudian psycho-analysis or Darwinian thought to undermine their reality and their contribution to knowledge of the human personality.

Chapter XV

THE OFFENDER

The medical student, before he is allowed to practise on any patient, has to study anatomy, physiology, medicine, surgery and affiliated subjects under supervision. He has to absorb lectures on social medicine, public health and so on. He has to watch bacilli and bacteria under a microscope; to look at the causes of many human ills.

Yet none of those sciences, individually or together, shows him what a human being looks like, talks like, feels. Only when he goes on to the wards in a hospital does the student begin to see that the examination of the skeleton and the organs in the classroom and in his textbooks, together with the study of the nervous system, the brain and the glandular system are only tools. These are means to enable him to diagnose the trouble of the fretful baby with projectile vomiting on the pediatric ward or how to deal with the old woman who has fallen downstairs and fractured her femur for the second time in two years.

Of course, he knows that without those disciplines he could neither have made a diagnosis nor recommended any form of therapy.

So it is with the sciences of psychology, ethics and metaphysics in studying the offender. By themselves, they do not breathe life into the warm, living, pulsating person in front of one, any more than the social studies of sociology, ecology, criminology or the law are more than tools to assist in a better comprehension of the causes of crime. Nevertheless, all are necessary for a fair assessment of an offender's problems and nature rather than a hit-or-miss grappling with difficulties. These, if beyond the understanding of the interviewer, will certainly be beyond that of his 'client'.

An 'individual' belongs to the clinic and the computer. A 'person' is someone alive like oneself; someone to be loved or hated, pitied or despised, helped or rejected, encouraged or condemned. No matter what the theorists say, it is impossible, unless one is a robot, to be other than subjective in dealing with a person. It is the warmth or frigidity of one's own personal response, the sincerity or falsity of one's attitude to another man or woman, which influences results in social work.

Sociologists are fond of describing the task of a caseworker as establishing a good case relationship. By this, they confirm, in clinical language, that one human being meets another and a spark of liking and trust springs between them. Then a frank discussion of problems becomes possible. If the social worker were not warm and outgoing, and prepared to respect and to listen to the other person, no such discussion could develop. This does not mean that pity and distress at another's pain are enough, any more than it is enough for the nurse to stand wringing her hands while a patient bleeds to death. She must keep calm and apply a tourniquet, pad and bandage.

The social worker must possess or acquire certain qualities if this relationship with the prisoner is to start. The offender is often called the 'inadequate', the 'deviant from the norm'. How insulting, how patronising! Who can claim to be the norm or non-deviant? Hidden in all of us from the public gaze are all sorts of inadequacies. The offender is never only criminal and nothing else.

A famous Archbishop wrote:[1]

'And while the community is bound for his sake (the criminal's), as well as its own, to treat him as a criminal if he is proved to be one, it is also under an equal obligation to treat him as a human being whose lapse into crime is no more than an incident, even though at the moment it be the chief

[1] *The Ethics of Penal Action*. The first Clarke-Hall Lecture. Delivered by His Grace, the Archbishop of York, The Most Revd. Wm. Temple, D.D., D.Litt., March 19, 1934.

incident in question. Unless a man is wholly identified with evil, which only God could know him to be, it must be more immoral and unjust to treat him as if he were.'

I myself know what such terms as 'inadequate', 'psychopath', 'delinquent', 'recidivist', even 'offender' or 'criminal', mean and to whom they refer. Yet I found it difficult, when first confronted with my men in Wandsworth, to tie, metaphorically, little tags on them. Too often these men would insist on being people, and as such would often contradict the labels which the academic disciplines informed me they should have. Classifications such as 'habitual drunk', 'alcoholic', 'inadequate', 'con (confidence) man', 'psychopath', 'homosexual', 'problem family offender', and 'fair prospect', seem not the complete truth when a real, live person sits in your office.

The Habitual Drunk

'The Four Musketeers' was the nickname I gave to four habitual old 'copperkits' after a certain incident. Their addresses were, alternately, local prisons, police cells, Salvation Army hostels, Rowton House and Waterloo Station waiting-room. What they did in this instance was, I suppose, wrong in some eyes, but it was not without humour and showed a touching loyalty to a mate. These so-called 'dregs of humanity' could still show traces of the better attributes of man: loyalty to a friend and thoughtfulness for others at considerable self-sacrifice to themselves.

One of the Assistant Governors on the Discharge board, on the morning when these four men were to be released, recommended that I should give them money from the Royal London D.P.A. funds, together with 'subsistence,' that is, bus fares to the nearest National Assistance Board. I gave them 5/- each. This was the amount allocated by the committee from voluntary funds to permit discharged men to have a cup of coffee or a glass of beer and sandwiches on release; a sort of celebration not technically necessary, as they were going to a hostel and would receive national assistance. The statutory subsistence was added to the voluntary contribution.

Next morning, when they were discharged, instead of going to the nearby pub to drink the money given them, they pooled their five shillings. Then one of them returned to the prison to pay the optional £1 fine for their 'mate', a fifth 'copperkit' who still had seven days of his sentence to serve.

When the Gate officer told me of the episode, we laughed together. The Assistant Governor later called at my office to ask if I was going to reprimand the men for spending the Royal London Society's money in this way. It had been given to them to help them till they reached the hostel, which had agreed to accept them.

I replied: 'No, C....... After all, the money, once I handed it over, was theirs. I think it's rather sweet that those old rogues should have spent it to release a pal instead of going off to their freedom, leaving him still inside.'

I must finish the story, for the sequel was probably no more than one could expect. All the five were back 'inside' the very next morning. They had decided to apply for the whole amount of National Assistance, instead of going to the hostel for cheap accommodation. The five had had a glorious 'binge' and two of them grinned quite unrepentantly at the Assistant Governor and at my colleague on the reception Board. My colleague, describing their behaviour to me afterwards said, 'If the A/G and Chief hadn't been there, I think they would have winked at me!'

What they did was wrong, but they were such personalities that they evoked smiles and tolerance of their rebellion against conventional sobriety. All five had an air of being happier inwardly than many of the rest of us. I personally would not choose that mode of existence, and have been saddened by the wreck which alcohol makes of people's lives. Yet somehow, I could almost feel a touch of envy for those five old 'copperkits', shiftless, thriftless and apparently useless to themselves and to society. I envied the lack of complexity of their way of living and felt affection for their roguish good humour. Two were Irish, and would have been fine comedians on the stage. Even the police, to whom they were, of course, well-known, treated them good-naturedly and tolerantly. The law said they could not go around being a nuisance, and they had to be 'booked' and sent back to Wandsworth, which did their drink problem no good at all. Yet this was a better home for them than the Embankment bench with a newspaper cover or an old air-raid shelter on a bomb-site.

This does not mean that I condoned drunkenness. Their case and others made me decide to see if something could be done inside Wandsworth itself. Otherwise these people would continue to stream in to 'reception'.

The Alcoholic

There is a considerable difference between the 'copperkit from skid-row' and the true alcoholic. Though it may be a difference only of degree, it is a vital one to anyone attempting their reclamation.

The core of the difference lies in the stage which their alcoholism has reached and also the level of their intelligence. A great many alcoholics have never seen a bomb-site except in war-time or, if they are young, in films. Often they come from 'good' families and drink either in hotels or in the privacy of their own homes. Some have been well-educated and held responsible posts before their sickness rendered them incapable of keeping any job.

Some 'copperkits', most of them less intelligent, from artisan backgrounds and capable when sober, of unskilled labour only, may be alcoholics; a great many, if not the majority, are not. They will not be reclaimable because they themselves do not wish to be any other than they are, however much the social worker considers that they ought to be different. No alcoholic can be permanently reclaimed by any means, medical, religious or social, unless he has come to acknowledge to himself that he wishes to give up intoxicating drink. Some have not yet reached that stage; others, by the time they reach the prisons have tragically sunk below it.

During the short sentences given to the 'copperkit' the specialists cannot assess what stage the man has reached. This is why the indeterminate sentence in Canada was so valuable.

Because of the emotional exhaustion involved, I found I had, for the men's sakes as well as my own, to spread these interviews which were more psycho-analytical than ordinary case-histories. They lasted over a period of a month to six weeks; and I gave only twenty-minute sessions to each man once a week. Men finally selected for the rehabilitation hostel had interviews with the psychologist and medical officer after they had been seen by the visiting Warden. Usually, such men were in for sentences involving crimes other than drunkenness.

Alcoholism was a social problem which had interested me ever since I had worked with it in Canada. The intense casework and teamwork which the problems demanded could not be tackled in the early stages of growth of our department in Wandsworth. All the senior staff from the Governor down, including the Senior medical officer and the Senior psychologist, were interested and willing to assist in providing treatment for those men while they were still in prison. The prison officers themselves, especially those working in the prison hospital, asked me if they could participate in any centre begun in the prison. A psychiatrist whose speciality was the treatment of alcoholics, a local probation officer and the warden of a rehabilitation hostel for alcoholics all offered their time and services voluntarily.

We held a meeting in the Governor's office and agreed that a plan for treatment could work if the men were placed in the prison hospital under medical care. In this grim prison there was an impressive atmosphere of friendly co-operation among the staff. A.A. (Alcoholics Anonymous) were willing to provide Associates for the men on release. I was delighted that at last something was going to be done. Alas! This was one of the obstacles I did not quite overcome. The Senior Medical Officer, whom we had agreed should make the approach to authority, received a blunt refusal from those higher than the prison staff. What the reason was is not for me to discuss, but we all considered that the authorities had missed a great opportunity of using Wandsworth for the rehabilitation of one group of criminals.

This did not mean however, that we did nothing for the alcoholic. The Governor agreed with me that the 'higher-ups' could not refuse to let one social worker refer cases to another, who would then contact the psychiatrist and others to start treatment on the men's release. So began my detailed case-histories for the hostel Warden, by which suitable candidates were carefully selected. As the hostel could deal with only ten cases at a time, we were very restricted in the amount of work we could do for this grave problem. At first too we had only a few Alcoholics' Anonymous visitors for those prisoners who expressed a desire to join. Latterly, before I left, I had arranged that the first meetings of A.A. with the men in a group began after my Pre-release classes. I was still dissatisfied, but at least some alcoholics on release obtained help hitherto unavailable to them from Wandsworth. Six months afterwards, a D.P.A. officer also interested himself in the 'copper-kits', which meant that another group was having something done for it.

Thomas

Thomas, as we shall call him. was a quiet little man aged forty. He was about five feet six inches in height, with neatly kept brown hair and soulful brown eyes. He had been orphaned when eight years old, as his mother had died of cancer and his father had taken to drink and died of it at forty.

Thomas, with five older sisters had been brought up by his maternal grandparents. They were Welsh, and were good to the children, but very strict 'chapel'. Grandfather, who owned his own small temperance hotel, was particularly stern. As children they had had to attend chapel three times on Sundays, going twice to a service and to Sunday school in the afternoons. When they came home from evening service, the whole family had supper and then went to bed. No reading or other activity was allowed on the Sabbath.

He did not particularly like school, but enjoyed mathematics and won prizes for English essays. He gave up school at fourteen to help his grandfather, who said he was going to leave him the business as he was the only boy in the family. He joined the army at eighteen, but was discharged two years later on medical grounds. He had a spot on his left lung, and was also near a nervous breakdown over his girl-friend, to whom he was deeply attached. While he had been in the army, she had met someone else and had written and told him so.

On return to his home-town he was very restless and upset. He met a much older woman, one of the hotel guests, who made a 'set' at him. He did not love her, and his family were dead against the affair. The woman was determined, however, and he married her, on the rebound from his jilting by the girl he really wanted, and to defy his grandfather who threatened not to leave the hotel to him. Within a few months, both were regretting their marriage. He had no job, as his family had forced him and his new wife to leave the hotel. In fact they left the town.

He obtained a job as a waiter in a large hotel in Cardiff. His medical record now showed that the patch on his lung had cleared up, and he kept quiet about his medical history because he felt this would prejudice his chances of employment. His wife found a job as a nursing aide in a hospital. They should have been quite comfortably off, but his wife was never satisfied, and kept nagging and taunting him about his inadequacy. He began drinking for the first time in his life, after a chance meeting with the girl to whom he had been previously engaged. At first she had not married and still loved him, but, on hearing that he had married and left his home-town, she, too, had married the man whom she had been seeing while Thomas was in the Army. 'The whole thing was a b...... mess' said Thomas, and he broke down during the interview, which had to be terminated for that day.

His wife, twenty years older, was also more sophisticated.

She kept egging him on to make more money so that they could have a home of their own instead of living in furnished rooms in a seedy locality. He started going for drinks, to other hotels in his off-duty periods, and also started posing as a hotel-owner. He was particularly bitter at his grandfather, who had in the meantime died and left neither business nor money to him. The grandfather had claimed the woman he married was only after Thomas for his prospects, which certainly seemed true.

Only one of his sisters kept in touch with Thomas. The others had all married and refused to have anything to do with him or his wife. They had been fond of his previous fiancée, and were annoyed that he had not married her. They were as strictly temperance-minded as their grandfather, and horrified at their brother's defection.

He found that by his posing, he could obtain money, and after six months received his first sentence for fraud and false pretences. His wife left him. On his release from prison he went on a drinking spree. He moved to the west coast for summer jobs as a wine-waiter, but lost each one because of his intemperance. He was arrested for thefts from automobiles, and served his second sentence. This, his tenth conviction, was a four-year sentence for fraud. He had been divorced for five years.

Now that he was forty, he had suddenly acquired the superstitious feeling that if he did not control his drinking after this sentence he would die at much the same age as his father and for the same reason.

He said that the one sister, who still kept in touch with him would be very pleased if he were accepted for the rehabilitation hostel.

On release, he was found a job as a clerk in a small import and export business. He started antibuse treatment, and met a girl in his office whom he wanted to marry. She knew of his weakness, and wished to wait for a year to see how he got on. Thomas had brought the girl to the hostel to meet the Warden. She struck him as very sensible, and he felt she would be a stabilising influence.

Thomas had not touched any alcohol for four months, the longest time that he had ever managed since he had begun drinking.

Prognosis: Doubtful.

The Inadequate

Walter received injuries in the First World War which had left him subject to frequent attacks of *petit mal* and occasional attacks of *grand mal* (epilepsy). He was a widower, aged 60, with no family. He was unable to work and was in receipt of 100% disability pension. Before his sister's death of heart trouble six years before, he used to live with her and she cared for him. Although he was admitted to Wandsworth with 'no fixed abode' to serve a twenty-one months' sentence, he claimed at the pre-discharge interview that he had lived for some years with a sympathetic landlady, who nursed him through attacks which occurred every few days. He had major blackouts monthly, and occasionally twice monthly. He was on drugs, but they did not seem to help much.

He indulged in petty shoplifting from the larger stores As soon as he had lifted, say, a bar of chocolate, he realised that he had done wrong. This at once brought on an attack of *petit mal*, which of course drew attention to him. He had had several previous convictions, the last only a few months before.

The social worker felt that this poor man was worthy of some interest and help outside the prison, and should be kept from his constant recommittals. He refused to go into an epileptics' hospital, and, in view of his age, it seemed that he might perhaps be happier with his landlady, to whom, he said he could return.

She had shown a genuine humanitarian interest in him, but the social worker was not satisfied, in view of the length of the sentence. Would the landlady still be willing to have him back? The poor man seemed at the interview to be not quite 'with it', and his desire to return to his landlady might just be wishful thinking. He could give no definite assurance by letter or otherwise that she was willing to take him.

Accordingly, the social worker asked for a home visit to be paid, and this confirmed her fear. The landlady had long before re-let Walter's room, and felt she could not have him back, as her own health was not now too good. S.S.A.F.A. (Soldiers', Sailors' & Airmen's Families Association) was contacted, but could not help. Norman House was then approached, and was willing to take Walter. The homely, protective atmosphere here should help him, and it was better for him to go there than to try to find lodgings unaided.

The Confidence Man

Of all offenders, next to the psychopath, the 'con' man is in my opinion the least rehabilitable. The criminal is a weak man, the 'con' man one of the weakest of all. He is a pathetic child who has never given up childhood play. All normal children play at being war-heroes or super-men or Florence Nightingales. This is healthy. What, however, is normal and healthy in children is not so in adults, and can in fact be dangerous.

If there were to be a maxim above the door of any social rehabilitation centre, the words of Shakespeare would be as good as any:

> 'This above all—to thine own self be true;
> And it must follow, as the night the day,
> Thou canst not then be false to any man.'

This is one of the most difficult of precepts for human beings to carry out. Very few of us have the ability to look at ourselves honestly. We shudder at the face that Mr. Hyde shows us when we expect our own Dr. Jekyll in the mirror. It is most difficult of all for confidence men.

These are the morally sick men in the prisons, because, after a time, they do not realise they are sick. The drug addict knows he must avoid the 'hypo' if he is to remain a human being, not a screaming, screeching animal, seeking bodily pleasures and the misty swimming world of phantasy. The alcoholic knows he must never touch a drink.

What of the confidence man? At first he knows he is telling lies about himself and his background because he cannot face reality. Pride has made him ashamed of his origins, and envy has made him seek one more to his liking. Later he finds, when people are fooled by his statements, that this is as easy a way of life as any. It is even worth a few terms of imprisonment during which he is always a model prisoner, attaining status as a red-band or 'trusty'. This puts him in contact with the senior members of the prison staff, whom he regards as his social equals rather than the other prisoners or the ordinary prison officer. He thrives on the jealousy or obsequiousness of other prisoners and laughs up his sleeve when prison officers or senior staff and visitors defer to him. If he has, at first, the odd moment of guilt, he shrugs his shoulders and consoles himself with the thought that if *he* did not do it, someone else would. People are 'suckers', especially hotel proprietors or voluntary-society agencies or M.P.s or town councillors.

Part of the 'con men's' stock in trade is to present a pleasing, even handsome appearance, a cultured accent, a great 'gift of the gab', an air of self-confidence in social work. While serving sentences, they somehow manage to impart an elegant air to the levelling battle-dress uniform for prisoners. They are the neatest of prisoners, with hair slick, neatly knotted ties and well-creased trousers.

Often they marry above their social beginnings, sometimes bigamously; or they get persons of high society or political status or the newspapers or television stations interested in them, and willing to take them at the value they have set on themselves. They are skilful and cunning in that they generally wheedle themselves into the regard of top men. They usually pose as self-employed company directors, and claim officer rank in the Services during the war. Many flaunt public-school ties or university blazers or medal ribbons to which they are not entitled.

Not for them a drink at the local. They frequent the lounge bars of the most exclusive hotels, where they hope their accent and air will win them a new 'sucker'. Very often, too often, they are successful.

Fortunately for society, the rot and weakness in their moral structure lead inevitably to collapse as they continue in their path.

The Criminal Psychopath

He is a contradictory, unpredictable personality. He is often suspicious of kindness; reacts to reasonable talk with unreasonableness and to sympathy with hostility. Punishment and threats are useless; an appeal to reason, conscience and thought for others is idle prattle to him. He is sulky and bad-tempered; has a grudge against society and trusts no one. He fails to establish normal social relationships in either his private life or his employment, and as a result is cast off by his wife, children and parents. He is either fired or walks out of job after job. This makes him more than ever convinced that he is right to have a grudge, and so he hugs himself within a vicious circle of suspicion and mistrust. He has usually a fear of being inadequate as a man, which may lead him into the paths of sexual deviations, even murder, to obtain satisfaction. Jack the Ripper was just such a one, and, in more modern times, so were Christie and Hanratty.

Yet deep down below this unpleasant crust which he wears, shivers the true man. Far from being unable to feel emotions or guilt, he feels them intensely. He makes use of the mechanism of depersonalization, denial of feelings and bravado to a pathological degree.

Psychopaths commit crimes as a gesture to deny and push away from themselves emotions which are intolerable agony to them, emotions such as affection, gratitude for kindness, feelings of sympathy, and all the warm social reactions which make life endurable in society. They prefer to retreat inside the hard shell of prison life and build up a reputation for callousness and viciousness, rather than face a relationship which calls for a response to gentler feelings in others.

They are the hermit crabs of humanity.

The Homosexual

Like the confidence man, the homosexual is usually very charming and polite, often of higher intelligence and in, or posing as belonging to, one of the professions. I never found that imprisonment did anything to help those men. In fact, I should say that, to them, as to the alcoholic, prison is useless from a reform point of view, however it may be as a punishment. It certainly does not achieve the third aim of imprisonment, namely to deter. As with other sexual abnormalities, there is, I suspect more of the idea of retribution, even revenge, in society's treatment of this type of criminal.

The Problem-Family Offender

This type is a great challenge to any social worker, and involves the closest of liaisons between various social-welfare bodies. Hence most local authorities have formed co-ordinating committees, which meet regularly to decide the best methods of handling such families within their communities. Here it is not only the husband who constitutes a serious social problem for society, but the wife also.

Charlie was aged 32 years, Irish, and worked as a hospital porter. He had had ten previous convictions, mostly for robbery, and his present sentence was of three years for robbery with violence.

At first Charlie, and his wife, Mary, aged 29 and three children of 8, 7, and 2, who lived in Surrey, posed a problem for rehabilitation where success seemed unlikely. Through a number of evictions from rooms during Charlie's sentence, his wife and children, two boys and a baby girl became known to the Children's Officer and the local co-ordinating committee, composed of medical officer, Children's Officer, area almoner, health visitor and N.S.P.C.C. officer. Charlie had expressed a fear that next time he would end up with a sentence of preventive detention, but did not know how he could avoid committing another crime. His wife, though a pleasant girl, was thriftless and just could not handle money. They had, over the years, got themselves hopelessly involved in debt, to meet which Charlie resorted to crime. He had also been an ex-Borstal boy, and claimed that his wife knew what she was taking on when they married. He had some doubts as to whether the first boy was really his. The child was born six months after they were married and this led both his and her family to disown them.

During Charlie's sentence a great deal of work was done with him and with his family by agencies inside and outside the prison, so that towards the end of his sentence the rehabilitation of this entire family looked more promising.

I attended a meeting of the co-ordinating committee, to which I had previously asked that Mary, Charlie's wife, be invited. This was arranged. After discussion, it was arranged that Mary should be sent to Frimhurst, already familiar to me from my medical social-work days, as an excellent centre where many families of this category were most successfully rehabilitated. Couples learned to run their homes and look after their children.

This effort of the co-ordinating committee was reported to the hostel board in the prison, and Charlie was selected as a hostel candidate. A job in a local factory was obtained for him by the hostel Principal officer and Charlie was allowed by both authorities to visit and to help his wife at week-ends. The change in Charlie was incredible. He said he felt he had only now 'grown up', and was determined to make use of all the help they were receiving. He had had numerous talks with his visiting clergyman (they were Roman Catholics) and decided to accept the elder boy as his and to believe his wife. This led to improved relationships in his marriage. A month before his release, Mary found a flat for them. The health visitor had been delegated by the co-ordinating committee to help the family for a time after Mary left the centre and

The offender

Charlie was discharged from Wandsworth. He had been offered another hospital job near their new home.

Prognosis: Hopeful.

The Fair Prospect

David aged 22 was single and an orphan. He was English but with 'no fixed abode', and he had had five previous convictions.

This young man, five feet eight inches in height, with fair hair and grey-blue eyes, was a pleasant, intelligent type. His talents, which were artistic, had somehow been turned in the wrong directions, and had led him into crime. He had been brought up in an orphanage in the north of London, having lost his mother when he was barely two years old. She was a chorus girl; his father, a private in the Royal Engineers had been killed in action.

David did not distinguish himself at school except in art; he had two pictures exhibited at an inter-schools art display. He left school at 14, and started training as a barber. He quite liked this career but admitted that he was a 'bit of a tearaway' with the local lads. He had had ambitions to be a 'ton-up boy', but was not really tough enough. He had committed several offences of wilful damage and petty thefts with a crowd and had been sent to Borstal.

At first this did not seem a hopeful case for rehabilitation. David was inclined to be sensitive and easily led; anxious to show that he was as tough as any other 'bad guy'. Yet there was good in him. It struck the social worker that, if he had been brought up in different surroundings, David might have been quite different. He was polite, bright, enthusiastic about the better things of life after which he hankered; but he felt that the only way he would ever obtain them would be dishonestly. Though he was not illegitimate, he was sensitive about being an orphan; his first offence was caused when one of the 'crowd' called him a bastard. There was a fight in which he got the worst of it. The other boy's acquaintances jumped on him when he had their friend on the ground and was 'bashing his head in' on the pavement.

Before his last offence he had been cohabiting with a girl called Susan, aged twenty-one, a typist in the city. Since his imprisonment she had moved to another district and was waiting for him in a flat in South West London.

At David's request, the social worker met this girl on a Special supervised welfare visit and was impressed by her maturity and strong will. Susan said that she had got this flat at the opposite end of London as she hoped that David would then be away from the influence of the gang, which made him commit offences to 'prove' himself. David wanted to marry her after his release and Susan was willing. Her parents who also lived in North London, did not know about David, but Susan felt that, if David proved that this time he was sincere, she could persuade her parents to accept him.

David was willing to go back to barber's work, but he really wanted to make more money at work which he enjoyed. He had produced several lampshades which he had himself designed. He wanted to take up this craft with Susan who had helped him, and to start a small business. This however needed capital and contacts, neither of which he had.

David was known to a probation officer, who like the social worker, thought that if he were steered in the right direction, David might still be rehabilitated. The probation officer felt that, if Susan were as strong a personality as she appeared to be, it might be best if the two married. David was obviously fond of her and she was devoted to him. She had a strong maternal streak, which would make her fight off anyone who tried to lead David astray again. This 'mothering' also seems to be what David enjoyed, as he had never known a mother. With Susan he did not have to prove how tough he was, as she did not want a 'tough guy'. He could therefore be natural with her.

In discussing their future, the probation officer said he would continue to take an interest in David, especially if he married. However, as David was not on probation, and this young couple would probably need, at least at first, a more regular friend and adviser than he could spare the time to be, it was felt that an Associate from Blackfriars Settlement would be better.

Susan still had hopes that, once David settled down, her parents would help them. Her father was a railway clerk and her mother owned a small hardware and china store which she had inherited from Susan's grandfather. There would not be room for the young couple with her parents, as these lived in a small flat above the shop. In any case, Susan, quite rightly felt that they should be by themselves and that living with others made many young marriages go astray. She believed that her mother might be interested in taking some of their lampshades as a side-line, and this would be a start in making contacts for the time when they would have their own business. She intended to go on working. She made £12 a week clear, and was going to save this and live on David's earnings if possible, so that they could acquire some capital.

David admitted that meeting Susan was the best thing that had ever happened to him, and he seemed sincere when he said he would not let her down. He had told her to sell his motor-bike while he was in prison. Susan got £56 for it, and this, she said, would help them to start married life.

A suitable Associate was interviewed by the social worker. He was very interested in this story of David and Susan, and said he would try to help them get on their feet. He managed to find David a job in a hospital, where he could continue his barbering. David accepted this rather grudgingly, the social worker thought. He felt there would not be much money in it, but agreed it would be a start. He would like to advance to hairdressing for women and take proper training, as this would lead to better prospects. The social worker felt that David was inclined to indulge in day-dreams of making his fortune; but he did see that he had to start afresh, which would mean humble beginnings. Susan said she would encourage David to accept this hospital job.

Prospect: Fair.

Chapter XVI

BILL

In this chapter I describe a typical day in a newly-discharged prisoner's life.

Though, like the case-histories throughout this book, it is a condensation of the experiences, feeling and conversations of numerous offenders, so poignant and pressing are the problems of newly released men that I felt compelled to write it in a more dramatic form. Such men leave our prisons in their hundreds in the chilly early hours of every morning throughout every year.

The incidents and emotions have been expressed to me by many exprisoners and by wardens of hostels. Bill may be fictitious; his experiences are realities.

The very air smelt different. The daylight was dazzling, and Bill felt as strange as if he had just been landed by rocket upon a new world.

For years he had not seen a tree. Locked up, as he had been, from everyday things, he had forgotten how freshly green they could be. This was not the first time he had experienced this sensation; yet each time it was new.

A dog crossed the road in front of him. He had almost forgotten what one looked like. A red London Transport bus passed slowly. Funny, how massive it looked! Two business girls passed on the other side of the road. Bill's eyes popped a little, and he began to feel less frightened. He gave a wolf-whistle, but quietly. His cell-mate's wife had told him one visiting day that skirts were going to be shorter this year, but really!

Here was his bus. He had had to ask the Chief who saw him off for the number. He climbed inside. He was still trembling oddly, but a couple of pints should stop this.

To steady his nerves and appear as though he was the same as everyone else, he took out his prison tobacco tin and started to roll a cigarette. He lit it with a sigh of relief.

A red-faced conductor came up to him and said truculently: 'No smoking inside, mate.'

Nervously, Bill stubbed out the glowing end and put the cigarette back into his tobacco tin. He remembered that it was only a twopenny ride to the 'public assistance'. Placatingly, he handed a threepenny piece to the conductor, who stood threateningly over him. The man reminded him of the b...... 'screws'!

'Twopenny one.'

The conductor looked insulted. 'You bein' funny, mate? Where have *you* been, Rip Van Winkle? The fare hasn't been twopence since 1957! Fourpence to next stage.'

By this time, all the other passengers were looking round at him—he felt suspiciously. Fumbling with shaking fingers in his pocket, Bill fished out another penny. He jumped off the platform at the stop, without waiting for the conductor's indignant: 'Hey!' as he turned the handle of the ticket machine with a tiny 'ping'.

Still trembling with humiliation, embarrassment and bitter anger which made his eyes smart and his nose develop a sniff, he started to walk across the road to the National Assistance Board office, which fortunately seemed familiar. The tyres of a car beside him screeched as the owner slammed on the brakes.

'Why the hell don't you use the zebra crossing? Ruddy jay-walkers! Pedestrians should be abolished. They're a menace.'

Bill didn't hear the rest. Over the years he had learned to close his ears to the shouting of the 'screws' inside. 'Keep quiet, there!' they would shout and he would think: 'Don't answer back! Just let them blow their tops. Let them think you're respecting every f......g word they're shouting. Do your bird, quiet, no fuss, no trouble. Do they think yer ear-drums have holes in them or somethin'?'

The fist-shaking motorist looked puzzled at the round-shouldered, pale-faced man in front of the bonnet of his car. 'You all right?' he asked, feeling suddenly, unaccountably, sorry for losing his temper.

Bill nodded and had to hurry across the road to avoid a rapid stream of cars coming the other way. He heard the 'screw' start up his car and move off.

God! How fast all this traffic moves! Was it as speedy as this three years ago? What about all this snarling up of London traffic that he had read so much about in the papers? Of course, it wasn't the rush hour. Come to think of it, that 'screw' in the car was in civvies. Probably wasn't a 'screw' at all. He must be goin' nuts! 'E'd 'ave to watch it! That's what three years of 'porridge'[1] did to a fellow. What them toffs, them socio . .—whatever they called themselves—said was being institutionalised!

Bill entered the National Assistance Board premises.

Under interrogation from a severe-looking man, who reminded him suddenly of someone he had not thought of for years, a particularly detested headmaster at his Council school, Bill stammeringly admitted that he had no job, but had been seen by the Labour man in the prison. 'Yes. He had been a joiner by trade, but he'd take any job offered! No. He had no address.'

The 'head' referred him contemptuously to the labour exchange. No. He would get no money here. The labour exchange would see him first.

Disgruntled and angry, Bill stalked out of the office. The labour exchange was nearly a mile further on. The 'head' had told him what bus to take, but he wasn't goin' to face more humiliation. He would walk. He could do with a drink, but the pubs was closed and he'd better get his 'public assistance' first. He had *better!* Or he'd create! It was his by right, wasn't it? It was only a spit in the eye anyhow. That was all 'they' thought him worth. The maintenance money that the prison had given him wouldn't go far.

Later, at the labour exchange they told him they had no

---

[1] Prison jargon for a stretch of imprisonment. By associated meaning, prison itself is "stir".

vacancies of any kind. It was not easy, they said, to fix up a man of his age—54.

Bill, with a shock of combined indignation and fright, realized that the outside world was tougher even than 'stir'. In there, age didn't matter. You were ordered to work. There was an old man of over 70 beside him in the carpenter's shop. He did better work than any of the young yobs in their twenties—and *he* still had another four years to do! Bill felt the loss of companionship, and a strange pang of envy for 'Grumpy', as the old man had been affectionately called by 'screws' and prisoners alike. What was the Exchange clerk saying now?

'No address?'

'No.' He was quite surprised when the clerk didn't pull him up with a sharp reminder,' No, *sir!*' as they did 'inside'.

'Any money?'

'The Assistance bloke sent me here.'

'We can't give you money, if you've no job and no address to go to. You'll have to go back to the N.A.B. They'll give you an address. We can't help. Sorry.'

Choking, Bill could hardly believe his ears! He had to walk the ruddy mile back! What were they muckin' him about for? Just because he was an ex-con! He felt like smashin' up something! But no! He had told the Gov. he was going to try to make a go of it this time. Who said punishment ended when you got 'outside' again? These ruddy do-gooders ought to try it sometime; then there'd be less of their airy-fairy notions.

His cell-mate, Jake the screwsman, who boasted about being the finest safe-breaker in Britain, had got out yesterday. He had given Bill his address and told him to contact him if he, Bill, was interested in doing a 'job'.

Bill smiled to himself as he remembered Jake's face when the third occupant of their cell, an Irish Paddy, had laughed and said: 'Sure, man! An' 'tis the foinest screwsman you are. How come you niver were able to open this can in two-and-a half years?'

Bill had intervened before Jake could give Paddy his

threatened 'punch up the bracket.'

Jake had been good to Bill, and Bill did not want to see his mate taken down to B.1.[2]

Good old Jake! But Jake meant trouble, and he, Bill, was going to go straight. He was getting too old for the game. If 'they' could give him a nice steady job and perhaps the address of an accommodating (in more senses than one!) landlady, he'd be all right! He wasn't too old for *that!* Or was he? After three years with a lot of pansies and queers, he wasn't sure, though he'd kept himself aloof from that muck. Oh! Let him get that public assistance and a job!

At long last! The Assistance office again! If that snooty official saw him a second time! Bill was in luck. A pleasant-faced young man with brown, wavy hair like his own eldest boy's greeted his weary return.

Funny! He hadn't seen Frank or either of the other two kids for over ten years, since Mabel walked out on him after his fifth conviction (and he'd had four others since then).

Couldn't say really, he blamed her! She'd divorced him and married some fellow he had never heard of. Bill hoped she was happy. Sue, the only girl of his family! She'd be eighteen by now; probably pretty and married too! Maybe he was even a grandad! He felt sad at the thought.

The young man excused himself and went to find Bill's file and papers that the snooty 'head' had had earlier.

William, their other boy, who had been called after him, had gone into the Merchant Navy. It had been just at the time that Mabel had been so upset. Bill had broken his promise that his fourth conviction would be the last. And Frank! He wished that this youngster behind the counter— here he comes back. He could have been Frank. Nice, respectable job!

But he could hear Mabel's voice shrill with anger in the 'visiting box' on her one and only visit to prison on his fifth conviction for theft. 'This is the last straw! First you and now Frankie! Followin' in 'is dad's footsteps! Goodness knows, I tried to bring 'im and the other kids up proper. Said you

2 Punishment Block.

was sick with TB in 'orspital, so they wouldn't know they'd got a gaol-bird of a father and the disgrace you put on us! An' now, 'e's in Borstal! And you 'ave the nerve to tell me this is the last time! You've said that, every time! 'Ave you any idea wot it's like for me, tryin' to bring kids up on Public Assistance? Not enough food, no clothes, no 'olidays? Who's bein' punished worse for your crimes? That's wot I'd like to know! You don't 'ave to worry about rent or H.P., or the tallyman in 'ere. You've got it easy! I think I'll do a spot of shop-lifting, and see if *I* can get a rest an' a decent 'oliday in 'Olloway!'

She had shaken herself angrily and refused to listen to his pleas. She had terminated the visit by turning her back quickly on him and asking the 'screw' to let her out.

Of course he had known she hadn't meant that bit about the shop-lifting. She was a good mum and would think of the kids, just like she said. Come to that, she had been a good wife! What a fool he had been when he was young! Still, the Gov. said it wasn't too late. If he got a job at his old trade, he could perhaps settle down with that landlady!

Bill saw the young man, looking questioningly at him.

Bill had been answering questions like an automaton, while his thoughts were in the past. He had learned to do this over the years, when he wanted to blot out his surroundings. He suddenly became aware that the young man was saying something with an almost apologetic air, as he pushed forward a piece of paper with an address written on it.

Bill looked at the writing and at the address. It was a hostel familiar to him, little better than a doss-house, full of tramps and lushes. He swore under his breath, and started to curse the young fellow, but was forestalled.

'I'm sorry. It's the only vacancy I have. I'll give you a voucher. They'll receive your N.A.B. money, and you'll get the balance when you leave.'

Bill knew the hostel routine. He nodded glumly. 'I know the gen. If I don't go soon, I won't get a bed there tonight!'

The young man indeed looked like Frankie. Bill felt sorry that Frankie had gone wrong. He did not know where the boy was now. The chaplain had found out for him some time ago that, after Borstal, Frankie had had two adult convictions. This young man must not go the same way. Bill did not feel angry any longer; only weary and hungry. He sensed that smarting of his eyes again. He sniffed.

'That's right!' replied the young man, 'If you reach there about noon, you'll be in time.'

Half an hour later, Bill booked in with the Warden of the hostel a Mr. A. What a memory those chaps had! Even remembered his Christian name was Bill: Remembered him from four years ago! Bill reluctantly admitted to himself that Mr. A was a good man. He was not one of 'them' who smile to your face, then land you 'inside.'

Bill was no snob, but what he could not endure were the other occupants of beds in the dormitory. Four years ago, he had not been able to sleep for the stench. The man in the next bed wetted the bed-linen, probably more than once. The man on his other side had had a 'skinful' and vomited on to the floor, groaning half the night till he fell into a snoring stupor!

Bill had pulled the bed-clothes over his head, trying to block out the noise and stink, but the blankets were thin and short and his feet then stuck out of the bottom of the bed, becoming colder in the winter night. The window had been kept open as a token gesture to fresh air.

However, it might be better this time. Perhaps tomorrow the exchange would have a job for him, and he'd get the rest of his Assistance. (He hadn't even seen any money yet!) He would try to find that landlady on his own.

With a resigned sigh, Bill turned from Mr. A.'s office and went out. He used the last of his subsistence money on a bowl of soup, a Chelsea bun and a cup of strong tea at the nearby A.B.C.

Next morning, after another terrifying and sleepless night which outclassed his previous stay at the hostel, Bill set out for the Labour Exchange.

One of the lushes had had an attack of D.T.s in the night and had wakened everyone by high-pitched, nerve-jangling scale screams. He had pointed, in between screams, and shouted that the floor was crawling with black widow spiders! The night warden had come in. Bill and another man, looking carefully at the floor before they put their bare feet out of their beds, had had to go over to help him.

By this time lights had flashed on everywhere and pandemonium had broken loose. Other drunks and some ex-cons had started shouting and cursing at the D.T. victim, at the warden, at Bill. Someone must have telephoned for an ambulance, for after an eternity of struggling with the victim, when Bill was feeling like a punch-bag after violent thrusts of the man's knees, two male nurses in white coats, one of them carrying a strait-jacket, tapes flying, had stridden up the dormitory.

Bill, the warden and the other man had been just beginning to get the upper hand. While the warden had held the drunk down on the bed by the shoulders, Bill had sat on the legs. The other man had seemed to be trying to smother the screams by attempting to sit on the maniac's head!

After the nurses had gone with their patient, the dormitory had settled down again, in the early dawn light, to sleep out the rest of the short night. Bill had not been able to sleep however. He had felt drained and hopeless. He was too old for work. Nobody wanted an ex-prisoner; only people like Mr. A. and all *he* could offer was a life like this! Even he didn't permit 'guests' to stay for more than two nights running.

Despondently, Bill arrived at the exchange the moment it opened. There would be no job, no landlady, no money. He had nobody who cared, who believed in him. He felt in his pocket for his tobacco-tin and found the piece of toilet paper which Jake had slipped into his hand a lifetime ago. He looked at the address in Jake's block letters. It was near Waterloo. He had seen a bus with that station printed on the front when he had been walking here.

Ruefully, he fished in the other pocket. He had the balance of the assistance money from Mr. A., as he had told the warden that he would not be returning that night: fifty shillings. Mr. A. had told him that if he got an address, and told the

N.A.B., they'd pay the rent. Christ! He couldn't give Jake's address! That for a laugh!

Too soon for a drink! He could get on that bus and take Jake out for a drink. Good old Jake! The only pal a man had in the whole world! And he *was* the best safebreaker in Britain. Bill felt honoured to be picked by Jake when Jake could have had anyone in the nick. Good old Jake! Drat! There was that watering of his eyes again! He sniffed and wiped his nose on his sleeve as he turned from the exchange, from 'them'. 'They' had no use for him. He a craftsman! He was too old, 'they' said. 'They' just didn't want to give him a chance. 'They' had no intention of ever letting him forget he was an ex-prisoner. Too old! Well, he'd show 'em! Jake, fond of phoney Americanisms, had leeringly told him about the 'broad' who was meeting him at the gate. He had offered to ask her for a pal for his mate Bill, whenever Bill chose to come to Jake's address, which was the 'broad's' apartment.

There would be money in the 'job' too. Jake had told him. No need to go crawling to 'them'—patronising b......s! Bill spat into the gutter and ran for the bus as it turned the corner.

Six weeks later, Bill was staring into the reproachful eyes of the Governor on the Reception board. He shuffled. Then stared back aggressively.

'Well, you did it *this* time, Bill. Five years P.D! And you won't be serving it all here. It's Parkhurst next. You've really come up with honours. Take him away, officer. Next man in.'

Bill's aggression faded. He walked out in front of the officer, his prison-rounded shoulders rounder than ever and his prison shuffle like that of a very old man. 'They' had got him again.

Chapter XVII

PROBLEMS OF REHABILITATION

There are thousands of Bills coming out of our prisons every day; Bills young, Bills old, Bills weak, Bills violent. The increase in crime is not all due to new criminals, but to the Bills of this country coming out once more into the world. Sometimes they are free for only a day, sometimes for a week, sometimes for months. Because they are unable, or do not wish to face the problems of living in and with society, they commit yet another crime. This they do sometimes for material needs, sometimes through greed, envy or anger against society, sometimes through unconscious desires of which they may not be aware. To such as Bill, a return to a tightly closed, high-walled and barred prison is a return to the shelter and security of the womb. How does one persuade a grown man that a return to ante-natal conditions is no good for him?

To the prison social worker, Bill's appearance means a multiple failure; of society, of the prison administration, of himself as a social worker and of Bill as a human being. By pre-discharge work starting well before Bill's release, some of his problems could be removed and others alleviated. However little preparation is made for these difficulties by the rest of the staff, including the psychologist, Bill goes out unchanged and unprepared. Every department is too overworked, too understaffed, too harassed and too much under strain from constant criticism by those who are not themselves involved. So the situation seems impossible and frustrating.

The Bills are fewer than they were because social workers now inside are spreading their nets more widely, to enlist the help of outside agencies. These reconcile Bill's family to him, or find a home before his release, for him to go to on that first daunting day, or a tolerant employer, who comes to interview him while he is still in prison.

There have been advisory committees and reports on after-care. Yet, though they have pointed out the problems, already too well-known to prison staff, and made suggestions, the burden of Bill's difficulties still settles on the tired shoulders of the prison social worker.

In spite of improved efforts, the hopeless, helpless drifters from one common lodging house to another are still too many and a reproach to all of us. However, it does not do to be over-sentimental. There are the Jakes also, who may occupy valuable time of Associates who could be better employed. That is why voluntary workers, no matter how good-hearted, should operate only with those men referred to them by the trained social worker inside the prison who knows which is Bill and which is Jake.

*　　*　　*　　*

Once the gate has banged behind him, the discharged prisoner has to face all the problems which society takes daily in its stride and a few more. These are due to his having been away from the world so long and to difficulties in his own personality.

This is the moment he has waited for, the day he has marked up on the wall of his cell. Suddenly, as he comes out of the gloom of the prison wings into the brighter daylight, something hits him like an electric shock. That something I once called 'gateitis'—a term which stuck as part of the prison jargon in Wandsworth.

All offenders, no matter how many times they have been imprisoned, experience this attack of nerves to a greater or lesser degree. Even the sophisticated 'professionals' have confessed to me that they have experienced it. It is far worse for some than others. Unfortunately, the majority feel it keenly. It depends on whether they are facing it alone or being met by patient wives or voluntary Associates or their probation officers.

Problems of rehabilitation

No ex-prisoner should be compelled to face this shock alone. For any man who has expressed the desire to make a fresh start, a solitary one should be unthinkable. Such a man should have already been broken gently to the outside world by means of a theoretical and practical training programme (and long before Bill's age of 54), including an extension of the hostel scheme recommended in an earlier chapter. If he is not met by his wife or parole officer (who probably has to wait in his office for all the other men coming from all the other prisons simultaneously) he ought to have an Associate selected by the prison social worker and parole officer.

Let us now look at some of the problems of discharge. The psychologist, during the offender's stay, may or may not have helped him to analyse his approach to life and to those he seeks to contact outside, yet there are still enough worries which might have been avoided to cause him stress.

Those problems are (1) physical; (2) socio-economic; (3) emotional.

The physical problems which beset him just before and after release often seem ludicrous to the outsider, but to a man still smarting from years of prison life they can swell to abnormal proportions.

One is increase or loss of weight during the sentence of several years. Men complain that they have put on a stone or more through prison diet, which, though nourishing, is inclined to be starchy. This is aggravated by lack of exercise. Two half-hour crawls round a prison yard morning and afternoon hardly remove that paunch or thickening neck. A man who came in with a shirt size $15\frac{1}{2}''$ collar may find that he has to be supplied (if he is lucky!) with one size $17''$. This happens on the day before his release, when he has been to check and sign for his clothes. They will be pressed and put ready for him to change into in 'Reception' the next morning.

It is too late on the day before a man's release to do anything about clothes problems which trouble men just as much as fashion-conscious women. A month or two beforehand would be better, to enable the medical officer to arrange a less starchy diet. It would also give time for alterations to be made in the tailor's shop of the prison, so that the man does not go out feeling as some say: 'A right Charley.'

This fear of looking a figure of fun, too fat, in clothes too small and too tight, affects the discharged prisoner when he goes to the labour exchange or to an employer, and diminishes his chances. The same applies to the man who has lost considerable weight. His baggy trousers and jacket hang on him as though on a scarecrow.

Although a man's clothes are taken care of by the prison staff and 'red-bands'[1] during the term of his sentence, a man admitted in summer with only a jacket, trousers and sandals may be discharged on a bleak January day with no pullover, no overcoat, no raincoat. A little change in administration could alleviate this problem.[2]

In the socio-economic field there are other problems. All men have the opportunity of seeing the Ministry of Labour representative a month before release. If a man is returning to another town, the Ministry agent, after enquiring what kind of work he is suited for, gives him the address of his local labour exchange and sends on his particulars to the manager there.

We never however, really felt that this was a satisfactory arrangement, and reports sent in weekly by the Labour Exchange showed us that a great many men slipped through the officials' hands and never appeared at all. Some found jobs on their own, but many, too many, drifted like Bill back to crime and returned to prison. (To us, one man would have been too many.)

A better arrangement is provided in some prisons by the prison social workers and Assistant Governors building up a register of employers willing to take on ex-prisoners. In my after-care classes, a popular evening always consisted of a panel discussion, with a group of employers and a trade-union

---

[1] Specially trusted prisoners, who work under supervision in various departments of the prison.

[2] The Governor is now responsible for seeing that prisoners released are adequately clothed.

official (Cf. appendix) sitting on the platform. Any employer interested in giving any of our men jobs was always asked to interview them before their release in the privacy of my office.

Hardened recidivists used to say to us that, if only this sort of spirit had been shown years before, perhaps they would not have had so many convictions. We accepted such comments with reservations, as we hoped sincerely that the men meant to take the opportunity given them, but we realised that more was necessary than having a job to keep a man 'straight'. Some left the jobs they had been offered after only a week, others stayed a little longer. Not nearly as many as we would have liked stuck out the initial difficulties and strangeness which everyone has to face in a new job amid new surroundings and new workers.

Perhaps the best method of commencing employment from prison was that arranged by the hostel staff. There the men, were on parole and under supervision of the prison staff. Employers reported to the staff and discussed the men's behaviour and problems. Those men tended to do better, but even then, there were failures. Hostellers stole from their employers or workmates or were found guilty of false pretences and fraud with the staff. This was partly due to wrong selection. In spite of such failures, employers were very good and understanding. They never refused to take further men from the hostel, although they had been disappointed, often more than once. Yet even this excellent method of rehabilitation was not without its failings.

As for finance Bill typifies the majority of men being discharged from the prison in the matter of having little or no money. Only the privileged hostel prisoner, about 1% of the total Wandsworth prison population, go out with a sum of money reaching £10 or over. Many, like Bill, are admitted penniless, and go out with only the prison subsistence and fares allowance—altogether less than £1. Formerly there was also a present from the Discharged Prisoners' Aid Society, but this being a voluntary society, did not have the funds to give more than a few shillings. Discharged prisoners' principal means of obtaining money is through the B.71 or B.79 forms to be handed to the N.A.B. officer.[3] The officer then gave Bill 50/- for food etc. and paid the rent of his room. If he was married, the N.A.B. would have supported his wife and family while he was 'inside'. On his release, his wife's book would be handed in and one given to him for the entire family until he obtained his first week's wage.

A great deal of criticism has been made about the amount of assistance which the law allowed to a prisoner's wife and family and later the prisoner, but there is another point of view—the taxpayer's. When an offender has committed a crime for which he has been imprisoned, the taxpayer has not only to provide for his 'keep' and clothing during his sentence, but has also to provide for his wife and family. Some prisoners' wives, though not well off, are better placed financially without their husbands (even if it is only with National Assistance[4]), because at least they are assured of a steady weekly income and the rent money. This is by no means certain for many wives, when their husbands drink, gamble and smoke away most of their earnings, honestly or dishonestly acquired.

By far the most intractable problem with which we had to deal in discharge discussions with the men in Wandsworth, was that of the man of 'no fixed abode'. This was nearly as bad in many other prisons throughout the country. Sometimes the man was a vagrant; often an alcoholic. If a suitable address were found for him, his disgusting personal habits and often lack of hygiene were more than any self-respecting landlady or landlord would have tolerated for long. So back he would drift to the doss-houses and the railway-station waiting-rooms or the bomb-sites, in between spells of imprisonment.

Others were not in this category. They were of 'no fixed abode' for two reasons. Their homes were in London, but they did not wish to contact their families or had been cast off by them. Or their homes and families were elsewhere in the

---

[3] Since 1964 this situation has improved, as the prison authorities are now authorised to give this allowance to the man before his release.
[4] Now Social Security Allowance.

country and the men had themselves gravitated to London either to seek employment, or because 'the pickings' in crime were better, or because they thought mistakenly that they would be less easily traced by police.

For such as these there are a number of alternatives. The man finds or knows an address on his own. The National Assistance Board[5] gives him an address. This is not always a hostel. Some offices have also private addresses. There are hostels of various kinds run by the Salvation Army, the Church Army, Rowton Houses Ltd and other voluntary agencies specially catering for ex-offenders, places which can often be located through the Voluntary Hostels Conference. All of those are run on a voluntary basis and usually staffed by men genuinely interested in humanity and its problems. Schemes are also run by some churches whereby vagrants and ex-prisoners may sleep in the church precincts. They include St. Martin-in-the-Fields and the Golborne Centre in London.

With the exception of perhaps a few of the excellent 'half-way' houses such as Merfyn Turner's Norman House, all alternatives must present a rather dreary and discouraging image to anyone just out of prison with no ties and no one to love or be loved by. (Cf. Chapter IV—figures in Annual report—Accommodation.)

The only possible improvement lies in letting a man out with sufficient money, which has been saved compulsorily for him so that he can pick and choose from a much wider selection of 'digs' advertised in the evening newspapers or local shop-windows. Some men, of course, because familiarity breeds not contempt in their case, but a sense of security, would still choose the seedy room in a slum street or the less presentable hostels, but at least the choice would be their own. At the moment, few have any real choice.

In our little slice of Bill's biography we saw how difficult it was for the offender to cope with problems that the rest of us take for granted. We are used to modern traffic conditions. We also know the current prices of goods and services, such as bus and train fares; the price of a cinema ticket; the cost of a cup

5 Ministry of Social Security.

of tea. A voluntary body in a town could help released prisoners by compiling a list of such useful information to be distributed to those who want it prior to discharge.

As for mixing with people, it is to be hoped that in any effective training programme, that the psychologist, the social worker and chaplain, combined with the prison officers, will have helped the offender to overcome many of his aggressions, and will have encouraged a less selfish outlook on living in society. In spite of this, he may at first feel tongue-tied and inwardly convinced that everyone he meets, even strangers, know he is an 'ex-con'.

A good voluntary Associate can often give a man this initial boost to his self-confidence. Meeting the ex-prisoner as a friend, he provides a more valuable relationship than a social worker can, once the man is free. Many more Associates of the right type are required. They should be people who understand that their function is not to preach or 'convert' to religion at an impressionable time, and still less to give gratuitous, usually inaccurate information about social work topics.

It often happens that not only are a man's problems many-sided, but the means for assisting with them are also. Among necessary aids are the 'half-way' houses, such as Norman House in London. Their value cannot, I think, be too often stressed as a means of assisting a man in his efforts to adjust and mix normally with other people. They provide an anchor, a homely atmosphere to which a man can return from a day's work, and he can stay until he feels confident enough to launch out on his own. Unfortunately, there are too few of them and too few of the right type of people to run them. If such houses were to be run by do-gooders, more interested in their own publicity than in the men themselves, or by unscrupulous persons taking advantage of human distress, the last stage of these men would be worse than the first, and they would bring the good houses into disrepute. Such houses, if they increase in number, should be under the supervision of the probation and parole service.

Other hostels, run by married social workers, some with

young families, serve the same purpose. Yet even the best of hostels are, as their wardens would themselves admit, but a poor substitute for a home, wife and family. This is so with any man, but even more so with an ex-prisoner.

Because of administrative difficulties and the number of men 'inside', it is not possible, as I have already shown in Chapter XIII to allow daily or even frequent visits of wives and families. Nor can a man discuss confidential matters in front of prison officers and other prisoners. There are often bitternesses and grievances on both sides which can be resolved only in the privacy of a man's home.

Many of the problems which afflict the married offender also concern his family. That is why it is so vital to have a closely related team of social workers inside as well as outside, the prisons, and to have sufficient of them to do the job properly with much lighter caseloads. It is impracticable, as I have already mentioned, to have the probation officer inside the prison (prison social worker) also making regular visits to the family while the man is inside. It may not even be advisable. The social worker even with the best of intentions and with the widest possible experience, may be biased. He will, in the nature of his work, see and hear the prisoner more often than his family and have a deeper knowledge of the man's point of view. A report on the wife's side by an outside parole officer, with an unbiased opinion, may be more effective.

Emotional crises also arise when a husband returns home after months or years away. Not only is the man touchy and unsure of his welcome. His wife may feel a mixture of emotions, including resentment that he has once more left her to take on all the obligations which should have been his; paying the rent and the bills, and supporting the children. She wants to give him another chance, and concedes, sometimes against her reason, that this time is going to be the last. Yet she is not sure that she will be able to stick to her welcoming attitude. She is also afraid of once more being left pregnant while her husband lands in further trouble with the law, and this conflicts with the natural desire of a woman to have her husband.

The children face problems which are familiar to all. If they are sons they may resent the intrusion into their life with their mother of this strange man who comes into the house. Previously he has done nothing except make 'mum' cry and sometimes be irritable with them. They have tried to comfort her while he was away. Now, mum is rushing around and making a fuss of this man who was the cause of her misery. They are ignored by mum and ordered about by this man who calls himself their dad. Who knows how many Borstal boys have landed there as a result of this near-Oedipus complex? Their resentment is aggravated by their father's frequent, inexplicable absences.

Again the answer to this problem may lie in an efficient system of parole, which would keep the family relationships in a more natural state.

* * * *

Social workers, probation-parole officers, Assistant Governors with social-study diplomas, prison officers, Associates, and wardens of hostels are all available to carry out rehabilitation. Such a heterogeneous mixture still requires to be more efficiently organized to avoid the duplication and chaos which all too often exist at present.

This could probably best be obviated if the recommendations of the Younghusband Report on 'Social Workers in the Local Authority Health and Welfare Services'[6] could be extended to the various people interested in prison social work, after-care and rehabilitation.

Discussing first the categories of human needs and trying to relate them to the functions of social workers, it points out:

(Paragraph 562) 'We have reached the conclusion that the content of the caseloads of social workers throughout the health and welfare services can broadly be divided into the following categories:

'(a) People with straightforward or obvious needs, who require material help of various kinds, some simple service,

[6] Op. cit.

or a periodic visit to see whether any change has taken place
or to provide evidence of the continuing support and interest
of the authority.

'(b) People with more complex problems, who require
systematic help from a trained social worker.

'(c) People with problems of special difficulty requiring
skilled help by professionally trained and experienced social
workers.'

The next section of value to us in prison rehabilitation is
contained in Paragraph 15.

'In view of the various senses in which the term social work
and social worker are used, and also the confused state of
training for social work in this country, we have inevitably
found difficulties of definition and terminology. For the sake
of clarity we indicate below the sense in which we use certain
terms throughout the Report.

Social Work
'The process of helping people, with the aid of appropriate
social services, to resolve or mitigate a wide range of personal
and social problems which they are unable to meet successfully
without such help. This process calls for both knowledge and
skill.

Social workers
'In the present shortage of trained social workers, however,
a large number of posts in which social work is the primary
function are filled by persons with no training or with some
other training. In order to avoid confusion we have found it
necessary to refer to these as social work posts or appointments,
and to those who hold them, as social workers. Nonetheless, we
hope that, in line with the situation in the teaching profession,
the term 'qualified social worker' will in future be applied
only to those who have entered the profession of social work
by taking a substantial and recognised qualification, that is
either a university or other related professional course or else

the general training which we recommend. We think that such workers should be clearly distinguished from those without either of these qualifications who nonetheless occupy social work posts.'

The report then suggests three classifications of workers to deal with the problems mentioned in Paragraph 562.

a) Trained social workers with advanced qualifications and experience. 'In our view, only persons so qualified should be eligible for supervisory, consultant and teaching posts.' This category would handle the people mentioned in (c) of Para. 562.

b) Those with a certain amount of practical experience and already employed by authorities, but with no academic training, or with academic training but in other unrelated subjects, or with academic training but no practical experience. Such workers could handle problems of those in (b) of Para. 562, but under supervision of trained social workers.

c) Those without either academic or practical experience. These usually came under the paragraphs about voluntary agencies and voluntary workers in the report. They would be known as welfare assistants. Under careful guidance of trained social workers they could handle many of the problems of (a) in Para. 562. They would still require 'training and careful selection if they are to give their services knowledgeably and acceptably and in order that they may recognise when a more highly trained worker is required.' Paragraphs 1052-1059.

How could those recommendations, and many others throughout the entire report, be applied to prison rehabilitation? Let us consider paragraph 562 and try to apply its clauses to after-care.

(a) People with straightforward or obvious needs could be handled by welfare assistants. The material is already there in the former Discharged Prisoners' Aid Societies after-care officers, the W.R.V.S., the New Bridge Society, Blackfriars Settlement and similar university settlements. The New

Problems of rehabilitation

Bridge Society and the settlements are the principal sources of voluntary Associates. Hostels for discharged prisoners already do capable work in handling the less complicated difficulties which beset their 'guests'.

Inside the prisons, carefully selected and trained prison officers, seconded to the Social work department, could treat the simple problems but would of course, have to record the applications and their solutions in the prisoners' social records. In this way duplication would be avoided. This help in social work would also give the officer a feeling of responsibility and participation in the programme of rehabilitation. It was my experience that a number of officers were interested in this form of social work, and with training would be quite capable of carrying it out and of referring more difficult cases to the prison social workers. Nevertheless I found that not all those attempting this in the prisons were suitable, partly because they had not been selected by social workers themselves engaged in the work, partly because they were attempting problems beyond their depth and capabilities. They were under the supervision of senior prison staff who were not social workers. The ideal for effective modern prison rehabilitation would be to appoint social workers of the supervisory and consultative grade mentioned in the Younghusband Report as the prison Governors. This is done in several prisons in Canada and was the reason of my pioneer appointment to an open prison there.

(b) As for people with more complex problems, there are outside the prisons a number of trained social workers who already have many of those cases referred to them. Such are the probation officers, and the medical and psychiatric social workers. Inside the prisons are some of the more junior prison social workers, and Assistant Governors with social study diplomas, some of whom have practical training in other fields of social work. Those who have only the extra-mural diploma or certificate would require further practical training outside the prisons.

(c) People with problems of special difficulty. Ex-prisoners could be referred to the Senior or Principal probation or parole officer for allocation. The psychiatric social workers of the mental hospitals might also be encouraged to take much more personal interest, not only in the certifiable prisoners but in those who are psychotic or psychopathic. Inside the prison, such men, together with alcoholics and drug addicts, should be the responsibility of the Senior Social worker, who would operate as one of a team with the medical officers and psychologists.

Chapter XVIII

ARE WE TREATING SYMPTOMS OR CAUSES?

It is possible in medicine to cure, or at any rate alleviate, the symptoms of fever (pyrexia, vomiting, headache etc.) without discovering the cause. Any doctor, however, will admit that this is not the best doctoring, because there is always the danger of relapse if the cause is something more serious than a cold in the head. The symptoms may be merely of a cold. On the other hand they may be the beginnings of measles or meningitis or typhoid, or other serious ailments which, if not diagnosed and given the correct medicine and nursing care, may leave incurable after-effects or lead to death.

So, when we are discussing crimes and essaying the rehabilitation of offenders, especially those who have had frequent relapses and are visibly growing worse in all three aspects of their nature—physical, mental and moral—it might repay us to make sure that we are really diagnosing correctly the causes of certain crimes.

In the Middle Ages, the church, art, poetry and drama all uttered dire and terrifying warnings of the most dreadful of evils to beset mankind, namely, the Seven Deadly Sins.

Plays were written for and performed in churches and in market squares by merchant apprentices at religious festivals. *Piers Plowman* listed the Seven Deadly Sins and church murals depicted the awful fate here and hereafter, of those who had been seized and possessed by these vices—Anger, Avarice, Envy, Gluttony, Jealousy, Lust, Pride.

In our modern sophistication we are apt to laugh at these bogeys and to dismiss them all as allegories, as part of a gullible superstitious era. The mediaeval scholars were however shrewd psychologists though they had no Freuds or

Jungs or McDougalls. Were they so far wrong? Or is it we who have drifted away from major truths?

Behind their somewhat exaggerated crudity of colour in paint, actions and words, (and they had to over-dramatise their message to an illiterate populace) might they not have been closer to the fundamental causes of man's most intractable sickness than we are today?

Instead of discussing the twelve questionable causes of crime which Baroness Wootton challenged and which I mentioned in a previous chapter, it might be worthwhile to pause in our study of modern theories, to take a look at older views.

Sociologists, clergymen and psychologists, puzzled by certain psychotic and psychopathic ailments, might do well to consider if we are indeed being confused by the symptoms and mistaking them for the real sickness. They might pause to wonder, whether by ignoring the Seven Sins altogether in modern treatments, we are missing the clues not only to crime causation, but to world and political unrest.

Let us look at any crimes and test them in the light of those deeper moral failings, rather than by explaining them as being caused by material lack or emotional deprivation. We may perhaps be able to see that at least one if not more than two of the Deadly Sins were the *real* instigators of the offence.

Psychoanalysis is a weapon, which though using modern phraseology, and even jargon, is trying to point out, by more devious methods, what moralists knew centuries ago.

(1) *Anger.* The French acknowledge this vice, together often with another, Jealousy, as an 'extenuating circumstance' in the *crime passionel.* It is often a cause of murder, sometimes unpremeditated. It may well be one of the causes of the violence among teenagers and football crowds.

(2) *Avarice or Greed.* This may well be the true crime for which certain offences such as larceny, housebreaking, theft, shoplifting are the outward evidence. Envy can act as its partner.

(3) *Envy.* Its destructive effects are the motivating power, often unconscious, of those who are unable to accept their

limitations. They refuse to face reality and be satisfied with their capabilities. Subconsciously, they probably realise the root of their sick outlook. They hate being failures and turn this passion on to those more successful than themselves.

The psychologist does not think of envy as a sin. He regards it as aggression turned against oneself. The victim not only hates the other party. In reality he is destroying his own moral, spiritual nature by hating himself for not being the successful person.

(4) *Gluttony.* Though at first glance this sin appears purely self-destructive, crimes of theft and robbery, even murder, have been committed by people, often in positions of power, both in feudal times and recently. The weeping of hungry children or peaked faces of their underlings meant nothing to feudal barons. The gluttony of the courts may have been one of the prime causes of both the French and later, the Russian revolution. The modern equivalent is an inordinate love of the acquisition of material things to the exclusion of higher qualities in mankind; the 'I'm all right Jack' outlook, which in the 18th and 19th centuries was rife as the doctrines of Psychological or Universal Hedonism, also known as Utilitarianism. The first expressed that an action was right or good if it gave the individual pleasure and wrong or bad if it caused him inconvenience or pain. The second claimed that the only actions which were right or good were those which produced the greatest amount of pleasure to the majority; minorities could go to the wall. Since the end of the second World War there has been a revival of both doctrines.

(5) *Jealousy.* This springs from over-possessiveness and lack of trust. It kills love and stirs up hate, a destructive emotion. Crimes of violence, from assault and grievous bodily harm to murder, can be caused by this sin.

(6) *Lust.* This comprises a multitude of sexual offences and aberrations.

(7) *Pride.* The Church teaches that, of all the Sins, this is the most deadly; the most destructive. This is not the natural pride of a mother for her children or of a craftsman doing a good job or creating something beautiful. Pride is a fatal

disease, a creeping blindness. The victims lose the power of self-criticism and are unable to admit they are ever at fault. Such a Sin causes the crimes of fraud and false pretences, including forgery. It is especially aggravated when combined with Envy and Avarice.

* * * *

In medicine, nature has provided an antidote to each poison. One cannot cure cyanide poisoning with another dose of cyanide. Just as the cure of poisoning requires antidotes and emulsifying treatment to soothe and to heal, so too violence and evil cannot be cured by violence and evil.

First, an attempt must be made to alleviate the effects of the Seven Deadly Sins.

Again, it was the mediaevalists who pointed out antidotes also numbering seven. They are Faith, Hope, Love (Charity), Prudence, Justice, Fortitude, Temperance.

The first three will be familiar to all Christians. The thirteenth chapter of Corinthians has never been bettered as an exposition of the powerful armaments which Good can summon against evil and was a constant source of strength to me in my work.

'Can they be used practically in the treatment of the offender?' it may be asked. The answer is that without using one, or all of them as occasion demands, one cannot hope to help him to become a 'new man'. Their mention is no mere dialectical exercise. They are actual, effective antidotes to the evil emotions which prompted the offender in the first place.

(1) *Faith.* This is a prime requisite at the start of *any* welfare policy, and essential in handling offenders. If prisoners are put on trust, they will respond with their own code of loyalty. This has been proved in the open, regional prisons and in the prison hostels. It is rarely that a man (even a recidivist), when put on his honour, will break faith, at any rate intentionally. The first part of this book also showed with what gallantry these men treated a woman alone in their midst. I had trusted them not to attack me or to rob me of either my money, which I never had to lock up or, still more temptingly, of my keys, their means of escape. I was small and

a woman. If one or more had tried violence, I should have been helpless. The prison officers were right in this. Yet never once did I receive anything but politeness. There was even grudging admiration for my working amongst them. My very helplessness and faith in their natural courtesy were my strongest weapons against any evil urges they might have had.

It is surely, therefore, not only good psychology but good social work to encourage an offender to lead a more honourable life by showing that one trusts him and relies on him. It is one of the greatest gifts a social worker can give to a prisoner; this opportunity to regain, or even acquire for the first time, self-respect. It has even been known to awaken in the dormant conscience the first pricks of guilt, which is the beginning of awareness in a man that he ought to do something about altering his mode of living.

On the social worker's side, it is equally important never to break faith. Never make promises which you cannot keep, or have not checked with the agency you are involving. Promise no more than you, at the moment, feel you can honour. As with children, never offer a sweet unless you are certain there is a bag of candies in the drawer. The psychological effect of ultimately giving a man more than you offered is better than the opposite of 'letting him down.' This can create resentment and may undo all your work. Over-offering is a weakness of some amateurs, who, in their desire to relieve distress, promise more than they have either the power or the authority to give.

Without his written consent, or at least his oral agreement, never divulge the fact that a man has been in prison, or any other of his social or medical problems, to anyone outside. It is not only a breach of trust but may lead the social worker into trouble, perhaps even legal complications. We should have as high a standard on this matter as a doctor has in his Hippocratic oath. It is this which distinguishes the professional from the amateur. Otherwise we are guilty of obtaining a prisoner's confidence and trust under false pretences.

The reader may think these principles are accepted by all,

but I have known them violated in prisons. They are not always implemented even by professionally trained staff. We cannot, therefore, be too careful about being on our guard about discussion on offenders.

(2) *Hope.* We must try to instil this into an offender. This is not by any means easy, especially with a man who has failed again and again to 'make the grade'—an offender whose only progress in life appears, to him and to others, to be expressed by a graph of rising sentences of imprisonment. We have, however the duty to show that we have hope in man's basic good no matter how thickly encrusted with his evident evil. We must have faith, hope and trust in a man, and must strive to awaken these qualities in him. Otherwise we shall not progress far in rehabilitating him.

We must also have faith and hope in ourselves and those who are working with us, together with loyalty. Rehabilitation of the offender is a long-term, sometimes wearisome, sometimes apparently fruitless task. Patience has sometimes to be summoned as the handmaiden of hope, we must adopt a nurse's outlook on a patient who has had a relapse. Despair is the death-blow to hope.

(3) *Charity.* By this I do not mean sloppy sentimentality which is more dangerous than indifference to the needs of these men, I mean a recognition that some at least may have become criminals due to extenuating circumstances, and that there may have never been any alternative but Borstal or prison for them. In dealing with distressed human beings, unless one is a monster, one cannot avoid feelings of affection, even love, for those who give to and take from us such deep emotions.

(4) *Prudence.* This is closely linked with Faith. Discretion is essential in any social work, but, when dealing with offenders, some of whom are pathological liars, one has to be careful not to accept their statements and intentions without making an independent check. Otherwise one cannot help them.

(5) *Justice.* This is a virtue which appeals to all men, honest or dishonest. Justice in the worker promotes trust in the offender.

(6) *Fortitude.* This is one of the most difficult of the virtues to practise unless one is born with natural strength. If, however, one can put the offenders' needs first and forget oneself, fortitude, strengthened by prayer, can enable one to stand against obstacles and to stick by one's principles and beliefs in the face of hostility.

(7) *Temperance.* This can mean moderation, the ethical *via media,* which I mentioned in a previous chapter. To be able to steer a middle course between two extremes of suggestions is a very useful virtue. It is also an important antidote against Pride, from which the social worker is no more immune than any other human being. When a man shows that he is able to stand on his own feet, the social worker must let him go, with a blessing. There will be plenty of others in need of help. It is only pride and selfishness to hold him, and certainly not for the man's good, which was the original goal of the worker.

Chapter XIX

CONCLUSION

In this book we have not been concerned principally with investigating the causes of recidivism. We have studied the means at present available for its treatment and suggestions for the future made by sociologists and others. We wanted to know how those means could be supplemented and what other methods could be employed to reduce the criminal population. We have decided which were practicable and worthy of attainment. Having selected the most feasible, we cannot, not being God, foresee the results, but, though the methods may be empirical, we can draw certain inferences.

One is that if we employ violence to treat violence, we shall only make matters worse. Another is that the present system of locking men away for years from society, from all they have known and loved, is as useless as locking a tuberculous patient in a sealed room without treatment. The patient may die; he is certainly unlikely to be cured, as the spontaneous healings of lesions are so rare as to be discounted. If released from the sealed room, he will only spread his infection. So it is with the recidivist in present circumstances. He may not die physically, but, much more serious, his soul may be dead to this world. If released untreated, he, like the tuberculosis patient, will only diffuse his ailment.

No social problem is ever isolated and unattached. Problems of the prisoner have high-lighted the difficulties facing his family. These are in many instances even greater than his, and to the local authorities and social workers, present problems more insoluble than those of the recidivist. Further, psychological, economic, religious and ethical problems have only a minor position in a penal policy which is faced with the difficulty of accommodating an increasing number of offenders when only a limited number of prisons is available.

Conclusion

Both in prison practice and in writings, the tendency has been to recommend and stress the material benefits required: better prisons, better conditions, more money on release, more Social Security money for wives and families, more money to permit relatives to visit. All these things are necessary, but alone they will not provide the answer to the problem of crime. They have concentrated too much on what should be done for prisoners rather than by them; too much on the objective rather than the subjective needs of man.

As with the Welfare State, prison reform, good though it is ignores the incipient danger of undermining a person's character, will and independence.

Of course some of the Victorian prisons are atrocious. Nobody could have been more shocked than I was at our older buildings, especially as I had come from Canadian prisons some of which, though of similar age have been modernised. Of course nobody approves of the keeping of three men in cells built for one man, or of the appalling insanitary conditions in our local prisons. Yet the thought more than once crossed my mind that John Bunyan wrote *The Pilgrim's Progress* in much less salubrious surroundings; and Oscar Wilde made use of his imprisonment to describe his feelings in *The Ballad of Reading Gaol*. Even today, some prisoners can lose awareness of their surroundings by writing or painting and using their minds; whether their writing or art is always worthwhile to the onlooker is not our concern here. It is the exercise of one of the other sides of man's nature which is of value to the person interested in seeing the birth of a new man. I treasure an oil painting and a pencil drawing presented to me by prisoners.

Another aspect of reform not often mentioned, perhaps not even consciously thought of, is discussed by Aldous Huxley in his *Ends and Means*. It is in a different context perhaps, as he is talking about political reform, but it is surely applicable to prison reform.

'No revolution can be regarded as successful, if it does not lead to progress. Now the only real progress, to quote Dr.

Marett's words, is "progress in charity". Is it possible to achieve this by means that are essentially uncharitable? No. Violence cannot lead to real progress unless, by way of compensation and reparation, it is followed by non-violence, by acts of justice and good will. In such cases, however, it is the compensatory behaviour that achieves the progress, not the violence which that behaviour was intended to compensate.

'No reform is likely to achieve the results intended unless it is not only well-intentioned but also (historically) opportune. To carry through a social reform which in the given historical circumstances will create so much opposition as to necessitate the use of violence, is criminally rash. A reform may be intrinsically desirable but so irrelevant to the existing historical circumstances, as to be practically useless.

'Change as such is to most human beings more or less acutely distressing. This being so, we shall do well to preserve even those elements of the existing order which are neither practically harmful or valuable but merely neutral. Human conservatism is a fact in any given historical situation. Hence it is very important that social reformers should abstain from making unnecessary changes or changes of startling magnitude. Wherever possible, familiar institutions should be extended or developed so as to produce the results desired; principles already accepted should be taken over and applied to a wider field. In this way, the amount and intensity of opposition to change and, along with it, the risk of having to use measures of violence would be reduced to a minimum.'[1]

*　　*　　*　　*

To obtain a correct moral or ethical balance a human being must, it seems to me establish a right relationship with Good in three directions.

(1) He must establish a right relationship with eternal Good, which has no boundaries of space or time or matter. Man, even those who deny it, have a deep, inborn awareness of their spirituality, which is the means of contacting that

[1] Chapter on "Social Reform and Violence".

eternal Good. Some men call it God; others Buddha; others Allah; others the Great White Spirit.

(2) He must establish a right relationship with society and the individuals in that society. This does not mean that one must agree with or approve, or like everyone or what people do. After all, Christ did not approve of the Pharisees' attitude, and used a parable to illustrate their wrong attitude to both eternal Good and to men. Nor did he approve of the money-lenders and stall-holders plying their trade within the temple precincts.

(3) He must establish a right relationship with himself. One should listen to that small inner voice. So often it is muffled by the blare and din of modern life. The Seven Deadly Sins are fatal not only because they cause harm socially but because they are utterly self-destructive.

*　　*　　*　　*

The individual is to both God and man as important as society. We must therefore equip ourselves, as well as circumstances and intelligence will permit. A man is like a diamond,

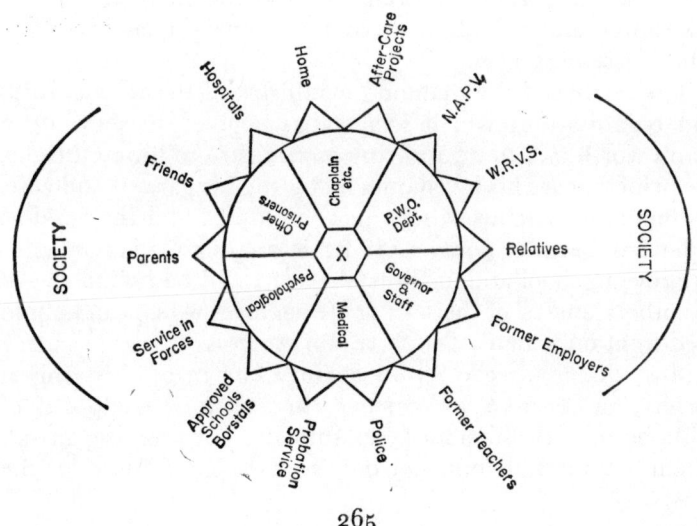

not only in value to his Creator but to society, and he should be so treated with the respect that such a jewel merits, no matter how dimmed his lustre nor how chipped his character. Of course, one has to be realistic, not sentimental. No amount of breathing hard on a one-third carat diamond and rubbing it on one's sleeve will magically turn it into the Koh-i-nor. All the same, the value is there even in the most degraded and in the most wretched setting.

Man is like this stone, too, in that, to have his beauty fully realized he must have first one facet, then another, turned to the light of knowledge, to be assessed and appreciated. He is not wholly a physical organism, not wholly a mind, not entirely a creature of emotions and nervous energy or of spiritual promptings.

Let me try to illustrate what I mean by applying this analogy to an individual prisoner X.

To understand X and assess his potentialities for re-education and rehabilitation to the fullest possible extent, we should have to study the following facets, each of which emits a different light. There would be the views of the Governor and his disciplinary staff, the findings of the medical officers and the psychologist, the investigations and case-histories of prison social workers, the reflections of the chaplain and his colleagues, and the often eyeball-searing light on him from others prisoners' eyes.

The setting of the diamond would be all the relationships and organisations which society has evolved to show up a man's worth and to try to bring more lustre to him. Of these, the principal are his loved ones including his parents and wife, his home, his friends, his former employers, and the Services if he has been a member. If he is a 'rough' diamond, his Approved School and/or Borstal record will be included. All the others 'spikes' of the setting are agencies which can help to shed light on a man's character and motives.

Most diamonds are set in a ring. For man, this ring is Society, rather like an eternity ring, as it is composed of millions of tiny diamonds, set into the surrounding metal. When a stone falls out, not only is it of less value than the whole ring, but society is itself the poorer. Society therefore has an obligation to see that as few as possible of its jewels work loose and are lost or so damaged as to be useless in a resetting.

THE VALUE OF
THE PRE-DISCHARGE CLASS

As we studied at Wandsworth the men's needs and fears as shown by their applications, a gradual pattern began to emerge, which I felt could be better dealt with in groups. Many men's queries concerned matters of general interest to them, such as housing, after-care, and the National Assistance Board,[1] about which they had often been wrongly advised by relatives and others.

From this pattern grew the idea of asking the men, several months before their discharge, to hold an informal discussion with me to see if they would be interested in having experts in various fields of social rehabilitation, both statutory and voluntary.

A number of men made excuses to themselves and to others as to why they could not go straight. They could not find a job, or there was not enough money from the N.A.B., or they had labour exchange difficulties, or clothing was unsuitable or the trade unions were hostile. We wanted to cut the ground from under their feet and to eliminate as many after-care difficulties as possible.

The hundred or more men for discharge each month discussed the subjects freely with me for nearly two hours; then chose the topics about which they wanted to hear. Later, when the idea of classes caught on, they chose the speakers also. I made the necessary contacts.

Thirty to forty men each month sincerely wanted information. I would not take those who were going to attend just for a night's entertainment. I excluded the latter by saying that once men had accepted, attendance would be compulsory for a

[1] Now Ministry of Social Security.

six weeks' course. Thanks to the wonderful co-operation I received from the Governor and the Tutor Organiser for night classes in the prison, I had no administrative difficulties in arranging my classes. These became so popular that some men who had completed the course before their discharge was due asked to attend the next course. As the various groups of men asked for different subjects, the courses were different and I permitted, with the Governor's approval, those men's requests to attend again, since it was not a duplication.

Six months later, the 'rehabilitation' wing, whose staff had not wished the men to participate in those talks on the Main block because, they claimed there were administrative difficulties in moving men from one block to another at night, began similar classes, often asking our speakers without consultation with me to repeat their talks. This request for classes came mostly from men who were being transferred to those pre-hostel wings before the completion of their lecture courses on the 'Main' and were disappointed at missing talks. The same applied to requests for Associates for those men isolated from us and the Main block.

Sample of After-Care Classes

A course of six talks on pre-discharge problems of After-care, to be given in the Mess-Room B.3. at 6.15. p.m. commencing Thursday 16th Nov.

Subject:	Speaker:
1 Problems of Housing and how they are handled by housing authorities	—, Housing Area Manager
2 The work of the — Discharged Prisoners' Aid Society	—, Secretary — Discharged Prisoners' Aid Society

3 'Any Questions' Panel

—, N.A.B. Area Manager
—, Deputy Area Manager, Ministry of Labour, — Labour Exchange
—, Personnel Manager, John Smith & Co. Ltd.
—, Asst. Group Secretary, X.Y.Z. Workers' Union
—, Managing Director, Messrs. — Electrical Engineers

4 The work of the Family Welfare Association—How they can assist prisoners' & their families

—, Area Secretary, F.W.A.

5 The work of—Settlement and the rôle of the Associate for the discharged prisoner

—, Warden, — Settlement.

6 The work of the Inland Revenue Dept. in connection with the Income Tax of prisoners

—, Inspector of Inland Revenue.

Speakers at other classes included a representative from the Shipping Federation, showing films; a Salvation Army Brigadier on hostels; a psychiatrist on the problems of alcohol.

Appendix 2

EMPLOYMENT IN PRISONS

(Extracts from Report of Prison Commissioners—1964)

There is still considerable misapprehension about how prisoners occupy their spare time, especially in what would normally be their working day. Although the desirable goal of putting all offenders in prisons to a full day's work, either inside or outside prison walls, has not yet been achieved in this country, the authorities do provide more opportunities than the sewing of mail bags or picking of oakum, as many inaccurate books and press reports would suggest.

The following is an alphabetical list of types of employment within the prisons of England and Wales for the year ended December 31, 1964, taken, by kind permission of the Home Office, from the report of the Prison Commissioners for that year.

Employment	*Total Persons employed daily*
Manufacturers: —	
Basketmakers	20
Blacksmiths	81
Bookbinders	146
Brush and mop making	144
Carpenters	582
Concrete moulders	53
Fitters	1,119
Heavy canvas work other than mail bags	297
Jam-making	11
Knitters and repairers	125
Mailbags (new)	2,053
Mailbags (repairers)	647

Manufacturers: —

Mats, matting, rugs	652
Mattresses (coir and hair)	283
Metal recovery	1,535
Moulders (iron foundry)	24
Needleworkers, dressmakers and repairers	217
Net makers	266
Pouch and leatherwork	136
Printers	86
Shipfenders	43
Shoemakers and repairers	429
Storemen	208
Tag makers	198
Tailors and repairers	1,345
Tinsmiths	131
Toy assembly and painting	524
Tubular steel furniture makers	42
Twine and rope makers	18
Weavers: cotton, linen and woollen	389
Wirefencing	49
Woodchopping	295
Miscellaneous (includes sorting, salvage and simple assembly)	721

Farm: —

Livestock and arable husbandry, market gardening, glass, land reclamation	1,257

Works Department: —

Bricklayers and masons	374
Carpenters and joiners	252
Electricians	141
Fitters	120
Labourers	1,027
Painters and decorators	550
Plasterers	35

Works Department: —	*Total Persons employed daily*
Plumbers	155
Quarrymen	43
Slaters	—

Domestic service: —

Cleaners, jobbers and labourers	5,144
Cooks and bakers	1,342
Gardeners	987
Hospital orderlies	744
Stokers	143

Outside work: —

For farmers, private firms and local authorities	293
For government departments	214

Vocational Trainees	1,342
Pre-release hostellers	167

Non-effectives: —

Untried prisoners who elect not to work	716
Certified unfit for labour	261
Sick	789
Under punishment	251
Others (includes inmates who are e.g. non-effective as a working unit on day of discharge: attending court: travelling between establishments: at summer camp.)	1,191

Grand Total	29,600

PROJECTIVE TECHNIQUES FOR REHABILITATION SELECTION AND PAROLE

Lady Wootton in comments already quoted in Chapter XV,[1] says that Schuessler and Cressey's researches on psychological tests showed that these proved little or nothing in the attempt to gauge who was criminal or had criminal tendencies. There is something in this, yet for the purposes of parole, one must accept that, even if tests may be of little value in application to the general population, they can be useful in prisons. Once a man has been proved, on other grounds that the purely psychological, to be a criminal, then surely tests come into their own as recording his degree of criminality and of normalcy for parole purposes. In fact, among the methods of treatment used to assist in a man's rehabilitation, the psychologists' techniques can play an important part.

Inside the prison, projective tests can provide a useful diagnostic means of assisting the prison staff to assess a man's eligibility for parole. Projective tests such as the Thematic Apperception Test[2] and the Rorschach inkblots[3] enable the psychologist to discover and gain insight into the motivations of offenders. They could also be an important aid to parole.

[1] *Social Science & Social Pathology*—Baroness Wootton.
[2] The Thematic Apperception Test comprises 30 pictures developed and arranged by Drs. Harry Murray and Christiana Morgan. Scenes involve single characters in repose, contemplation or sorrow or multiple characters of the same or opposite sex. Some of the scenes are ambiguous and allow characters to be designated either as men or women. The subject is asked to make up a story about each scene, to describe the feelings of the characters, to tell the conditions antecedent to the story, to outline the plot and the relationships between the characters and to tell the outcome.
[3] Developed by Dr. Herman Rorschach some 45 years ago, this is a collection of 10 ink blots on cards. A person is asked to tell of what the blots remind him. Each response is as different as each individual.

Appendix 3

Louis Cohen[4] states that parole preparations can be divided into three functions:
a) the investigation or collection of all data to understand the problem.
b) the development of a parole plan and
c) the continued supervision of the man on parole until he can manage his own affairs competently.

a) Psychological tests could provide a valuable and objective assessment of various attitudes of the potential 'parolee' towards his home and community. They would supplement social case-work interviews and help to give an accurate picture. It has even been demonstrated, as Cohen emphasises, that 'deliberate attempts at faking the Rorschach have been unsuccessful. What seems to happen in the projective techniques when the subject tries to fake or distort the material is a modification of detail but not of the essential elements.'

From both types of tests, not only might we be able to perceive the attitudes of the subject in relation to himself and to his world but, as Cohen says; 'we may well find the particular motivation for the crime and we can frequently find resources for future growth and development.'

b) Planning the prisoner's future placement involves a study not only of his emotional needs, but also of his impact on prospective employer, relatives and neighbours. These can seldom be found out only in case-work interviews. Social workers who have seen men relapse, leave home or give up jobs are aware of this. Cohen claims, with some justification, that 'those areas can frequently be exposed through the projective tests. A rejected lad may want and need a warm environment, an uncertain one may want authoritarian régime. These needs may be frequently worked out in planning.'

If Cohen's claim is valid, the tests would be invaluable to the social worker and to the parole officer when they discuss with the future 'parolee', where he is going to live.

[4] Louis D. Cohen, 'Psychological Techniques in Probation & Parole Work'. (1950 Year Book of N.P.P.A.). *Advances in Understanding the Offender*. (National Probation & Parole Association. American Publication.)

c) Cohen makes an even stronger claim for projective techniques in parole supervision. 'It is,' he writes, 'difficult to avoid bias in evaluation of progress of the probationer or parolee. The overtly compliant subject who seems to do as he is told may be actually in greater difficulty than the rebellious violator. It takes considerable experience to judge accurately the progress of the subject. The projective techniques may be of value here.'

Cohen's final suggestion that projective techniques would be useful for predictions about the success of an individual's parole might be a worthwhile line for prison psychologists to pursue. Such ideas, though novel and startling in Britain, are yet worth considering. They would also encourage psychologists to take a more active interest in the future rôle of the offender in society.

BIBLIOGRAPHY

Reports, Journals and Letters

Adult Offender, The. White Paper, 1964   H.M.S.O.
Advances in understanding the Offender   National Probation and Parole Association, 1950. New York

After-Care, Annual Report of Central After-Care Association   1961
Criminal Justice Act, 1961   H.M.S.O.
Commissioners of Prisons, Report of   1959, H.M.S.O.
Daily Express, June 30, 1961   Article on H.M. Prison, Wandsworth

Daily Mail, June 26, 1961   Article on H.M. Prison, Wandsworth

Daily Telegraph, Letters to the Editor,   Nov. 18, 1964; Nov. 27, 1965

Maxwell Report, Report of the Committee on Discharged Prisoners' Aid Societies   Reprinted 1957, H.M.S.O.
National Assistance Board Leaflets
Welfare Facilities Available for Discharged Prisoners   No. 1293, 1/6/60
Help for those in Need   July 1960
Welfare Facilities   No. 1293, (3), 23/11/61
National Association of Discharged Prisoners' Aid Societies, Annual Reports   1959, 1960, 1961, 1962
National Association of Discharged Prisoners' Societies, (Incorporated)   Handbook, 1957
Norman House Report   1959-1960
Organisation of After-Care   Report of the Advisory Council on the Treatment of Offenders, 1963, H.M.S.O.

Prisons & Borstals, England & Wales   1957, 1960, 1962, H.M.S.O.
Prison Service Journal   No. 4, Jan. 1962
Probation, A Handbook of   National Association of Probation Officers, 1960-1965

Problems of the Ex-Prisoner, A Report   Pakenham/Thompson Committee, 1961

Social Workers in the Local Authority Health & Welfare Services, Report on	Working Party (Young husband) 1959, H.M.S.O.
Social Services, Guide to the	Family Welfare Association, 1963
Work for Prisoners, Organisation of,	Report of the Advisory Council on the Employment of Prisoners. 1964, H.M.S.O.
Work of the Prison Department, Report on	1964, H.M.S.O.
The Probation Service, R. Morison Report on	1962, H.M.S.O.
Work of the Probation and After-Care Department, 1962-5	1966 Cmnd. 3107, H.M.S.O.

Dictionaries and Encyclopaedias

Britannica Encyclopaedia.
Chamber's Twentieth Century Dictionary.
Nuttall's Standard Dictionary of the English Language.
Thesaurus of English Words and Phrases by Mark Roget, M.D.
Webster's New International Dictionary of the English Language.

Ethics

Bradley, F. H.	*Ethical Studies*
	Collected Essays, Vol. I. Chaps. 4, 5, 6, 7
Broad, A. K.	*Five Types of Ethical Theories*
Broad, C. D.	*The Mind and its Place in Nature*
Butler, Joseph	*Ten Sermons*
Hume, David	*Inquiry concerning Principles of Morals*
	Treatise of Human Understanding, Pt. IV, Sect. 6
Lillie, Wm.	*An Introduction to Ethics*
Longford, Lord	*The Idea of Punishment*
Mill, J. S.	*Utilitarianism*
Moore, C. E.	*Ethics*
Rashdall, Dean	*Theory of Good and Evil*
Simpson, J. Y.	*The Spiritual Interpretation of Nature*, Chaps. 3 & 15
Taylor, A. E.	*The Faith of a Moralist*
Temple Wm., The Most Rev., Archbishop of York	'The Ethics of Penal Action' (Clarke Hall Fellowship Lecture, 19/3/34)

Logic and Metaphysics

Bradley, F. H.	*Principles of Logic,* Vol. I
Cornford, F. M.	*Plato's Theory of Knowledge*
Descartes, René	*Meditations*
Jowett, B.	*Dialogues of Plato*
Lindsay, A. D.	*The Republic of Plato*
Locke, John	*An Essay concerning Human Understanding*
Sinclair, Angus	*The Traditional Formal Logic*
Spearman, A.	*Psychology Down the Ages*
Taylor, A. E.	*Plato, the Man and his Work*

Psychology

Conybeare, Sir John ⎫ Mann, W. N. ⎭	*Textbook of Medicine*
Drever, J.	*An Introduction to the Psychology of Education*
Lebon, Gustave	*The Crowd, A Study of the Popular Mind*
McDougall, W.	*The Group Mind*
„ „	*Physiological Psychology*
Spencer, W. W.	*Our Knowledge of Other Minds*
Stout, A. K.	*Manual of Psychology*
„ „ „	*Studies in Philosophy and Psychology*

Sociology and Criminology

B.B.C. Publications	*The Social Workers*
Banks, Frances	*Teach Them to Live*
Book L., Dorothy	*The Corrective Institution from the Viewpoint of the Social Agency*
Clayton, C. F.	*The Wall is Strong*
Cronin, Harley, M.B.E.	*The Screw Turns*
Glover, Elizabeth	*Probation and Re-education*
Jones, Howard	*Crime in a Changing Society*
Klare, Hugh	*Anatomy of Prison*
Page, Leo	*Crime and the Community*
Penguin	*Survey of the Social Sciences,* 1965
Rose, Gordon	*The Struggle for Penal Reform*
Turner, Merfyn	*Norman House, The First Five Years*
„ „	*Safe Lodging*
Wootton, Baroness Barbara ⎧ ⎨ ⎩	*Social Science and Social Pathology* *Crime and the Criminal Law* *Socrates, Science and Social Problems*

INDEX

281

INDEX

INDEX

DELINQUENCY AND CHILD NEGLECT
Harriett C. Wilson

This is the first comprehensive study of a group of families often referred to as 'problem families'. Harriet Wilson shows that they are not a homogenous group, and furthermore, that they do not possess any unique personality traits. On the contrary, the disabilities which are found among the families who took part in this investigation are also found in the general run of the population. The main disabling factor turned out to be the social isolation to which these families are subjected.

This isolation affects not only the personality of father and mother but it has also a profound effect on the character formation of their children, who tend to become delinquent. The child from this environment has not learnt to control his impulses effectively enough to take part in social life on a normal basis. He is handicapped from an early age.

Harriett Wilson concludes that the delinquency found in this environment is a symptom of a total family situation which can only be treated at the family level by preventative family services.

'This is a lively and stimulating book and is well worth reading by every teacher in a densely populated area.'

Education

'A valuable and careful sociological study . . . not only a solid but an attractive study.' *New Society*

MALADJUSTED BOYS
Otto L. Shaw

'. .. teachers and social workers who are intimately concerned with this problem will find this book of great professional interest, but it deserves a far wider readership.'

Teachers' World

'. . . We can be grateful to Mr Shaw, not only for the work he is doing, but also for making a readable book of it.'

New Society

PRISONS I HAVE KNOWN
Mary Size

In 1947 Miss Size was recalled from retirement and appointed Governor of Askham Grange, the first women's open prison. This was the peak of her career during which she played a considerable part in the many changes which have revitalized the prison and borstal systems of this country. The case histories gathered during her forty-two years service provide an absorbing fund of human stories. We learn a great deal about the women prisoners, their problems, behaviour and daily routine. She maintains that every criminal should be regarded as potentially a good citizen and she has played an important role in the elaborate process of moral and industrial training.

PRISONERS AND THEIR FAMILIES
Pauline Norris

'A source book of the utmost importance to penologists welfare officers and lawyers . . . should be taken very seriously by anyone concerned with the law or its administration.'

Sunday Time

'This most competent and meticulous study will provide incontrovertible ammunition for all those concerned to reform a wretchedly unsatisfactory aspect of our national life.'

The Times Educational Supplement

'This book is of major significance. It needs to be considered seriously by everyone concerned with sentencing, and by all social workers who may work with prisoners' families.'

Social Service Quarterly Autumn

LONDON: GEORGE ALLEN AND UNWIN LTD.

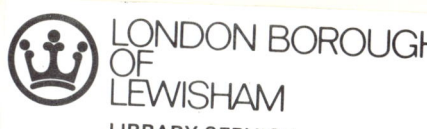